D0257144

WALKING THE
COUNTY
HIGH POINTS
OF ENGLAND

WALKING THE COUNTY HIGH POINTS OF ENGLAND

Summersdale Publishers Ltd
46 West Street
Chichester
West Sussex
PO19 1RP
UK

www.summersdale.com

Printed and bound by CPI Group (UK) Ltd, Croydon

ISBN: 978-1-84953-239-6

Substantial discounts on bulk quantities of Summersdale books are available to corporations, professional associations and other organisations. For details contact Summersdale Publishers by telephone: +44 (0) 1243 771107, fax: +44 (0) 1243 786300 or email: nicky@summersdale.com.

WALKING THE
COUNTY
HIGH POINTS
OF ENGLAND

DAVID BATHURST

summersdale

Counties of England

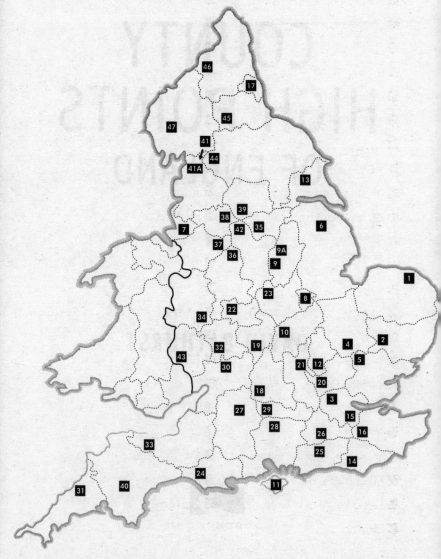

Numbers indicate approximate location of high point within county

Counties ordered from lowest to highest high point:

1. Norfolk
2. Suffolk
3. Greater London (Inner)
4. Cambridgeshire
5. Essex
6. Lincolnshire
7. Merseyside
8. Rutland
9. / 9A. Nottinghamshire
10. Northamptonshire
11. Isle of Wight
12. Bedfordshire
13. East Riding of Yorkshire
14. East Sussex
15. Greater London (Outer)
16. Kent
17. Tyne & Wear
18. Oxfordshire
19. Warwickshire
20. Hertfordshire
21. Buckinghamshire
22. West Midlands
23. Leicestershire
24. Dorset

25. West Sussex
26. Surrey
27. Wiltshire
28. Hampshire
29. Berkshire
30. Gloucestershire
31. Cornwall
32. Worcestershire
33. Somerset
34. Shropshire
35. South Yorkshire
36. Staffordshire
37. Cheshire
38. Greater Manchester
39. West Yorkshire
40. Devon
41. / 41A. Lancashire
42. Derbyshire
43. Herefordshire
44. North Yorkshire
45. County Durham
46. Northumberland
47. Cumbria

Acknowledgements

I would like to thank the team at Summersdale, especially Chris Turton, for their support, suggestions and enthusiasm; my walking companions for their company and their forbearance; the many kind strangers who have helped me locate a particular landmark or path to assist me on my travels; and lastly, but most importantly, my wife Susan and my daughter Jennifer, who have endured my frequent 4–4.30 a.m. starts and weeks away from home with stoicism and understanding.

Contents

Introduction

I'm standing on a Sussex station platform waiting for my train and it's 4.50 a.m. I've had a busy week at work and it's Saturday. I've left a long-suffering family behind at home and I don't expect to reach my day's objective for a good six and a half hours. I'm at the mercy of Southern Railway and, later on, South West Trains and I think two bus companies. I'm hopeful, but by no means certain, of finding a cafe or station buffet open and having enough time to buy a cup of coffee before the next train's due. I hope the weather forecaster was wrong when they talked of showers merging to form longer spells of rain. And if I miss a bus connection at the other end I'm not sure I'll make it home in time for *Match of the Day*.

But, to paraphrase the slogan for a certain beauty product, I think it's worth it. I'm off to explore another 'county high point' – the highest ground in an English county – and it's all contributing to a journey, or series of journeys, of discovery, taking me by the hand and leading me up to the highest point of each and every county in England.

Why do I think you might be interested, and, therefore, why this book?

Well, three reasons really. Firstly, most walkers would agree that a walk up a hill or series of hills provides greater drama, excitement and satisfaction than sticking to the valleys or levels. Some might say that a walker's natural inclination is to seek out the high places and, in any day's walk, it will be the attainment of the higher ground that will provide the highlights. There can be few more exhilarating feelings for a walker than that of reaching a hilltop and gazing across a vast panorama of land, be it countryside, towns, villages or further hilltops – even more so when a thoughtfully placed topograph provides indicators of distances to landmarks which may or may not be visible on a clear day. While England may not boast the highest mountains in the world, it still possesses a large number of very

9

impressive mountains, hills and ridges, and there is tremendous pleasure and satisfaction to be gained in climbing them; and even more satisfaction from knowing that the summit is the highest ground in the whole county. Some of the high points featured in this book are truly breathtaking: Scafell Pike, Worcestershire Beacon and Ditchling Beacon are three examples which, despite their very great differences in character and geographical situation, provide fantastic views and great memories for the walker. While not all county high points can match the scenic splendour of these three, the majority do offer great views and great walking; one of the joys of this quest is the huge variety of walking experiences it offers, thanks to the astonishingly varied scenery in this country. Some walks will be little more than a stroll up a gentle hillside while others are very much tougher, and will require considerable navigational skill and proper equipment (more about that later.) There really is something for everyone, from the novice to the skilled fellwalker.

Secondly, the book is also intended for those who may lack the physical resources or inclination required to do the walks, but may wish to enjoy a 'virtual' tour and, in doing so, learn much about the geography and character of England. At its most basic, this book will act as a useful reference source, but it seeks to do far more than that, taking you to a very diverse range of landscapes, and places which tell a great deal about England and the English. The walk to the summit of Wiltshire offers the largest stone circle in Europe, a burial mound dating back 5,500 years, a carved white horse visible for 22 miles, and the possibility of sharing your pub lunch table with men in Druidic costume. And that's just one walk out of more than forty covered in this book. Read of the unique refreshment opportunity on Surrey's high point, the peat wilderness which conceals the summit of Derbyshire and the miner standing proudly atop the roof of Nottinghamshire. Imagine standing on Cleeve Hill, the summit of Gloucestershire, as a rain belt sweeps in from the Vale of Evesham; picture the floral glory of Hidcote Gardens, just ten minutes from the heights of Warwickshire; and spare a thought for the writer whose zeal for the task is often blunted by excessively early starts and irregular bus services.

Thirdly, you may be one of an ever-increasing number of walkers who enjoy 'bagging' landmarks boasting particular characteristics. The huge increase in popularity of 'geocaching' (a form of treasure hunt in which an item is hidden somewhere in the world and its co-ordinates or map reference posted on the Internet) shows that many walkers like to have some objective to aim for in the course of a journey on foot, and achieving a 'collection' of walks with some common thread running through them may hold a certain attraction for you. As Jenny Walters wrote in *Country Walking* magazine (February 2009 edition), each of the county summits is 'the roof of its kingdom, which means an Everest-sized chunk of satisfaction at standing taller than everyone else'. If there's an anorak in you struggling to get out, look no further than what lies beneath – there's every chance you'll get addicted.

For all the reasons given above, I wanted this to be more than just a guide book – you can get directions easily enough by pressing a few buttons on your computer. I'm keen that you should share with me the frequent exhilaration, the occasional frustration, and the determination and single-mindedness that goes with a quest of this nature – and, when you come down off the top of your last county high point and sit in a cafe slurping your tea and polishing off a slab of celebratory cake, think what a great journey it's been. Computers can't get inside any of that.

Having sold you the idea of getting started, we next need to identify what the counties are. Historically, England was divided into thirty-nine counties, each with their own county council. As a result of local government reorganisation from 1974 onwards, the picture has changed considerably; what we now effectively have are forty-seven counties; some have lost their county councils and now enjoy only ceremonial status, there being a number of different authorities providing local government within their boundaries. It's to be hoped, however, that wherever you live you will be able to identify your own county, and derive pleasure and satisfaction from reaching its peak.

There have been numerous changes to county borders over the years, so I have identified the highest ground in each county as it is at the time of writing. This means, for instance, that I have identified the highest point in Lancashire as either Gragareth or Green Hill (previously its highest point was the Old Man of Coniston, but this is now part of Cumbria) and North Yorkshire as Whernside (previously its highest point was Mickle Fell, but this is now part of and indeed the highest point in County Durham).

When you reach one of these high points, you may see some nearby ground which appears to be higher than the designated high point. This is because in each case the officially designated 'high point' is the highest natural ground in that county. It does not take into account artificial constructions such as buildings, earthworks or railway/reservoir embankments, which have been added by man over the centuries. I have made one concession, and one only, to a man-made construction, and that is Nottinghamshire. The man-made green mound in Silverhill Wood in this county provides a massively better view and more rewarding walk than the official high point a few miles away, and it is branded and signposted as the 'highest point'; it offends against common sense to ignore it. The walk in Nottinghamshire incorporates visits to both the natural and artificial highest points.

It should also be pointed out that some of the high points are on private land with no public right of access. The highest point in Kent is in the grounds of a private residence, and some other high points, namely those of the Isle of Wight, West Midlands, Warwickshire, Northamptonshire, Rutland, Cambridgeshire, Berkshire, Hampshire, Wiltshire, Lincolnshire and Tyne & Wear, are on land with no public right of way enabling access to the points concerned.

If you wish to access any high points that are not on either public access land or on public rights of way, the safest course is to seek permission from the landowner concerned. I recognise that this may be impracticable, in which case you will have to decide whether you wish to take the risk or content yourself with viewing the high point, to quote Bette Midler, 'from a distance'. You may have no choice but to do the latter where the summit point is physically inaccessible – those of the East Riding of Yorkshire and the West Midlands being two such examples. But if you do take the risk, you lay yourself open to being challenged for trespassing, which may be a criminal offence in certain circumstances – and neither my publisher nor I can accept responsibility for the consequences. Note that permission is routinely required to access the highest point of County Durham, and there are some restrictions on access to the summit of Devon due to military firing, and that of Leicestershire because of blasting. Further details are contained in the relevant texts.

Many of the high points are marked by Ordnance Survey triangulation points: stone pillars which were constructed as a means of facilitating the mapping of Great Britain. For convenience I have in the descriptions that follow referred to them by their traditional abbreviation 'trig points'.

The walks have been arranged throughout the book in height order, starting with the lowest high point and ending with the highest; some walks incorporate two high points. Each walk begins with a heading showing the name of the county high point(s) covered in it, with heights in metres and feet, and a full OS grid reference, then a preamble as follows:

1. **The approximate length of the walk in miles.** An inexperienced walker should allow at least one hour for every 2 miles walked. More experienced walkers will be aware of their capabilities. Note that in especially hilly country any walker's average walking speed will decrease significantly.

2. **The start and finish points of the walk.** Wherever possible, these will be served by public transport. I am anxious to promote the use of public transport rather than private vehicles, for obvious environmental reasons, but I have to be realistic and accept that for some walks, public transport access will be impracticable. This will be made clear in the relevant walk headings and descriptions.

3. **Public transport information.** This is intended to provide a brief summary of rail lines and bus routes serving the start and finish points of the walk, but you will need to enquire before you travel in order to ascertain information on services and times. Be aware that information on some websites may be out of date and it may be best to phone rather than simply rely on the Internet.

4. **Refreshment availability.** The abbreviations P, C and S are used. P denotes pub or pubs, C denotes cafe or cafes, and S denotes shop or shops. Please note that while the information given was accurate at the time of writing, things can and do change. You should never rely on a given establishment being open at any given time and if the availability of a pub, shop or cafe is a significant factor in planning your walk, you should check its opening times in advance.

5. **Difficulty rating.** These are split into easy, moderate, strenuous or severe. Walks described as easy or moderate require no special equipment (although if rain is forecast, you should have some waterproofs) and the shorter, easy walks will be ideal for inexperienced walkers and/or families with children. However, a number of the walks are extremely tough. Any walk described as strenuous or severe, whether in full or in part, should not be undertaken

by inexperienced walkers; all walkers attempting them will require decent boots, adequate supplies (refreshment opportunities en route may be limited or non-existent), proper mapping, compass or GPS navigational device, mobile phone and, if rain is likely, weatherproof gear. On a number of the walks described, there are some very stiff climbs and drops, and it is essential to be both careful and patient when ascending or descending steep rocky ground, and to allow more time than you think you'll need. Many avoidable accidents happen through carelessness caused by rushing or tiredness, often towards the end of the day. Don't put yourself at risk.

6. **Rating.** This consists of a one- to five-star assessment of the walk as a whole. I appreciate how subjective this is and, while I've tried not to be prejudiced too much by the conditions or my own state of mind as I was doing the walks myself, I acknowledge my ratings may not be agreed by everyone. My star rating is as follows:

- 1 star * – a pleasant and undemanding walk.

- 2 stars ** – a reasonably enjoyable walk with some features of interest.

- 3 stars *** – a generally enjoyable and rewarding walk.

- 4 stars **** – a really enjoyable and satisfying walk with lovely scenery, great views and many features of interest.

- 5 stars ***** – an exceptionally good walk with spectacular and beautiful scenery; if the weather is right, it will rank among the best of all walking experiences in England.

On occasion, the route directions will involve making a detour and then returning to a particular location to continue with your end-to-end walk. Where this happens, a number e.g. **1** will be inserted against the start and finish point of the detour.

It just remains for me to say, happy county high point bagging!

David Bathurst
Chichester, West Sussex

Norfolk

Beacon Hill (Roman Camp) – 105 metres / 346 feet – TG 183414

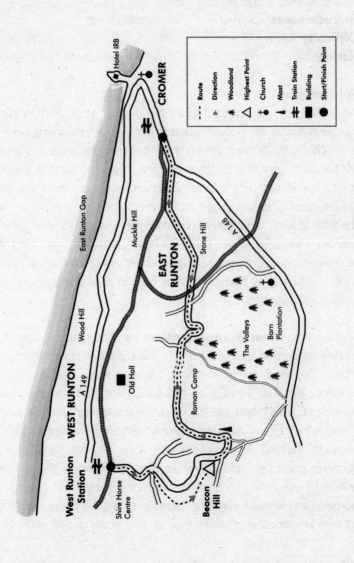

Length: 3½ miles
Start: West Runton station
Finish: Cromer
Public transport: Regular trains serving West Runton and Cromer on the Norwich–Sheringham line
Refreshments: Cromer (P, C, S); none en route
Difficulty: Easy
Rating: **

Pole position

Put it this way: you needn't blow the dust off your crampons or visit your doctor for altitude sickness pills before embarking on this one. This is the lowest county high point in the book and gives itself up with very little struggle. Not that I was complaining hugely, having spent most of the previous seven hours on the train, and very aware I'd be spending most of the following seven hours on the train as well; hoping that, unlike on the way up, the seat which had been allocated to me somewhere in cyberspace was not two seats away from someone with an intrusively loud iPod, while every other carriage was quieter than a Trappist monastery during an outbreak of laryngitis.

Starting from **West Runton station**, join the road crossing the railway line immediately to the west of the station and follow the road inland. The road kinks to the right, then to the left, and very soon reaches a junction, with Calves Well Lane going off to the right. Turn right into Calves Well Lane, taking care not to be sidetracked along Renwick Park East; Calves Well Lane is the track heading off at right-angles to the road. As the lane shortly veers very sharply right, you continue straight on uphill along a narrow sandy track. You've now entered the wooded area known as West Runton Heath, which is home to an extensive variety of birds, including the green and great spotted woodpecker, great tit, blue tit, coal tit, robin and wren. You may also see butterflies such as green hairstreak, speckled wood, red admiral, grayling and gatekeeper, and you should look out too for adders, common lizards and slow-worms.

Shortly, you reach a junction of paths with a pictorial sign indicating no cycling or horses; turn left here and proceed on a clear undulating path, keeping the houses to the left and good views to the sea beyond. You drop down to a further 'no cycling/horses' sign and reach a wooden post with arrows indicating Route 16 straight ahead, and Route 1 to the right. Immediately before this wooden post, turn right onto a path which goes uphill through the trees, quite steeply in one or two places, and arrives at a grassy clearing with a flagpole in the middle. The flagpole marks the summit of Norfolk. My GPS device suggested a height of around 355 feet compared with the 'official' height of 345 feet; whatever it is, it's not going to have you reaching desperately for your oxygen mask.

As well as being the highest point in Norfolk, it's also the climax of the Cromer Ridge, a ridge of glacial moraines near the coast. This area is known as **Roman Camp**, although no evidence of Roman occupation has been found here. As long ago as 1329 money was being paid to maintain a beacon hereabouts, which would have been lit at the time of the Spanish Armada, and during the Napoleonic Wars a signal station was built on the site. The views are restricted, but you can clearly look out to sea; going north from here, amazingly, there is actually no land between here and the North Pole!

From the flagpole, go on across the grass to a driveway and turn left onto it, you are now on the **Peddars Way & Norfolk Coast Path National Trail**, which you will remain on for the rest of your walk. This is one of the easier National Trails, wending its way for just over 90 miles from Knettishall near Thetford to end its journey at Cromer, as you will be doing. Go forward to a junction with a road, crossing straight over and almost immediately bearing left as signed along a track through the woods, downhill. This is also an approach road for a large campsite, so don't be surprised to share the road with a posse of cars and camper vans. Just to the right of the entrance to the campsite, carry on along an obvious path which enters open country. You reach an area of rough grass, on the other side of which is a crossing track, which you go straight over – the signpost is concealed here and you won't see it until the last minute – and continue along Cross Lane. You soon negotiate a sharp left-hand bend, then a sharp right-hand bend, going forward to cross a metalled road and pass under a brick-arched railway bridge. Beyond it, you follow a clear track eastwards, veering north-eastwards and going forward to reach another metalled road. Bear right onto this road and arrive at a busier road, turning left here to follow it to **Cromer station** which is on the left. If you wish to visit the centre of Cromer, just carry on down the road.

Cromer has been a popular resort since the end of the nineteenth century when the railway arrived; its church tower at 160 feet (49 metres) is the highest parish church tower in Norfolk. During World War Two it was a front-line lifeboat station which saw 450 people rescued, and Henry Blogg, Britain's best-known and much-decorated lifeboatman, was the coxswain here for more than fifty years. Fishing continues as it did before the arrival of the tourists, and Cromer is particularly famous for its crabs; the first edition of the official Ordnance Survey guide to the Peddars Way & Norfolk Coast Path suggested that the conquest of the route might be celebrated with a crab sandwich. Being short on time before the start of my seven-hour return journey, my more modest 3½-mile walk had to be celebrated with two bananas from the self-checkout at Morrisons next to the station, costing me 38p. And paid for – having pressed one button too many by mistake – by debit card.

Suffolk

Great Wood – 128 metres / 420 feet – TL 786558

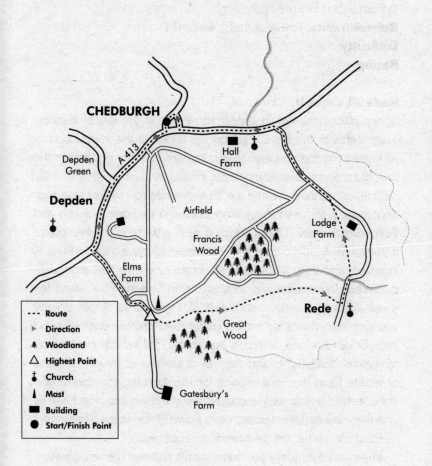

Length: 5 miles
Start and finish: Marquis Cornwallis pub, Chedburgh, near Bury St Edmunds
Public transport: Regular buses serving Chedburgh on the Bury St Edmunds–Haverhill route
Refreshments: Chedburgh (P); Rede (P)
Difficulty: Easy
Rating: **

Rede all about it

At first glance this would appear to be one of the less demanding assignments in this book. Not only is it one of the lowest county high points in the country, as you can tell from its position in the text, but the walk itself is very easy; in fact, although a 5-mile circular ramble is described, it can easily be shortened to a simple 'out-and-back' walk with minimal aggravation caused to existing blisters and ingrowing toenails. The problem is getting there in the first place. If you're using public transport you could take the train to Bury St Edmunds and then a bus to Chedburgh, or a train to Cambridge, then a bus to Haverhill and another bus to Chedburgh. Cambridge is certainly more central, so unless you live in East Anglia already you may find the latter option preferable. That is, until you find yourself on bus one, which is then halted for twenty minutes by temporary traffic lights and then by a phalanx of travellers, none of whom have the right money for the journey; the connection at Haverhill for bus two is consequently missed and you have to wait fifty-nine minutes for the next. I didn't have these problems; I cheated and cycled the 14 miles from Sudbury.

When you eventually get there, you'll find the scenery pleasant rather than spectacular. Once you've left the main road, however, there is a real sense of peace and surprising remoteness, even though the big towns of Bury St Edmunds, Colchester and Chelmsford aren't far away. Everything is green, which may disappoint if you yearn for the heather moorland of Kinder Scout or Dartmoor, but it's rural, it's unspoilt and it has its own special charm. If you have access to a bike, I would certainly recommend you do what I did and incorporate this walk into a day's cycling exploration of Suffolk's villages, with churches which seem cathedral-like in size compared with the often modest size of the villages themselves, and colour-washed cottages with extravagant gables, exposed timbers, thatched roofs and decorative plasterwork, known as pargeting. The picture-postcard villages of Long Melford, Clare and Cavendish are close by, and Sudbury makes an ideal starting and finishing point, with its railway station and excellent range of independent cafes and shops. (Whisper it softly so the locals won't hear, but if you don't find what you want there, there's a spanking new Waitrose five minutes from the station.)

Assuming you've come by bus and are starting from the bus shelter at **Chedburgh**, near the **Marquis Cornwallis pub**, turn left out of the bus shelter, make your way to the immediately adjacent main **A143** and turn right to follow it. If you want a drink at the pub before starting, turn right out of the bus shelter, along to the T-junction, turn left to arrive at the pub and beyond the pub follow the road to the A143, turning right. You then have a frankly pretty uninspiring walk beside the busy A143 for just under a mile, although there is a pavement initially. Relief arrives with a left turn along the no-through-road-signed **Elms Farm** – and you follow this road for a little over a quarter of a mile to the farm. Immediately beyond the farm buildings the road kinks left. The highest point in Suffolk is in the field immediately to the right just beyond the left kink; to enter the field you may need to continue to just short of the mast you see ahead, and then hop up the bank to access the field. The OS map suggests that the magical 420 feet (128 metres) highest point is actually on the road, but the field is just that bit higher. The reality, as you will see, is that you're on a plateau, with no ground

23

around you that is noticeably higher than any other. The field gives the best views southwards, across miles of delightful rolling Suffolk countryside dotted with little villages and, as I've said above, there is a great sense of peace and remoteness.

If you were pushed for time, you could simply retrace your steps from here, following the road back past Elms Farm to the A143 and then turning right. Rather than slog all the way back to Chedburgh, you may be able to pick up a bus back to Bury St Edmunds or Haverhill from beside the road coming in from Depden in just under half a mile up the A143 – there's a bus stop and timetable – otherwise, just keep on to Chedburgh. But if you want to make this a circular walk, carry on along the no through road as far as the right bend, with the mast immediately in front of you. Then veer right with the road very briefly, and just before the sign indicating the road has become a footpath, turn left along a concrete way which passes just to the right of the mast, veers right and reaches a junction with a wider concrete way. Turn left onto this wider way, aiming for the right-hand top end of it, and you'll see a signed footpath going straight on ahead, with a reservoir to the right. Possibly its banks may put it on a par with or even higher than the highest point, but as it's an artificial construction it doesn't count!

Keep along the path, which shortly reaches a field with a sign cautioning you to keep to the bridleway. Follow the left-hand field edge round until you reach the near corner of the woodland ahead (**Great Wood**) where there's a signed footpath junction; you need to take the left-hand yellow-signed footpath, not the blue-arrowed bridleway. You at once pass over a wooden plank bridge, then bear right along the north side of Great Wood. Continue briefly in the same direction along the right-hand field edge beyond the wood, then in obedience to the path sign, veer left and strike out across the field, looking back for a good view of Great Wood. It has to be said that despite its name, the wood is certainly not large. At the end of the field, proceed as signed through a small area of trees, then through a field near the right-hand edge, heading eastwards. This could be rather squelchy in wet weather. Continue into the next field following the right-hand field edge; this is a particularly attractive part of your walk, in lovely tranquil Suffolk scenery. Now you look out for and take a signed path to the right which, beyond the vegetation, bears left and continues eastwards following a left-hand field edge. You reach a hedge and take the path along the left side of it – right-hand field edge – and now veering very slightly south-eastwards, go forward onto a clearer path and then the metalled Church Close to reach a T-junction with the Rede–Chedburgh road. You are now on the edge of **Rede** village. To continue the circular walk, you turn left onto the Rede–Chedburgh road but I recommend you turn right and then immediately left past two fine colour-washed cottages to visit Rede church. (The centre of the village, including a pub at the time of writing, lies just round a sharp bend beyond the turning off to the church.) The church dates from about 1170 and the tower was added in the fourteenth century. It is unremarkable but very peaceful inside; note the well-carved misericord-type seats at the east end of the choir stalls and the painted organ pipes. The local guide says the organ was dismantled and restored in 2009 by 'Messrs Boggis of Diss'. They've done a fine job.

Whether you took the detour or not, you now follow the Rede–Chedburgh road downhill, a little east of north, to a sharp right-hand bend just beyond a bridge. Leave the road here and join a signed footpath, taking exactly the direction shown across the field, just west of north, aiming for the bottom left corner of a horse paddock, indicated by some exposed fencing in the field boundary (if you're unhappy crossing the field, follow the right-hand field edge round to reach the same point). Continue just west of north immediately alongside the paddock, keeping the hedge to the left and **Lodge Farm** beyond the paddock to the right; then at the far left corner of the paddock veer round to the right with the paddockside path and shortly reach a stile in the hedge to the left. Cross the stile and then negotiate a series of stiles over the field ahead to arrive back at the Rede–Chedburgh road. Turn left to follow it back to the A143 and turn left again to follow this road past Chedburgh church and some industrial works to arrive at the junction with the road leading to the bus shelter. It's a pretty tame end to what has been an attractive walk. The Marquis Cornwallis pub is reached by walking past the bus shelter then turning left at the T-junction just beyond it; the pub is a short way along on the right-hand side. Then it's back to the serious business of keeping local bus companies solvent.

Greater London (Inner)

Hampstead Heath – 134 metres / 440 feet – TQ 263865

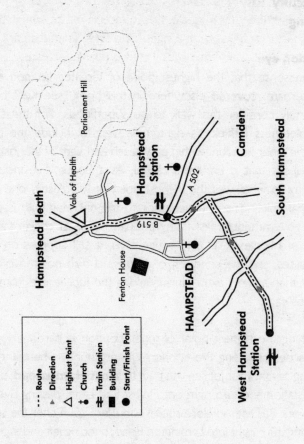

Parliament Hill

Vale of Health

Hampstead Heath

Hampstead Station

Camden

South Hampstead

A 502

B 519

Fenton House

HAMPSTEAD

West Hampstead Station

Legend

--- Route
▲ Direction
△ Highest Point
✝ Church
⇥ Train Station
■ Building
● Start/Finish Point

Length: 2 miles
Start: West Hampstead station (Jubilee line)
Finish: Hampstead station (Northern line)
Public transport: Regular Jubilee line trains serving West Hampstead; regular Northern line trains serving Hampstead
Refreshments: Hampstead (P, C, S)
Difficulty: Easy
Rating: **

London eye

In the sense that the highest point of Greater London is near Westerham, covered elsewhere in this book (see Kent below), you may consider this walk to be superfluous. For the sake of completeness I think it's right, however, to include the highest point in inner London, within easy reach and sight of the vast urban metropolis that is England's capital. As a bonus, I've included a journey to what was the highest point of Middlesex, one of the 'original' thirty-nine counties prior to the tinkering with England's local government areas. Many people, not least cricket fans, still think of Middlesex as very much alive, it still appears on postal addresses, and the conquest of its original high point involves no more than a short extra journey along the Jubilee line from West Hampstead.

Reaching the highest point of inner London is hardly a logistical headache, providing the London Underground is behaving itself. Having caught your Jubilee line train to **West Hampstead**, exit the tube station and turn right onto West End Lane, passing over two Network Rail lines in close succession. Very soon after the second crossing, turn right into Lymington Road, bending left and ascending to Finchley Road; cross more or less straight over into Arkwright Road, climbing to a T-junction with Fitzjohn's Avenue; bear left and go straight on to Hampstead's main street. **Hampstead** was no more than a country village until the eighteenth century, when the discovery of a mineral spring turned it into a resort of high society. It boasts some magnificent Regency architecture, although its oldest house, a beautiful brick mansion called Fenton House, dates back to the late seventeenth century. Residents of Hampstead have included John Constable, John Keats, Lord Byron, H. G. Wells, Sigmund Freud, Michael Foot, Glenda Jackson and Enid Blyton.

Walk up the main street, continuing on uphill over a crossroads, immediately beyond which is another road junction with a pond in the middle, White Stone Walk coming in from the left and the **B519** Spaniards Road going off to the right. As it does so, there's an obelisk, which marks the highest point of inner London. Following the B519 away from the obelisk, and maintaining height, you have **Hampstead Heath** immediately to your right, with fantastic views beyond to the City of London, including the highly distinctive 'Gherkin'. You may wish to enjoy a walk on the Heath before returning to the centre of Hampstead. The Heath is about 700 acres and, with its sandy hills, secluded valleys and broad stretches of grass, it is like a giant recreation ground for Londoners; arguably its greatest building is Kenwood House, a fine Georgian mansion with a magnificent art collection.

Then it's back to Hampstead, where Northern line trains can whisk you back into central London. Of course, you may feel you've earned some refreshment and might want to relax in a pavement cafe, reflecting, as you sip your iced tea and nibble on your choux pastry, on the wealth of authors, politicians, scholars and artists who have sat on this very spot and left a timeless legacy of genius that still hangs almost tangibly in the refined air of this corner of the metropolis.

If you want to follow this walk up with a trip to the former summit of Middlesex, you need to make your way to West Hampstead station and catch a Jubilee line train to its terminus at **Stanmore**.

Emerge from the Underground station and turn left onto the A410 London Road, in a few hundred yards reaching a crossroads with the A4140 going away to the left and Dennis Lane to the right. Bear right up Dennis Lane – it's a bit of a slog, but the road isn't too busy – to a T-junction at the top. Turn right onto Wood Lane, then opposite an Islamic centre turn shortly left into Warren Lane.

Follow Warren Lane, looking out carefully on the right after a few hundred yards for a signed footpath going off onto **Stanmore Common**. It's easily identified as it advertises the Bentley Priory Circular Walk (BPCW). Stanmore Common hosts a remarkable variety of plants, and as you walk you should look out for the heath spotted-orchid, marsh pennywort, marsh speedwell, St John's wort and Devil's-bit scabious, while insects include the jewel beetle and a number of rare crane flies. Follow the path, shortly taking the left fork and going forward to a metalled crossing track; go straight over and fork immediately left, passing through pleasant woodland, to enter a parking area. Proceed directly across the parking area almost to the far end, but just before the end bear right onto the signed BPCW path, following the BPCW discs carefully to arrive at the A4140. Turn right and follow the road as far as a crossroads junction with the A409 at Bushey Heath. During the 1930s the London Underground planned an extension of the Northern line to this point, which never materialised – and it would certainly have shortened this walk had it gone through. The crossroads junction is the highest point in Middlesex and, as if to mark this, there's a house called 'the Alpine' on the crossing. But don't be too disappointed if you fail to spot any snow-covered ski slopes or tail-wagging St Bernard dogs bearing liberal supplies of warming brandy.

Turn left to follow the A409 Common Road for a little more than a quarter of a mile, getting to within sight of a sign advertising a left bend in the road. However, before reaching the sign, look out for and turn left onto the signed **London Loop** path. The London Loop is to walkers what the M25 is to motorists, albeit with fewer traffic cones, describing a 150-mile green ring route around London via Essex, Hertfordshire, Buckinghamshire and Surrey. Just here, it's a very clear concrete path which proceeds through attractive common land, the securely fenced Bentley Priory to your left. Bentley Priory, originally built in 1766, was acquired by the RAF in 1926; it was a non-flying RAF station and was the HQ of Fighter Command during the Battle of Britain. It was only in May 2008 that the RAF vacated it, but the secure fencing remains. Follow the concrete path for just over half a mile, through what is the **Bentley Priory Nature Reserve**, a patchwork of woodland and open space. It is extremely rich in grasses, wild flowers including the greater burnet-saxifrage, betony and harebell, and birds which include the garden warbler, chiffchaff, willow warbler, siskin, redwing and fieldfare.

At the end of the concrete path you reach a T-junction of paths with a clear green signpost; turn right here to follow a path downhill through the trees, and past a field where cattle graze. Go forward through a gate into Old Lodge Way, following this road to a T-junction with Church Road. Turn left to enter and pass through the pleasant village of Stanmore, with its pretty church, soon going over the Dennis Lane/A4140 crossroads and continuing back to Stanmore station. Probably then wondering whether the money, well, some of the money, London Transport has extracted from you to make the journey would have been better spent on the complete DVD collection of Julia Bradbury Wainwright Walks you happened to see in your Oxfam shop yesterday lunchtime.

Cambridgeshire and Essex

Great Chishill – 146 metres / 480 feet – TL 427386
Chrishall Common – 147 metres / 482 feet – TL 443362

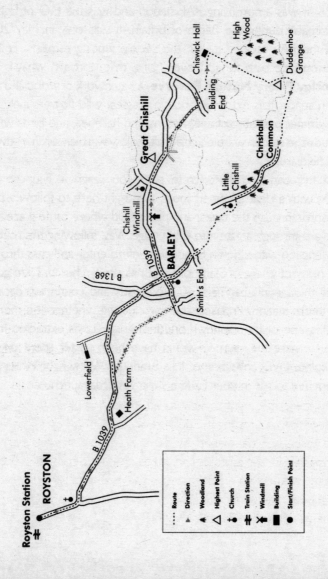

Length: 13 miles
Start: Barley
Finish: Royston station
Public transport: Regular trains serving Royston on the London–Cambridge line; regular but very infrequent buses serving Barley on the Royston–Hertford route; very infrequent buses serving Great Chishill on the Royston–Chrishall route
Refreshments: Royston (P, C, S); Barley (P, S)
Difficulty: Moderate
Rating: ***

Lowbrow entertainment

Despite the fact that you'll bag two county high points that are less than 3 miles apart, I have to say it's unlikely you will set about this walk, through two of the flattest counties in England, with anything approaching red-blooded enthusiasm. Cambridgeshire now incorporates the old county of Huntingdonshire, but that contains no ground higher than was in Cambridgeshire before. Indeed I spent one Saturday seeking out the highest ground in the old county of Huntingdonshire; the high point was described in *Country Walking* magazine as 'field near Covington'. It is acknowledged to be by no means certain where this highest point actually is, and it was never going to be any more than a paltry 260 feet (80 metres) high; when I did get to what I believed to be these dizzy heights, I was challenged by a peculiarly irate young man who, despite my backpack, map and camera, clearly saw my minor deviation from the public right of way as an arrestable offence. My eager anticipation of sampling the delights of present-day Cambridgeshire and Essex was dampened by the cancellation of the train I had earmarked for the journey, and the day was then completely ruined by my overhearing a passenger on the next train announce to his neighbour the solution to the fifteen-letter anagram clue in my hitherto untouched *Times* crossword puzzle.

But this is actually a really enjoyable, as well as a moderately easy, walk. Although the countryside is unremarkable, its flat nature means that from such rises that there are, the views are generally quite extensive and there are some delightful buildings, particularly at **Barley**, your starting point, and Chiswick Hall.

Although your walk starts from the village of Barley, it is likely you'll be arriving by train from Royston. Walk up the slip road from **Royston station** forecourt, turning right to follow the road into the town centre, and keep straight on into the main precinct. (Precisely the same walk, incidentally, as that undertaken by Marcus and Ellie in Nick Hornby's About A Boy, just before Ellie uses her boot to smash a window containing a Kurt Cobain poster.) To reach the bus station, with the possibility of buses to Barley and Great Chishill, go straight up the narrow shopping street (keeping the Natwest building on the right), to the top end, and cross the road to reach the bus station. If buses are unavailable, or you want to walk it all – and as it is all road walking via Barley to Great Chishill windmill, I suggest you probably will not – turn left halfway up the narrow street into Angel Pavement, a covered shopping mall. Emerging from it, turn right to pass the market area and walk up to the T-junction with **Market Hill**. Cross over Market Hill and turn left, then at the T-junction at the end cross to the far side, turn right and follow the pavement round to the left, taking the signed **B1039** Barley road. Follow this road all the way to Barley, a distance of some 3 miles on top of the 13 miles required by the walk described below. I told you it wasn't a great idea.

Barley is a delightful village, getting its name not from the crop but, it's believed, from 'Beranlei', describing a Saxon lord's clearing in woodland. The village has a number of interesting buildings, and if you've walked all the way from Royston you'll have deserved a rest and a chance to enjoy them. They include a church, which has retained its Norman chancel arch; the Town House opposite the church which was built in about 1530 and now serves as the village hall; the Old Forge which was used to shoe horses but which latterly has been used to repair veteran cars; and the seventeenth-century cage and lock-up next to the war memorial, built to deter local criminals.

Your walk proper starts at the **junction of the B1368 and B1039** in the centre of Barley. From this junction head south-eastwards on the B1039 Saffron Walden road, soon veering east and following the B1039 as far as the splendid **Great Chishill windmill**. The first authentic record of a mill here appears in 1592; the structure you see today was acquired by the county council in the 1960s and you may be lucky enough to find it open when you visit.

To continue your walk, turn right immediately beyond the mill onto a signed path, which shortly veers left to proceed gently uphill along a left-hand field edge, clearly defined throughout. At the top you reach a T-junction of paths, and turn left to walk down to the road, bearing right here to enter and pass through the village of **Great Chishill**. You pass the church – the original village church was built in 1136 but it collapsed and was subsequently rebuilt – and continue along the main road, rising gently. When I passed through the village my impression was of a rather straggly, unremarkable place but at one time it supported a baker, a butcher, a wheelwright, a bricklayer and a dressmaker. In September 1983 two local men set a world record by producing loaves of bread from the wheat in a field in just under forty-one minutes!

On reaching the top of the rise you pass a thatched cottage to the left and, just beyond, you pass a driveway guarded by stone lions; immediately beyond that, you bear left along a rough track to reach what looks like a substation. Bear right just before the locked entrance gate to follow the perimeter fence of the substation round and you are, in fact, now on the highest ground in Cambridgeshire. It's also private ground, so in theory you should acquire permission to walk from here to the locked entrance gate. The views across the rather flat Cambridgeshire countryside are certainly pleasant but hardly spectacular. Return to the road, turn left to continue along it, and shortly reach a left bend, just beyond which you turn right onto a signed path. Follow it in the direction shown, aiming for and proceeding immediately to the right of a pond guarded by vegetation and, keeping this to your left, follow the left-hand field edge, going on beyond the pond in the same direction, and dropping down to reach a track.

Keeping in the same direction, you join the track and go gently downhill to reach a road, now leaving Cambridgeshire and entering Essex. Turn left to follow the road for a couple of hundred yards, passing the lovely pinkwashed and thatched Drury Cottage. The road bends a little left and, as it does, turn right as indicated by a clear footpath sign at a house called the Well, going forward as signed to a gate; beyond the gate you follow the left-hand side of a meadow on a clear green path. After 150 yards or so, turn left onto an unsigned path which goes forward through some bushes to a footbridge and path junction. Go straight over and walk uphill through the field, then drop gently to enter another field, bearing left to follow the left-hand field edge round and enjoying lovely views to the fine Chrishall church. You pass to the right of **Chiswick Hall**, a Grade II listed building, timber-framed and plastered. It was built in approximately 1600 by Sir John James in a park of 300 acres, and was later converted into a farmhouse.

Immediately beyond Chiswick Hall you reach a path junction. Turn right and follow a delightful green path, rising steadily and going more or less in a straight line across **Chrishall Common**, with areas of woodland across the fields to the left. In just over half a mile your clear path is joined by a strip of woodland to the right; follow immediately parallel with and to the left of this strip to reach a footpath sign showing an arrow pointing half-left – this is the highest point in Essex. Disappointingly, but not uniquely, this one is wholly undistinguished. You might almost feel moved to do as I did and try looking for a particular hump or bump in the nearby woodland, setting one distinct spot above all the rest, even if it can't provide that sweeping panorama of the county you might have longed for, from the scenic shores of the River Blackwater and the abundance of wildlife within its creeks and estuaries, to sightings of the lesser-spotted 7.49 Shenfield to Liverpool Street.

Moving on, pass through a narrow strip of woodland in obedience to the arrow, enjoying views across the pastures of north Essex, which are again attractive rather than stunning. Beyond this, bear left to follow the winding left-hand field edge and drop gently to soon arrive at a very obvious path junction sign with the church of Langley within sight ahead. Turn right at this sign to follow a good clear path just north of west, which gently rises then falls to arrive at a narrow road. Join the road, keeping the same direction, and follow it north-westwards for about a mile to reach the charming hamlet of **Little Chishill**. The church of St Nicholas here is thought to date back to the twelfth century – the first recorded vicar was John Martyn in 1333.

When you reach the church, turn left to follow the signed path through the churchyard, passing the church door (or, if you feel you've deserved a rest and it's unlocked, popping in) and going forward to a stile at the top end of the churchyard.

Cross the stile and walk half-left downhill, aiming just to the left of the road ahead, negotiating two or three further stiles to reach a clear field path striking out north-westwards (left) away from the road. Follow the path, crossing a ditch and climbing steps, then bearing left to follow a narrow field-edge path gently uphill. It's worth pausing as you climb, to look back and enjoy the excellent view back to Little Chishill. Bear left as signed just before a house and its grounds, and at the footpath junction just beyond the grounds turn right; follow the path along the right-hand field edge, then strike out across the field, along what is a very clear green path, to arrive at a track which takes you immediately to a road.

Turn right onto the road, then bear immediately left onto another road, which you follow, gaining lovely views to Great Chishill windmill, arriving at a road junction at the end of Barley's village street. Turn left to follow the street, going forward past the church and a shop to reach a pub and another road junction. Don't turn right onto the signed road to Royston but go straight on, joining the B1368 and soon passing **Smith's End Lane**, which is to the left; just beyond that on your right, immediately before Horseshoe Close and Farm, there's a signed footpath. Bear right to follow this path: a lovely clear track, for over a mile. It's almost a shame to reach the B1039, as that's the end of the path walking, and it only remains for you, on arrival at the road, to turn left to follow it back to Royston.

Having made it back to base camp, with plenty of trains back to London and forward to Cambridge, you can relax and enjoy the town which grew up at the crossroads of the prehistoric Icknield Way and the Roman Ermine Street. James VI had a palace here in the early seventeenth century, and there are some fine Georgian houses and inns. If the name Royston seems familiar you may be thinking of the BBC comedy *The League Of Gentlemen*, where the town was named Royston Vasey. Sorry to disappoint; the town was named after the comedian Roy 'Chubby' Brown, who was born Royston Vasey, and the actual town used was in Derbyshire. I was certainly happy to linger here after what had proved a surprisingly energetic walk, deciding that my available funds were better spent on a coffee and sticky date cookie than on a copy of an alternative cryptic crossword puzzle-carrying newspaper and pair of earplugs.

Lincolnshire

Normanby Top – 168 metres / 551 feet – TF 121964

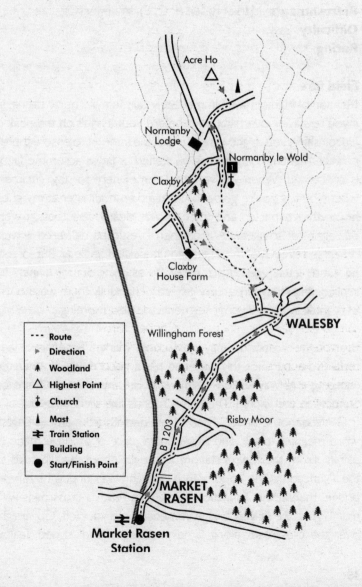

Length: 11 miles
Start and finish: Market Rasen station
Public transport: Regular trains serving Market Rasen on the Newark–Lincoln–Cleethorpes line
Refreshments: Market Rasen (P, C, S); Walesby (C)
Difficulty: Easy
Rating: ***

Field fare

Mention of Market Rasen immediately calls to mind horse racing, so if you're staying overnight here before your assault on the peak of Lincolnshire, you might want to check the Internet to ensure there's no race meeting, or you may be stuffed as far as accommodation is concerned. When you've found somewhere to stay, get there when you say you're going to. I arrived an hour later at my guest house than expected and my host was clearly very cross; I went out again for a takeaway and when I returned delivered a well-rehearsed speech of mortified and unqualified apology. But, oh no, he wasn't letting me off that easily. 'I was going out for dinner,' he replied. 'Had to get in a curry instead.' Thankfully there was no hint of cyanide in my grapefruit segments the next morning.

Even if the hospitality may be lacking, Market Rasen is a very picturesque base for this walk and has a good range of amenities including a railway station – although note there are no trains on Sundays in the winter. The name sounds like something out of a P. G. Wodehouse novel, 'Rasen' here derived from an old English word meaning 'plank' and suggesting a place of a bridge made of planks. From the town's station, turn right down the slip road to the T-junction at the bottom; turn right and walk under the railway bridge, then at the T-junction turn left to reach a crossroads with traffic lights, the railway bridge immediately to your left. Go straight over the crossroads along Jameson Bridge Road, signed Tealby, and follow this road, the **B1203**. After half a mile turn left onto a road signed Walesby. If you wonder why so many places on this walk end in 'by', Lincolnshire was part of the Danelaw, the area of eastern England settled and largely ruled by the Norsemen from the ninth century, and settlements of Scandinavian origin are identifiable by the suffix 'by' on their names. Walesby, for instance, means 'farmstead or village of a man called Valr'; Normanby, which you'll meet later in your walk, means 'farmstead or village of the Northmen or Norwegian Vikings'.

Initially there's a paved path running parallel with the road, but this peters out and you then have a bit of a road slog, although at least the road is quiet and the woodland surroundings pleasant. After 2 miles' walking from the B1203 you reach **Walesby** and pass the church, then take the next left road turning and go straight over the crossroads, walking up a narrow road. In 100 yards or so, just beyond the right-hand bend, turn left along a signed footpath by the house 'Farthings'. Follow the footpath along a right-hand field edge (some maps show it following the other side of the field boundary, but this is not correct) then continue north-westwards over a field, aiming for a little cluster of buildings. Ahead of you is the tall green hill that you'll shortly be scaling. Cross over one track, then almost immediately reach a junction with another; turn right as indicated by a bridleway sign, then in a few yards turn left, as indicated by a bridleway arrow, and cross a little footbridge.

At last your taxi-ing is over as you begin to climb, following a narrow green path uphill along a left-hand field edge. You reach the top of the hill and continue north-westwards on the plateau along an obvious path, with splendid views to the west. In due course you're joined by the **Viking Way** coming in from the left, its logo a black Viking helmet on a yellow background; it runs for 147 miles from Barton-on-Humber to Oakham in Rutland and crosses an area which was occupied by Norse invaders. You cross a metal stile built into a gate, kinking right and then immediately left, then go forward northwards along grass, aiming just left of the beautifully sited church of **Normanby-le-Wold**, the highest church in Lincolnshire. The name reminds you that you're on the edge of the Lincolnshire Wolds. As stated in the description of the walk to the summit of the East Riding of Yorkshire, the wolds are rolling chalk uplands characterised by steep-sided dales, the result of erosion of the chalk; the Lincolnshire Wolds are effectively a geological continuation of the Yorkshire Wolds. Your walk to the summit of Lincolnshire takes you along the western fringe of the Lincolnshire Wolds, and you can contrast your lofty position with the flat fields and lowland villages of the county further west, enjoying grandstand views across huge tracts of Lincolnshire and Humberside.

Join the road which passes just to the left of the much-restored thirteenth-century church and continue along the road past the turning to **Claxby** ◼, going on just west of north along the road to reach a T-junction. Turn right along the road and in about a quarter of a mile you reach a field on your left which contains a radar station. You're now very close to the highest point in Lincolnshire, but to get there you need to go onto private land, and for that you should seek permission or risk being caught trespassing. Field-edge walking is now to dominate for a while. To access the county high point, enter the near corner of this field – there was no difficulty of access at the time of writing – and follow the left-hand field edge, taking care not to damage crops. Go to the far corner of the field and continue straight over into the next field, via a rather half-hearted metal/wooden obstruction. Bear left along the left-hand field edge to reach the triangulation point marking the highest point of Lincolnshire; the views aren't panoramic, but they are extensive to the north and to the west.

Retrace your steps all the way to the Claxby turning ◼ above, and bear right onto the road signed for Claxby. Shortly the ground seems to fall away in front of you and the views ahead are magnificent; for an even better view you could detour onto a signed footpath going off to the right, just before the road begins its downward plunge, but you will need to return to the road. Whether you've made the detour or not, descend steeply to a T-junction, turning left to walk past the village of Claxby. You could divert into the village and visit the church, which is believed to date back to the twelfth century, but I have to say it isn't the prettiest or most photogenic of villages.

Continue south-westwards along the road beyond the village, swinging sharp left, south-eastwards, along Park Road, then where the road swings sharp right you continue along a public byway south-eastwards, heading for **Claxby House Farm**. Just before the farm buildings, turn left along another signed public byway, soon veering right, south-eastwards, along the right-hand edge of **Claxby Wood**, the views improving all the time.

Head uphill, contouring the hillside, then drop down, the path a little less distinct. The Viking Way path comes in from the left; turn right at this path junction and drop down to a gate, then veer left with the path to arrive at another junction of paths. Turn right here to shortly arrive at a road onto which you turn left, entering **Walesby**, and after 150 yards or so, just beyond South View, you turn right onto a signed path pointing to a tearoom. You follow a driveway, then go forward along a grassy path through an overgrown field, then left along another driveway; as you follow this, you'll see the tearoom to your right, which will provide some well-earned refreshment – seasonal opening variations permitting. Just beyond it you reach a T-junction; turn right and follow this road back to the B1203, bearing right again to return in half a mile to Market Rasen – and woe betide you if you're late for supper.

Merseyside

Billinge Hill – 179 metres / 586 feet – SD 525014

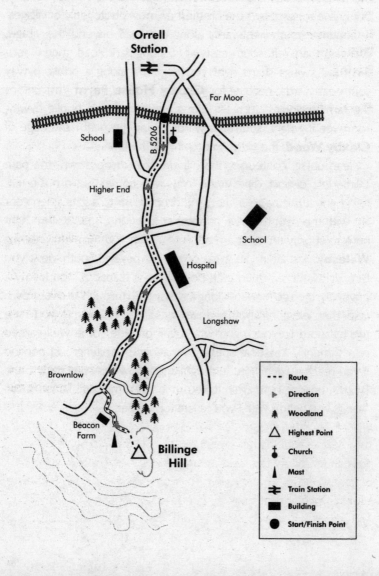

Length: 5 miles. NOTE: Could be shortened to 2½ miles by starting from Crank Road turning
Start and finish: Orrell station or junction of Upholland Road with Crank Road
Public transport: Regular trains serving Orrell on the Manchester–Kirkby line; regular buses serving Orrell and Billinge from St Helens
Refreshments: Billinge (P, C, S)
Difficulty: Easy
Rating: **

Mersey mission

It was local government reorganisation that brought Merseyside into being in 1974, mainly from areas that were previously part of the administrative counties of Lancashire and Cheshire; although the county council was abolished in 1986, Merseyside still exists legally and ceremonially. Contrary to what the name might imply, the region is not simply an urban jungle beside a great river, but incorporates many miles of attractive countryside, albeit hardly elevated enough to have mountaineers quaking in their crampons. This is a nice straightforward walk and certainly one of the easiest of the northern county high points to conquer; for a short walk there's a splendid range of facilities, too, with lots of drinks and sweet treats available.

If you're coming by train, get out at Orrell and having exited the station, turn right over the railway bridge. Immediately beyond the railway bridge turn right onto a footpath – it's very popular with dog walkers so expect some attention from inquisitive canines. The path runs parallel with the railway and ends at the **B5206** St James Road. Turn left to follow this road, passing the Roman Catholic church of St James with its elegant tower, to your left, and then the **Running Horses pub** on the right. St James Road becomes Gantley Road and arrives at a mini-roundabout junction: go straight on here, along

Upholland Road, passing further amenities in the form of a garage with a shop and cafe. A couple of hundred yards up the road you reach Bispham Methodist Church and Crank Road going off to the right beside the church. There is a bus stop here so if you're coming by bus you could start your walk at this point.

Follow Crank Road uphill past the **Holts Arms**; it's not hugely exciting walking, but it's hardly demanding either, and two roadside pubs in barely a mile is certainly good going. The road becomes more rural in character and, in a little under a mile, you pass the attractive whitewashed Beacon Cottage to your left. Now you need to sit up and take notice; ignoring an initial signed path to Billinge Hill to the left, you continue to a point just before a right-hand bend and prominent sign welcoming you to the St Helens district. Here, immediately before the bend, you do turn left onto a lane which soon bends right and passes **Beacon Farm**. Don't continue on past Belvedere Barn but, immediately before this house, veer left and shortly fork right as per the footpath sign. The lane is now a narrower path which leads you to a T-junction with another path. Here you turn left and now your objective comes into view, namely the top of **Billinge Hill** (known locally, apparently, as 'the Lump'), decorated with a honey-coloured square tower and rather more diminutive trig point just behind it.

The path to its summit is very obvious. The tower has perhaps predictably become a target for graffiti artists but this is still a splendid spot; a considerable gain for, it has to be said, not a lot of pain. Your main focus of attention is likely to be the huge urban sprawl of Liverpool and its suburbs, starting with St Helens just below you, but there's plenty of rolling countryside, too, and a lovely open feel. I conquered the summit in the rain and the views were still good; this is indeed a county high point to save for a rainy day.

Having lingered here a while, simply retrace your steps to the road and then bear right to follow it back to the junction with Upholland Road. Then a choice: a bus or return to the station via

Gantley Road, St James Road and the trackside path, with hot and cold drinks on offer at various points. I went for a coffee at the cafe, and was rewarded with a very inexpensive mug of caffeine, a two-day-old copy of the *Daily Star* and a free weather forecast. The latter was, as it turned out, not among the cafe's strong points – they got it completely wrong and the promised persistent rain soon cleared. I wasn't going to ask for my money back though.

Rutland

Cold Overton Park – 197 metres / 646 feet – SK 827085

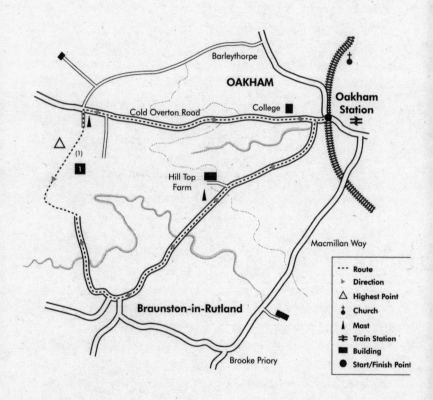

Barleythorpe

OAKHAM

Cold Overton Road

College

Oakham Station

Hill Top Farm

Macmillan Way

Braunston-in-Rutland

Brooke Priory

--- Route
▷ Direction
△ Highest Point
† Church
▲ Mast
⇌ Train Station
■ Building
● Start/Finish Point

Length: 5 miles
Start and finish: Oakham station
Public transport: Regular trains serving Oakham on the Leicester–Peterborough line
Refreshments: Oakham (P, C, S); Braunston-in-Rutland (P)
Difficulty: Easy
Rating: **

County caught

Poor Rutland – does it exist? Until 1974 it certainly did, the darling of trivia buffs everywhere as the smallest of the 'traditional' thirty-nine counties of England, just 147 square miles, until the spoilsports of Whitehall dictated that it be swallowed into Leicestershire. However, it remained a county for ceremonial purposes and, on 1 April 1996 it became a unitary authority – known as Rutland County Council. This means that the correct legal name for the authority is Rutland County Council District Council. One gets this vision of Rutland residents suffering writers' cramp just applying for a reassessment of their non-domestic rate.

Rutland has a proud history: it once supplied iron ore to the Corby steelworks in Northamptonshire; it's home to two RAF bases; there is a dukedom of Rutland (whose family seat is at Belvoir Castle); and Rutland Water, an important nature reserve, is by surface area the biggest man-made lake in Britain and among the biggest in Europe. A circular walk, the Rutland Round, runs for 65 miles, remaining in or on the border throughout. Rutland has even had a sketch show named after it, *Rutland Weekend Television*; starring Eric Idle, it was first broadcast in 1975 and spawned a spoof Beatles-style band called the Rutles! The walk to Rutland's highest point isn't a classic, but logistically it's very easy and, especially round the middle, it is most rewarding, with views across much of the RCCDC's empire.

Emerging from **Oakham station** – there is only one exit – turn right along a road which runs parallel with the railway down to the level crossing. Turn right to go over the crossing and along **Cold Overton Road** which you follow for just under 2 miles uphill, initially past the neat housing on the western outskirts of Oakham and then into more open country. As you reach the top of the rise, you pass a mast to your left and, just beyond that, there's a junction with a minor road going off to the right. Turn left onto a track immediately opposite, keeping the mast to your left. Go straight on, passing through a gate, as signed, onto a path through a large field, close to the right-hand field edge, south-westwards. In 300 yards or so you reach a field boundary and gate **1**. Note that the walk from here to the high point is not on designated rights of way, so technically you should seek permission to undertake it. Pass through the gate and, almost immediately, you'll see another gate in the fence to your right; go through this gate, turn half-right and you'll see the trig point marking the highest point in Rutland on the top of the incline by the field boundary to the right. The views aren't panoramic, but at least they are extensive to the east, across large areas of flat Rutland and Cambridgeshire countryside dotted with farms and villages.

Return to point **1** and now continue south-westwards, keeping the field boundary close to your right, observing the yellow-painted waymarks. The views across Rutland remain extensive; Rutland Water can be observed just east of Oakham. The path, well defined and still going in the same direction, enters a strip of trees and, as you proceed through the trees, look out for a signed path junction, with a path going off to the left. Take the left path here and follow it just south of east, getting closer and closer to the right-hand field boundary. Shortly before reaching the far end of the field, turn right onto a signed path, accessing it through a gate guarded by tall wooden posts on each side; follow this quite narrow path, just east of south, heading downhill. In roughly half a mile you reach a sharp left-hand bend and, having negotiated this bend, you shortly reach a road onto which you turn right to reach the centre of **Braunston-in-Rutland**.

This village, with its lovely old stone cottages and (at the time of writing) two pubs, contains a number of features of interest. All Saints' Church dates back to the twelfth century and has significant remains of medieval wall paintings, while just outside the church is a stone grotesque carving, which is probably an ancient fertility goddess. There is a tiny village green guarded by two splendid cedars and through the village runs a continuation of the River Gwash, which proceeds on to Rutland Water.

It now just remains for you to get back to Oakham, and this couldn't be easier. Backtrack along the village street to the place where you joined it and plough on along the road for 2 miles. Although it's unclassified, it can be quite busy, there's no pavement and sod's law dictates that all the traffic will be moving on the side of the road chosen by you. Initially you face a bit of an uphill slog, but then you drop downhill, getting fine views to Oakham, and arrive at a T-junction with Cold Overton Road. Turn right here to return to the level crossing. Having crossed the tracks, you could simply proceed to the station, which is up to the left, but you may wish to continue straight on to look at the centre of Oakham, the former-county town of Rutland. Its two most interesting features are the Rutland County Museum of rural and agricultural life in Rutland, and the Norman motte-and-bailey castle which, although mostly ruined, still boasts a splendid great hall. There are plenty of small independent shops and places to stay, and you may well want to lodge here for the night after your conquest of the high point in order perhaps to visit Rutland Water the next day. Who knows, in this era of burgeoning cable channels, the day may come when pressing a few buttons on your hotel room digital remote will get you the genuine *Rutland Weekend Television*.

Nottinghamshire

Newtonwood Lane – 204 metres / 669 feet – SK 456606
Silverhill Wood – 218 metres / 716 feet – SK 471622

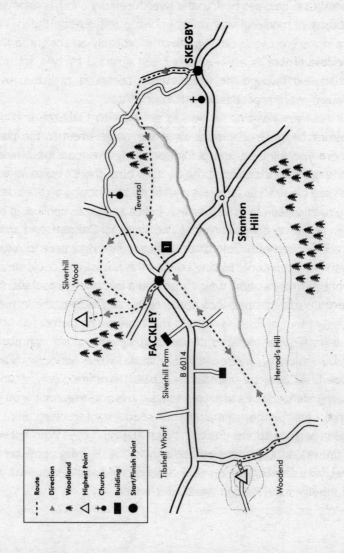

Length: 7 miles
Start and finish: Skegby
Public transport: Regular buses serving Skegby and Fackley from Sutton-in-Ashfield
Refreshments: Skegby (P, S); Fackley (P)
Difficulty: Easy
Rating: ***

Double Notts

So, what is the highest point in Nottinghamshire? The official answer is: a rather unremarkable spot on a hillside up against an anonymous security fence off an anonymous lane near the M1. The much more satisfactory answer is: a superb viewpoint in Silverhill Wood with a very photogenic and poignant sculpture boasting panoramic views, and loftier than the official high point by nearly 50 feet. The trouble is, it's man-made so technically it doesn't count. But it's so close to the official high point, it's so easily reached and so many herald it as the summit of Nottinghamshire that it would be an affront to miss out on it. I would have been very disappointed to have missed it after a long overnight coach journey from London, which was further delayed at Nottingham while police assistance was summoned to facilitate the ejection of a passenger for smoking in the coach toilet.

In fact, the conquest of both the official and unofficial high points in a single half-day expedition is logistically very straightforward. Your best bet is to aim for **Sutton-in-Ashfield**, which has a railway station (albeit a 'parkway' station, inevitably meaning it's an awfully long walk from there to anywhere) and a large number of bus services. Find the one going to **Skegby** and ask the driver to drop you at the **Greyhound pub**; from there, follow the **B6014** Old Road downhill, as the road dips and curves left. At the bottom of the dip you turn right onto a signed railway path, immediately before and parallel to Buttery Lane. Follow the old railway line, part of the line linking Nottingham with Shirebrook, just west of north, soon reaching a railway path fork with different coloured surfaces on each path as they diverge. Take the left fork here which soon goes over Buttery Lane and heads westwards. You're on the site of the old railway line which used to link Mansfield with Alfreton; it boasted three westbound trains a day, and if you missed the 7.17 a.m. train you'd have to wait till 2.28 p.m. for the next. Quicker to walk. In the twenty-first century this is in fact absolutely lovely walking through unspoilt attractive countryside; perhaps I'm biased as I love old railway walking anyway, but to me, seeing it on a cloudless early-July morning, it was perfection.

Continuing along the old line, you pass the sign to the Teversal Trails Visitor Centre, having now walked 1½ miles from Skegby. Shortly beyond the visitor centre you veer left with the railway path, soon crossing the B6014 at **Fackley** ◘ and now heading south-westwards for just over a mile, passing the site of **Teversal station**. The surroundings are peaceful and, surprisingly, delightfully rural; the urban sprawls of Mansfield and Sutton-in-Ashfield, although only a few miles away, seem very distant. Another railway path comes in from the left, and you carry straight on, signed Tibshelf, soon approaching a brick-built arched bridge. Just before it, you turn right up a path signed Woodend; it soon veers left and brings you out onto Chesterfield Road, onto which you turn right, then take the first left into Newtonwood Lane. Turn right at the first stile, half hidden, just a short way up the road on the right, and walk round the left-hand field edge, then alongside the boundary fence with the secure area, just west of north. The official county high point is roughly level with the chapel-like structure in the enclosed area; the fence in fact marks the border between Nottinghamshire and Derbyshire. The views are very disappointing, the plaque which one or two guides suggest is there has been removed and, in short, it's a big anticlimax after the lovely railway walk you've just enjoyed. So let's go and be unofficial.

Retrace your steps back to the bridge crossing of the B6014 at Fackley, indicated by point ■ above, and continue as though going back towards Skegby, but shortly beyond the bridge, you arrive at a signed path junction. Take the fork signed 'The Miner – Highest Point' veering off left, ignoring the path leading back to Skegby. Shortly you take another fork left, again signed 'The Miner – Highest Point,', avoiding the Pleasley turning. You arrive at a pair of lakes, where on the occasion of my visit the signposting was non-existent, but an information board provided the necessary directions; you need to take the left-hand path on the nearside of the left of the two lakes and walk along the edge of **Silverhill Wood**. At the next path junction, actually a crossroads of paths, bear right uphill along a wide track through the woods. Following a brisk climb, you reach the top of the rise and find yourself at the foot of a tall grassy mound to your left. On top of the mound is 'The Miner' – a memorial statue which commemorates the men of the nearby mining communities, and which marks what the authorities are now keen for you to regard as the highest point in Nottinghamshire. The views are quite magnificent, the most rewarding ones being to the west, where the hills of the White Peak, the southern part of the Peak District, are clearly in evidence. However, there is great variety in every direction, rolling countryside contrasting with sprawling villages and towns.

Now retrace your steps to the bottom of the hill but this time go straight on to arrive at Silverhill Lane. Turn left to arrive at Fackley and cross straight over for the **Carnarvon pub**, from where there are regular buses available back to Sutton-in-Ashfield. I was behind time and anxious I might miss my train from Alfreton, but I happened to spot a taxi and the driver not only agreed to carry me, but ended up taking me to another viewpoint near the village of Huthwaite, just south of the official high point and infinitely superior to it, with no extra charge for the detour. If I'd been a few minutes earlier I'd have missed him. So maybe there's something to be said for coach toilet smokers after all.

Northamptonshire

Arbury Hill – 225 metres / 738 feet – SP 540587

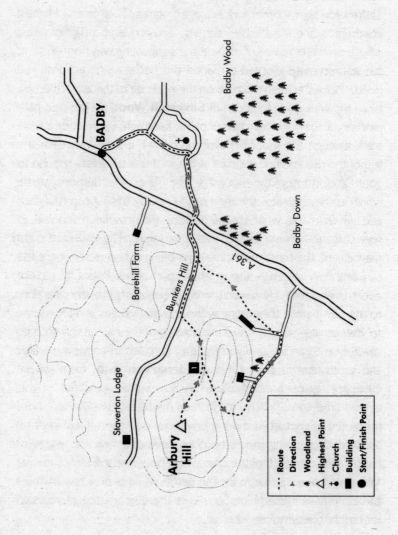

BADBY

BADBY

Badby Wood

Badby Down

A 361

Barehill Farm

Bunkers Hill

Staverton Lodge

Arbury Hill

Route	...
Direction	▲
Woodland	♠
Highest Point	△
Church	✝
Building	■
Start/Finish Point	●

Length: 3 miles
Start and finish: Badby
Public transport: Regular buses serving Badby on the Rugby–Banbury route
Refreshments: Badby (P, C)
Difficulty: Easy
Rating: **

Luncheons and dragons

To be honest, I didn't find this the most spectacular county high point walk I've ever done and, even if you regard Northamptonshire as the jewel in England's crown, I doubt you will either. That said, the village where you start and finish, Badby, is certainly pleasant enough, enjoying an attractive setting, with thick woodland on its south and east sides, and, at the time of writing, ample refreshment opportunities. It's actually regarded by the AA as being interesting enough to feature in its *Book Of British Villages*, a selection of 700 of the most interesting villages in Britain, which appeared (the book, not the villages) in the early 1980s. My first visit to it was in August 1981 as part of my mission, duly accomplished six years later, to explore every one of the villages featured in the book. Relieved that my visits to this – plus 699 other villages from Abbots Bromley in Staffordshire to Zennor in Cornwall – were not enough to render me terminally certifiable, I have to say my return visit to Badby this time was barely less surreal, interrupting a Cotswolds family holiday to motor up from Chipping Campden via the Fosse Way starting at 5.30 a.m.

If you're coming by public transport, the bus stop to alight at is at **Pinfold Green**, at the northern end of the village, and you need to proceed southwards up the main street past the convenient **Windmill Inn**. You could detour left to visit the church of St Mary the Virgin, which dates back to the fourteenth century, and its war memorial window shows St George and St Michael, complete with swords and flaming wings, slaying two dragons. However, to continue your walk, you need to bear right up Bunkers Hill to reach the **A361**; just before the road crossing there was at the time of writing a cafe on the left-hand side, if your Rugby or Banbury breakfast seems rather too long ago. At any rate, you shouldn't need to leave Badby hungry. Cross straight over the A361 onto a very narrow metalled road and follow it, soon passing a footpath turning to the left. Just under half a mile beyond the A361 crossing, look out for a gate on the left-hand side, set back a little from the road, and also a bridleway sign. Follow this bridleway as signed, walking along a clear path on a left-hand field edge and arriving at a gate; go through it and follow a clear path on an embankment, descending gently to reach another gate **1**.

So far, so good, but now you need to leave the right of way and, theoretically, you ought to obtain permission to proceed along the route described below. If you haven't got it, you proceed at your own risk, and while I saw no signs along the lines of 'Trespassers will be eaten' – unlike in Live and Let Die, there aren't too many crocodile farms in the area – being challenged by an irate landowner isn't the best reward for your long bus ride. We'll presume you've got permission, but you've still got to do the walk, and as you proceed from **1**, remember you will need to retrace your steps to this point later. Turn right at **1** to walk along the left-hand field edge, keeping a barbed-wire fence to your left; in 100 yards or so you reach a gap in the fencing and turn left, climbing steeply up the grassy bank. Keep looking to your right as you ascend and, when a post comes into view up to the right, bear right and make for that post.

Once you reach it, you find yourself on the edge of the **Arbury Hill** plateau, and you simply now continue along the delightfully peaceful plateau to its highest point by the edge of the trees, enjoying views which, while not in the Worcestershire Beacon class (the comparison was inevitable as I'd done it three days previously), are still good. When I walked across the plateau there were no physical obstructions but there were posts suggesting the possibility of fencing being erected at some point. It is believed that there was an Iron Age fort on the plateau, the evidence for which is in the form of a square ditch and embankment about 650 feet (200 metres) across.

Now you need to carefully retrace your steps to ■ above and go through the gate, walking along the right-hand field edge to shortly (less than 200 yards) reach another footpath sign where a byway comes in from the left. Turn left to follow this byway, crossing a field and soon reaching a junction with a track going off to the left; turn left to follow this track, shortly passing a pond and then a house. Just beyond the house, turn left along a signed footpath, following the left-hand field edge, then bearing half-right along an obvious path through a corn field. You then need to follow the footpath signposts carefully through horse paddocks; you may engage the attentions of the horse in residence, but if he decides to do to you what he did to me and chase you off his land, be philosophical and, as you up your speed to a brisk 8 mph, think of the extra drinking time back in the Windmill Inn. Thus propelled, you'll shortly find yourself back at the narrow metalled road onto which you turn right to return to the A361, crossing over into **Bunkers Hill** and descending to Badby.

Having completed your walk you may wish to spend some time in the village and its surrounds. It's bordered by Fawsley Park with its Tudor great hall and ruined dower house, formerly the homes of the Knightley family. In the village itself you'll find two greens, with a Gothic-style village hall in the centre of one of them, and, while there is a good deal of modern development, some of the stone cottages date back to the seventeenth century. A youth hostel was housed in one of these old cottages back when I was exploring my 289th AA British Village, and the Youth Hostels Association unusually boasted a property with its very own cottage garden, which as a guest there I could admire, while steaming my Heinz tinned syrup sponge pudding, freshly purchased from the hostel shop. Perhaps I should have counted myself lucky that I wasn't thereby deemed a public nuisance and put to work pruning the hollyhocks.

Isle of Wight

St Boniface Down – 241 metres / 790 feet – SZ 569785

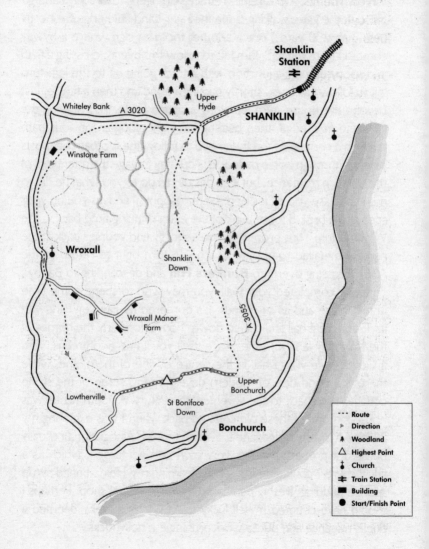

Shanklin Station

SHANKLIN

Upper Hyde

Whiteley Bank   A 3020

Winstone Farm

Wroxall

Shanklin Down

Wroxall Manor Farm

A 3055

Lowtherville

St Boniface Down

Upper Bonchurch

Bonchurch

- - -	Route
▷	Direction
♠	Woodland
△	Highest Point
♱	Church
⇌	Train Station
■	Building
●	Start/Finish Point

Length: 6 miles
Start and finish: Shanklin station
Public transport: Regular trains from Ryde (nearest ferry port to the mainland) to Shanklin
Refreshments: Wroxall (P, S); Shanklin (P, C, S)
Difficulty: Moderate
Rating: ***

On the Wight lines

The Isle of Wight became an island after the end of the last Ice Age, when the rising sea flooded the Solent, separating the island from the mainland; it has actually had a separate county council since 1890, surviving the 1974 reorganisations. Known to the Romans as Vectis, it did not come under full control of the crown till it was sold to Edward I in 1293. The island has some interesting royal connections: it was heavily fortified by Henry VIII, using stone from the monasteries dissolved at his command, and Queen Victoria made Osborne House her summer home for many years. In 1944 the world's first undersea oil pipeline (PLUTO) was laid between the Isle of Wight and France. One other interesting fact about the island is that it is the only place in England with a stable population of red squirrels – there are no grey ones to be seen!

It may seem a little incongruous that the walk from virtually sea level to the highest point on the island involves a trek along a disused railway line – railways traditionally preferring to keep to the lowlands and avoiding steep climbs – but the old Shanklin–Ventnor line really is the nicest and most convenient way of starting the assault on St Boniface Down. I may be slightly biased, as I am a lover of disused railway walking, but perhaps after following this particular piece of old line, you will be as well. Quick railway history lesson: the Isle of Wight enjoyed an explosion of railway building in the latter part of the nineteenth century, with the Ryde–Shanklin line opening in 1864 and being extended to Ventnor in 1866. The Ventnor extension closed exactly 100 years later, although the line from Ryde to Shanklin survived. The section of old line between Shanklin and Wroxall is now almost all available for walking; thus it is that having left the train at the Shanklin terminus and exited onto the station forecourt, you can turn right down some steps to a road, cross straight over it and find yourself on the old line. Signed to Wroxall, it's actually designated as the Sunshine Trail, but I doubt an action under the Trades Descriptions Act will be successful if it's raining.

Now follow the old line, passing initially to the left of an industrial estate, and stay on the old line all the way to the village of **Wroxall**. It's a lovely and very easy walk, with splendid views towards your ultimate objective, St Boniface Down, once you've pulled away from Shanklin's suburbs. Jeff Vinter, describing the line in his *Railway Walks* guide, remarks that the route is very good for wild fruit, with an abundance of elderberries and blackberries, and possibly even wild strawberries: tiny but tasty. On reaching Wroxall, roughly 2½ miles from Shanklin, the path leaves the old line and you go up to meet a road by the village church. Turn right onto the road to arrive at the main village street; now turn left along the street, passing a shop on the opposite side, and go forward to the **Four Seasons Inn**, which is on the left hand side. Leave the main road here by taking the road going up past the left-hand side of the pub, effectively heading in the same direction as you were before. Go uphill to a fork junction and continue into Stenbury View, going forward from there onto a bridlepath which keeps climbing. Carry on along the obvious path uphill, noting a signed path coming in from the right as you gain height; there's a helpful map board which you'll see as you reach **Wroxall Down**. Keep on the bridlepath, aiming for the highest ground on the down, heading south-eastwards, then veering gently just north of east to arrive at a road.

Turn left to follow the road, arriving at a trig point which isn't the highest point, as will be obvious from the surroundings.

Immediately beyond it is a large enclosed area, signalling your arrival at **St Boniface Down**, the climax of your journey, and with plenty to interest the naturalist and historian. It's home to the largest cricket in the British Isles, the great green bush-cricket; there is reputed to be a wishing well on the south slope, requiring the wisher to climb from the south without looking back; and in 1545 there was an attack on the Down from the south by a French invasion force which was routed by the local militia commanded by Sir John Fyssher. The Down played its part in repelling a much more serious threat to our islands, with a radar station being built here shortly before World War Two. The station was bombed by Stukas on 12 August 1940 and suffered extensive damage.

The Down is not a particularly pretty sight nowadays. The now derelict radar station paraphernalia within the enclosed area all looks rather sad and, at the time I explored it, appeared to serve no purpose. I realised I would have to find a way into the area to claim I had 'done' the highest point on the island, and to begin with felt sure I would be beaten back by the forbidding mesh fencing. But then, to my surprise, staying on the road beyond the trig point, with the perimeter fence immediately to the right, I shortly reached a gate in the fence which was open; there were large gaps in the fencing immediately adjacent, making me think entry into the enclosure would not set off an alarm and summon all available police manpower across the island. That said, it is private land so I technically had no right to be there and you, too, will enter at your own risk. If you do, then just beyond the gate is a tall grassy hump which is arguably the highest point of all. Superb views are to be found to the north on a clear day to Fawley oil refinery, the Solent and the sprawling conurbations of Southampton and Portsmouth, as well as much of the eastern half of the island.

If access to the hump isn't possible, don't worry, as there is another area a little further on which could compete for the honour of highest point. Return to the road and follow it on; the road becomes a track and you can now look half-left to a splendid ridge heading away to the north. Join an obvious path just beyond the northernmost tip of the enclosed area, this path now joining the ridge, and you'll see little hillocks in the heather to the right, which could be said to match for height the hump in the enclosure. Looking back from further along the ridge I could see there was really very little in it. So if they've locked that gate, mended the fencing and perhaps put a few strands of barbed wire round it for good measure, it's probably not worth risking ripping your trousers trying to vault over the top.

Now enjoy a magnificent walk along the ridge, actually Luccombe Down, with splendid views to Shanklin, Sandown, Culver Cliff and even the chalk cliff faces of West Wight. As you proceed, look carefully for a wooden signpost to the right advertising 'Shanklin 1 (mile)' and detour right here to walk to a trig point which provides one of the best views to be had on the Isle of Wight, particularly towards Shanklin, Sandown and the sea, but also miles of rolling countryside, albeit you've come down a little from the highest point on the island. Return to the path you've been on and continue; very shortly the main path veers north-westwards but you continue northwards on a narrow path which hugs a fence that is just to the right. Drop down, going forward to a strip of woodland, and descend some very steep steps. Beyond the steps, keep hugging the fence to the right and continue just east of north on a very clear path to arrive back at the old railway line you followed earlier. Turn right and retrace your steps to **Shanklin**.

Trains back to Ryde are fairly frequent but it's not the most inspiring place to have to wait any length of time for the next one, especially if you've just missed one, as I had, by thirty seconds. I might have known my hunger for those wild strawberries would come back to bite me.

Bedfordshire

Dunstable Downs – 243 metres / 797 feet – TL 008194

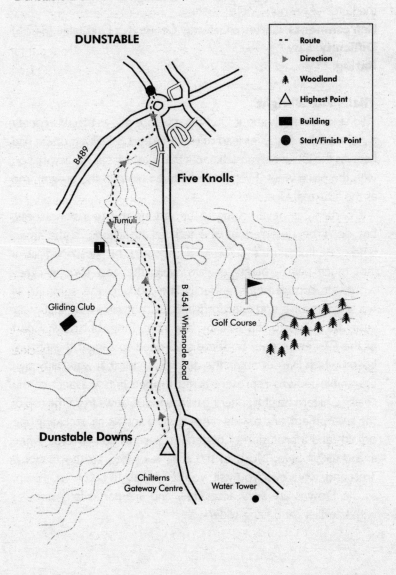

Length: 2 miles
Start and finish: Junction of B4541 Whipsnade Road with B489 near Dunstable
Public transport: Regular buses serving the above junction on the Luton–Aylesbury route
Refreshments: Chilterns Gateway Centre (C); Dunstable (P, C, S)
Difficulty: Easy
Rating: ***

That's kite all right

I didn't know much about Dunstable before my visit to this county high point. My first ever lead role in a Gilbert & Sullivan opera had been as the Duke of Dunstable, but that was as far as my association with the place went. Even there I'd been billed in the programme as the 'Duke of Unstable'.

It certainly is never going to be among the tourist hotspots, but don't be deterred by the lack of attractions in the town below Bedfordshire's summit. This could be described as a 'not much pain – plenty of gain' walk; the best sort, in other words. It complements perfectly the walk to the summits of Buckinghamshire and Hertfordshire, as not only can that walk easily be linked to this one by bus from Tring, but it's still part of the Chiltern scene. So there's no need to repeat the history lesson which I've set out in the description for that walk, although Dunstable Downs represent a more open grassy aspect of the chalky Chiltern heights, offering tremendous views from the top of the escarpment, and a wide range of flora and fauna, including bee orchids and a profusion of butterflies, such as the marbled white and chalkhill blue. Much of the area is owned by the National Trust and, whenever you visit, you're unlikely to be on your own, as the Downs are very accessible, and are particularly popular with kite-fliers and hang-gliders.

If you've come from Tring by bus, it's worth asking the driver to drop you at the bottom of **Whipsnade Road (B4541)**; but if they refuse, or you are so absorbed in your *Harry Potter* you don't press the bell in time, you'll find yourself in the centre of Dunstable and will just have to backtrack along the B489 to the Whipsnade Road junction. Anyway, follow Whipsnade Road away from the junction but almost immediately bear right along the signed **Chiltern Way** path uphill, beside an avenue of trees, keeping the backs of houses to the left. Continue uphill, ignoring a left fork, aiming for and arriving at a gate, which you pass through, and beyond it you keep on in the same direction, aiming for the highest ground.

At the top, the ground suddenly falls away ahead of you ◼. It's a superb spot, the enjoyment of the extensive views heightened by the splendour of the Downs themselves, rising impressively from otherwise unremarkable Bedfordshire countryside; although as a freezing fog had set in on my visit, reducing the visibility to 100 yards or so, it came as something of a shock. Fortunately I didn't fall off the edge and managed to recover my composure sufficiently to bear round to the left; you need to do this, too, keeping along the top of the escarpment to reach a proper surfaced path coming in from the left. Bear right to follow it along the hilltop, aiming for a very conspicuous 'wind catcher' which in the summer provides air conditioning for the nearby and equally prominent **Chilterns Gateway Centre**. Bear left at the wind catcher up to the Centre and, by following the approach road back to Whipsnade Road, you'll reach the trig point; the little ridges close by the trig point are slightly higher than the ground on which the trig point is built, and can be regarded as the highest point on **Dunstable Downs**, and therefore the highest ground in Bedfordshire. I undertook this walk on a freezing cold November Saturday and, having scrunched my way over the frost-capped hillside, had to scrape a layer of ice off the trig point to view it properly. But at least I had the outside tables provided by the visitor centre cafe all to myself.

Now using the wind catcher as your guide to picking up the surfaced path again, retrace your steps all the way back to the start, remembering to turn left to keep to the escarpment edge at point **1** above, then bear right to head downhill, aiming for the gate. Once back at the start point, you may prefer, rather than waiting for the next bus on the Tring–Aylesbury route, to turn right at the B489/B4541 Whipsnade Road junction and follow the **B489** into Dunstable. The town does contain a splendid Priory church, containing a magnificent Norman nave dating from 1150. Buses from here to Luton are very frequent, although the bus journey has to be one of the most boring you're ever likely to have to undertake. And the less said about Luton station, the better.

East Riding of Yorkshire

Bishop Wilton Wold – 246 metres / 806 feet – SE 821570

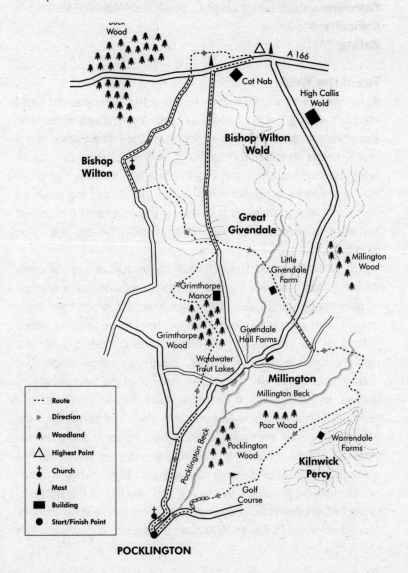

Length: 16 miles
Start and finish: Pocklington
Public transport: Regular buses serving Pocklington on the York–Market Weighton route
Refreshments: Pocklington (P, C, S); Bishop Wilton (P, S)
Difficulty: Moderate
Rating: ***

Top of the Wold

As far as this walk is concerned, the adage that 'it is better to travel hopefully than to arrive' could not be more appropriate. The scenery for much of the way to and from the highest point of the East Riding of Yorkshire is magnificent, with extensive views across large areas of both East and North Yorkshire, but the high point itself is a massive anticlimax. Do this walk because of the views en route and for the satisfaction of scaling the heights of this part of Yorkshire, but don't ask for your money back at the end of it – you have been warned.

This particular walk passes through a section of the Yorkshire Wolds – chalk uplands carved as a result of erosion into a number of deep steep-sided dales. The dales, many of which have been clothed with attractive tree plantations, tend to be used for sheep grazing, as the hillsides are too steep to be cultivated, while the high ground is extensively farmed, chiefly for cereal crops. The chalk grassland as a whole contains many colourful wild plants and flowers, including hawkbit, scabious, salad burnet, crosswort and harebell. The attraction of this walk is in the fact that it follows the western fringes of the Wolds, thereby offering some superb views from the hilltops to lower ground to the west, but also seeks out a number of the exceedingly picturesque dales. While it could be shortened significantly by starting and finishing at the delightful village of Bishop Wilton, you would miss out on some great scenery. Moreover, buses to Bishop Wilton are infrequent (and non-existent on Sunday), and Pocklington, the base town for this walk, is a delightfully old-fashioned country town with an excellent range of amenities and independent shops, and without the lifeblood and character having been sucked from it by huge supermarkets and bland chain stores. That said, if you get here after the independents have shut for the day, you'll doubtless be grateful for the Co-op.

From the centre of Pocklington, head north-westwards from the bus station up the road past the west side of the church, turning at the first right beyond the church into Chapmangate. As Chapmangate veers right, bear left at the junction up the road signed 'Bishop Wilton 5 (miles)'. Go up to the mini-roundabout and take the right exit along 'The Mile;' follow this road for, appropriately enough, about a mile, passing the left turn to Meltonby and, a little further on the right, Woodhouse Lane. A short way beyond this right turn, look out for and take a signed path going off to the left. This is part of the **Chalkland Way**, a 40-mile tour around the Yorkshire Wolds, which starts and finishes at Pocklington, and of which you will see a lot during this walk. Initially your path heads off to the left, at right-angles to the road, then shortly veers right and strikes out just east of north. Follow the obvious path forward north-eastwards, soon crossing Miller Lane and taking the direction shown by the arrows, including one in the middle of the next field, going uphill to reach a stile at the entrance to a wood.

Walk through **Grimthorpe Wood** on a path which is a little narrow in places, and emerge on the north-east side of it, veering left to follow the edge of the wood. The wood recedes to the left and the path, sticking to the left-hand field edge, veers right, but very shortly look out for and take a path going left, crossing a footbridge and rising to reach a field boundary. Turn left here, as signed, and follow the field edge round, soon veering right, then right again, north-eastwards, still on the Chalkland Way, and enjoying excellent views back to Pocklington and its very conspicuous church tower.

The path heads north-eastwards, then dives into **Brimlands Wood**, heading just north of east along the edge of the wood to rejoin the road. Turn left onto the road, passing the sign welcoming you to **Great Givendale** and reaching a road junction where you bear left, signed Bishop Wilton. Just beyond the houses of Great Givendale, turn right onto a signed path, actually the **Minster Way** which runs for 50 miles, and links the minsters of Beverley and York.

Your path here starts as a track, veering left then right, and proceeds just west of north along the hillside, providing grandstand views, which should include York Minster on a decent day, while nearer at hand, you can look north-westwards to Bishop Wilton and its soaring church spire. Your path then veers left and shortly right, before going left again and crossing a fence, curling right to follow the left side of a field boundary and then veering sharply south-westwards, downhill. It drops down to reach a road onto which you turn right, going forward to **Bishop Wilton**. This is a charming village, with its wide green bisected by a stream, and you may be lucky enough to find refreshments here, too. The St Edith's Church has a Norman chancel and ironwork screen, and the black-and-white mosaic floor is based on a design in the Vatican.

Go straight through the village, north-westwards, along the road and, having passed through it, you reach a crossroads. Take the right-hand turn, signposted Fridaythorpe, along Worsendale Road; it climbs quite steeply, with good views to Bishop Wilton behind you and Worsen Dale to the right, and reaches the **A166**. Go straight over onto a path, then in about 150 yards turn right onto a path heading east, parallel to the A166 and passing a mast. At a field corner the path appears to die, but follow the field edge briefly round to the left and very shortly you'll see a path going off to the right through the trees; take this path, which goes forward to veer right and become a very badly overgrown path through a gully, returning to the A166. Turn left to shortly reach a road junction on the left and then a mast inside a securely enclosed area, within which you'll also see the trig point marking the county high point. This really is the most desperate anticlimax after the hard work you've put in to get here; there are no views to speak of because of the breadth of the plateau, and you don't even have the satisfaction of being able to touch the trig point. You could venture into the field immediately beyond and gain some slight elevation (albeit artificial) by climbing onto the wooded earthwork in the middle, but even that will be impossible if there's mature corn growing in the field in question, and, in any event, this is private land so you should have permission to be there at all. Pretty disappointing all round then.

Walk back alongside the A166 and, almost opposite the first mast referred to above, turn left along a road which you follow for 1½ miles, enjoying great views to the right, arriving back at the Great Givendale turning again. Turn left here along a track which passes a little chapel, heading north-west initially, then veering very sharply south-eastwards and more gently south of east, ignoring two forks going off to the left. Beyond the second fork you go through a gate to follow a clear path just south of east, then veer right along it, south-eastwards, through the valley of Givendale. You drop down to a footbridge, meeting **White Keld Dale**; don't take the track going half-right from the gate beyond the footbridge, but go straight uphill very steeply, still south-eastwards. At the top go forward to a gate straight ahead, veering gently right along an obvious track which passes to the left (east) of **Little Givendale Farm** and goes forwards to a road.

Cross straight over the road and follow a road marked on maps as the Balk, down to Millington, signposted as a quarter of a mile away. You reach a crossroads and go straight over onto what is **Millington** village street. However, a little before it bends right, turn left along a signed path, heading for College Farm; shortly fork right and drop down along a path through a gate and along a boardwalked section, sticking to the Minster Way. Beyond the boardwalk you climb very steeply up the hillside just north of east to reach a stile. Don't cross this stile but instead follow the path to the right of it, keeping the fence to the left, heading south-eastwards. Climb quite steeply, going forward through horse paddocks, keeping **Warren Farm** to the left and reaching a signed junction with the **Yorkshire Wolds Way**, a 79-mile National Trail linking Hessle (near Hull) with Filey. Turn right to follow the Yorkshire Wolds Way, getting great views of the countryside, including Millington and its part-Norman church, heading south-westwards. Veer sharp left, as signed with the Yorkshire Wolds Way, then shortly veer right and right again, still on the Yorkshire Wolds Way, descending beside a wood and heading south-westwards.

At the foot of the hill and beyond the woodland you reach a road, now leaving the Yorkshire Wolds Way and going forward along the road in the same south-westerly direction. Follow the road for just over half a mile, keeping the Kilnwick Percy estate – which contains a hall, park, lakes and Norman church – to the left and passing the corner of woodland on the right, veering from south-westwards to south-eastwards. Shortly after your veering south-eastwards beyond the wood, turn right onto a signed path, now on the **Wilberforce Way** as well as the **Chalkland Way**. The Wilberforce Way is a 60-mile linear trail from Hull to York devised to mark the 200th anniversary of the abolition of British involvement in the transatlantic slave trade, the campaign for its abolition of course being spearheaded by, who else, William Wilberforce. The reason for Hull being chosen as the start of this route as it was Wilberforce's birthplace, and indeed the route passes through Pocklington where Wilberforce attended grammar school. There's actually a place named Wilberfoss between York and Pocklington, and you may pass or have passed through it on your bus journey to or from this walk.

Having left the road and joined the Wilberforce Way, take the direction indicated by the signpost just south of west, across the golf course, aiming for the right-hand side of woodland ahead; the path isn't clear and you're at risk from low-flying golf balls, but in due course an arrow reassures you. Follow the right-hand side of the wood, then beyond it kink left, as signed to the south (left) side of a fence. Follow the clear path which drops down, crossing a road and reaching another road, with a sign pointing back the way you've come saying **Kilnwick Percy** is 1 ¼ miles away. Bear right here, onto a road through a housing estate, then take the first road turning left and follow this road round to the left. Between houses 15 and 14 on the right, turn right onto a concrete path leading down to another road. Turn left at this road, shortly arriving at a T-junction with a busier road; bear right onto this road which takes you back into the centre of Pocklington.

There's an excellent variety of cafes and food shops in the town, which will doubtless welcome your custom, but you may prefer to bide your time and catch a bus straight back to York to celebrate your completion of this long walk in one of the bewildering variety of eating places there – where a slice of fruit cake and knob of cheese in a posh tearoom in the tourist quarter will definitely set you back more than a full McDonald's Happy Meal. I resolved the dilemma of choosing by opting for both: a cream tea in the legendary Bettys, with immaculately dressed waitresses and Gilbert & Sullivan being played on the piano, and then a cheeseburger and fries among the youth of Leeds to the piped strains of Lady Gaga.

East Sussex

Ditchling Beacon – 248 metres / 813 feet – TQ 332131

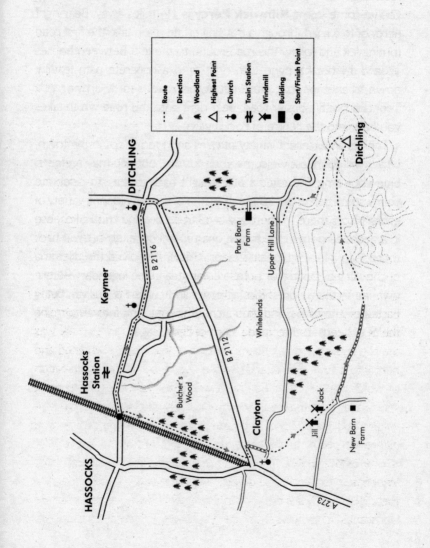

Length: 6 miles
Start and finish: Hassocks
Public transport: Regular trains serving Hassocks on the London/Gatwick Airport/Haywards Heath–Brighton line
Refreshments: Hassocks (P, C, S); Ditchling (P, C, S)
Difficulty: Moderate
Rating: ****

Weald meet again

No logistical problems, not too long or arduous a walk, great view from the top, things of interest on the way out and on the way back, a lovely tearoom and at least three pubs – this is a super walk, which the determined bagger can complete in less than two hours, but which you could be forgiven for turning into a full day's outing, enjoying every minute. Just pick a decent day – and this being the balmy south, there are plenty of those.

Ditchling Beacon is the highest point on the South Downs, the lovely chalk hills which run from East Hampshire south-eastwards to reach a grand finale at Beachy Head. The South Downs do not, in fact, provide the highest point in West Sussex, as they are dwarfed by the wooded Black Down some way to the north, but in East Sussex they look down on everything else. The rocks forming the South Downs are made from sediments, of which chalk was the top layer, laid down many millions of years ago, then lifted and bent into a large dome, and eroded over time by the combination of wind and rain. The South Downs provide some of the most spectacular countryside in south-east England and are a haven for wildlife and plant life; of particular note are the huge numbers of different types of butterflies and orchids. The South Downs Way is one of the oldest National Trails, running for 100 miles from Winchester to Beachy Head (yes, that is the way to walk it, begging the official guide's pardon) and each section of it offers majestic landscapes. The views from the heights are magnificent, especially to the Weald, the once heavily wooded area sandwiched between the North and South Downs. Alhough lower, obviously, than the Downs, the Weald is certainly anything but flat, and once supported a flourishing iron industry.

Your walk starts at **Hassocks station**. Walk briefly down the station approach road, then opposite the pub on this road turn right down a flight of steps to meet the main street (**B2116**). At the bottom, cross the road, turn right and walk towards the railway bridge; as you reach the bridge you meet two signed paths in close succession going off to the left. Ignore the first but take the second, which for just over a mile runs parallel to and just to the left of the railway, ending by the junction of the **B2112**, coming in from the left, with the **A273**. Cross straight over the B2112 and follow a signed path over a sports field, aiming for the right-hand side of the clubhouse – I suspect the football team would appreciate your walking round the side of the pitch rather than straight over it – then beyond the clubhouse join the approach road taking you very shortly to **Clayton** village street.

You need to cross straight over onto a signed bridleway heading southwards, but it's worth detouring to the right to see two features of Clayton. One is the extraordinary brick baronial entrance to Clayton Tunnel on the London–Brighton line, and the other is the village church, which boasts a pre-1066 chancel arch and superb medieval wall paintings. Keith Spence in his *Companion Guide to Kent and Sussex* bemoans the fact that they have 'had to contend with being spattered by bat droppings'!

Now proceed along the bridleway south of the village street. Ignore a signed (yellow arrow) footpath going off to the left, and continue along the obvious signed (blue arrow) bridleway, which now gains height quickly, heading steeply south-eastwards. Now look out for the two windmills, **Jack and Jill**, to your right, and aim for the clear path skirting the north-east side of the mills. Of the two, Jill, the right-hand one as you look at them, is undoubtedly the more attractive and photogenic, with its sails and bright white colour; the darker, Jack, to the left, is something of a poor relation, lacking any sails! Jack is the tower of a smock mill, a type of windmill consisting of a sloping horizontally weatherboarded tower usually with six or eight sides, topped with a roof or cap which rotates to bring sails into the wind; it got its name from its resemblance to smocks worn by farmers in an earlier period. Whereas Jill is a post mill, one in which the whole body of the mill that houses the machinery is mounted on a single vertical post around which it can be turned to bring the sails into the wind. They were built in 1821 and actually hauled here from Brighton in 1850 – by oxen.

Having paused to enjoy the mills, keep along the path, arriving at a T-junction where you turn left onto a clear track heading south-eastwards. Very shortly the **South Downs Way** comes in from the right, and you now follow the South Downs Way all the way to **Ditchling Beacon**. Initially you continue to climb, keeping the fence to your left, then you veer gently left, from south-eastwards to just north of east, now on top of the scarp. The East Sussex/West Sussex border spur of the Sussex Border Path comes in, also from the right (although it isn't signed) and then shortly goes off to the left. Now enjoying magnificent views, continue along the top of the scarp, passing just to the right of clumps of bushes and one of the characteristic dew ponds of the South Downs Way; you shortly pass to the left of another dew pond, then begin a very clear and quite stiff climb, signalling your approach to the climax of the walk. As you climb, you keep a fence to your right. The fence bends sharply to the right and immediately beyond this bend you'll see the trig point above you to the right. Simply make your way to it, and note the small grassy hump just to the side of it, which is a little higher than the ground on which the trig point is built.

The field behind the trig point appears to be slightly higher again than that, but if you make your way round to enter it (accessible by heading a little south-eastwards from the trig point to reach a gate and using that to enter the field), you'll see that really there is nothing to choose between it and the hump. The trig point does provide a tremendous panorama, stretching across the Downs for miles in both directions – the Weald to the north and the sea to the south. In 1588 one of a chain of big fires was lit here to warn of the Spanish Armada's approach.

Return to the South Downs Way and turn left, keeping the fence to your left and heading downhill, coming to a path heading away to the left, signed Heathy Brow to the left and Keymer Post ahead. Here you turn right, opposite the Heathy Brow path, and walk downhill across the grass to a narrow path running parallel to a fence from right to left. Turn left to follow the path beside the fence, until it reaches a sharp right-angled bend to the right. Bear right with the fence, then at the fifth post look left and you will see a sunken/ gullied path going away to the left, and a green path on the right-hand bank of the gully. Follow the green path on the bank, which goes very steeply downhill just north of west, swinging to the right (northwards) and then, just beyond the point where the gullied path peters out, veer left and climb some steps. You then veer right, downhill again, to reach a junction of paths with stiles. Go straight over, not left, and continue steeply downhill through the trees to arrive at a road junction, with Underhill Lane coming in from the left. The road going off to the right is the main road leading uphill to the car park below the Beacon, the one already hot, sweaty and tired cyclists have to slog up on the closing stages of the London to Brighton Bike Ride each June.

Turn left to follow Underhill Lane briefly, then shortly bear right via a stile onto a signed footpath heading north-eastwards away from the lane between fences; be warned that this, another overlap with the Sussex Border Path, can be extremely squelchy. The signage is very clear and the ground underfoot improves as you pass stables and through a field where horses are kept. Pass through a gate and continue on just east of north along a right-hand field edge, veering a little west of north through a field as signed; there's no sign at the next field boundary but you now veer a little to the right to proceed to a footbridge, with housing to the right. Cross the footbridge and go forward to a mini-roundabout, possibly one of the smallest mini-roundabouts in existence. Pass round the near side of the mini-mini-roundabout and follow a narrow Sussex Border Path-signed footpath (there's also a No Cycling sign) which takes you to the top end of Beacon Road, and from here you go forward in the same direction beside the B2112 South Street into the centre of **Ditchling**.

Ditchling, the sometime home of the artist Sir Frank Brangwyn and the sculptor Eric Gill, and at the time of writing the home of the singer and 'Forces' Sweetheart' Dame Vera Lynn, is a delightful village. It boasts a fine church with Norman and Early English features, and, over the road from the church, there's a Tudor house named Wings Place with some excellent timberwork, while Eric Gill's calligraphy designs and woodcuts have been housed in the former village school. There's also a very nice cafe; although at the time of writing it had changed its name to the Ditchling Tea Rooms, previously it was known as Dolly's Pantry, and did the most fantastic bacon and egg doorstep sandwiches. Ask them for a round – they can only say no.

Turn left at the crossroads in the village centre along the B2116 West Street. This road proceeds past the village church and goes on to **Keymer**, where there's a church and a pub, then continues to Hassocks, about 1½ miles from Ditchling. There's pavement all the way and, at journey's end, you'll see the station clearly signposted to the right preceded by an excellent range of amenities on the main street. If you missed out on the sarnies in Ditchling there are lots of eateries and, if the 6 miles of Downland tramping have taken their toll on your feet, I'm sure you'll find it Hassocks for sale as well. Well, someone had to say it.

Kent and Greater London (Outer)

Old Fort Bungalow, Betsom's Hill – 251 metres / 823 feet – TQ 435563
Westerham Heights – 245 metres / 804 feet – TQ 436564

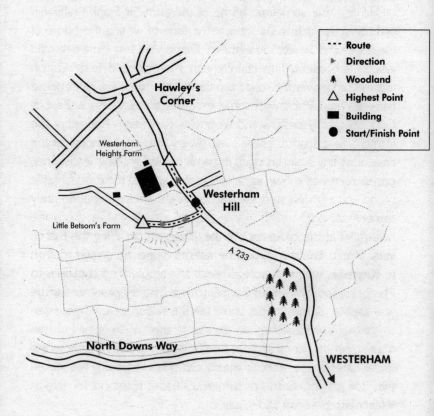

Length: 0.3 miles
Start and finish: Graham Hall Coachworks bus stop on A233 just north of Westerham
Public transport: Regular buses serving Westerham Heights on Westerham–Bromley route
Refreshments: None. NOTE: There are ample refreshments in Westerham, a very short bus ride away
Difficulty: Easy
Rating: *

No head for heights

Oh dear, oh dear. Kent, the Garden of England, is a county blessed with much beautiful scenery and many magnificent viewpoints on the North Downs Way National Trail, which reaches its climax at Shakespeare Cliff just west of Dover. Which makes it all the more ironic that its highest point provides only very limited views and it's on private land to boot. Not that you need a boot, or pair of boots, for this one and you'll wonder if even your flip-flops were excessive.

There are some consolations. Firstly, it is indeed an extremely short walk and certainly not a case of tramping miles from the nearest village or town for no real reward; secondly, on the same very short expedition, you'll be able to bag another county high point, namely that of Greater London (Outer); and thirdly, there's a fine town and stately home just a couple of miles away. So maybe at the end of it you will feel it's all been worthwhile.

It all starts by your catching a bus on the Westerham–Bromley route, getting off at the **Graham Hall Coachworks** bus stop – yes, it really is called that, but if your driver's not sure, mention **Westerham Heights** and you may elicit a spark of recognition. From the bus stop walk very briefly southwards along the **A233** Biggin Hill–Westerham road towards Westerham, then turn right into a lane. Follow the lane and bear left off it, as if making for the coachworks, but turn left again and walk along the driveway for the Old Fort Bungalow, climbing up to reach the bungalow itself. The Old Fort Bungalow is a private house; it's unclear how it got its name as there appears to be no evidence of a fortification on or around this spot!

This, and the area immediately outside it, marks the summit of Kent. You may be disappointed to find that the vista to the north is non-existent, but there are good views southwards down to Westerham and surrounding villages. It is important that, if you wish to linger here, you ask permission of the owner, and you may, in fact, prefer to contact them in advance. You don't particularly want to chance it and then, when challenged, find yourself forced into a spurious claim to door-to-door encyclopaedia salesmanship or to be conducting a house-to-house survey on locals' preferred types of dog food.

Having left the bungalow area, retrace your steps to the A233. In order to get to the highest point in Greater London, turn left and, staying on left-hand side of the road, walk the very short distance to the turning on the left with the sign **Westerham Heights Farm**. Cross the road just here; the thick vegetation bordering the road on the other side marks the highest point, but this time there are absolutely no views. You may think there's a certain irony in the name Westerham Heights, as vertigo sufferers have absolutely nothing to fear, and you may even feel a slight sense of unreality as you stand here. This is supposed to be Greater London, for goodness sake. Where are the houses, the apartments, the office blocks, the shops and the restaurants? No: it's a reminder that Greater London, covering an area of 607 square miles and boasting thirty-three boroughs (including the County of the City of London) stretches far out into the countryside. Which may serve to emphasise the richness and diversity of the capital, but which will sorely disappoint if you were hoping to round the corner and find a conveniently placed Starbucks or M&S Simply Food.

Now you've a choice. You could return to the bus stop and head London-wards, an uninspiring bus journey conveying you to the joys of Bromley and its Bromley South station with frequent fast trains into the capital. You could walk down the A233 south-eastwards towards Westerham and, if you wanted to extend your walk, you could join the **North Downs Way National Trail** heading eastwards towards Chevening and Otford, or westwards towards Oxted. A third option is to proceed either on foot or by bus to explore Westerham, the most westerly town in Kent. On the village green there are statues of General James Wolfe, who spent his childhood here, and Sir Winston Churchill, who lived at nearby Chartwell. There are a number of fine buildings in and around Westerham, including the National Trust-owned Quebec House, where Wolfe spent his childhood, and the late seventeenth-century mansion Squerryes Court, while the seventeenth-century church boasts a fourteenth-century spiral staircase running up into the tower, which in design is Early English, a style of architecture which succeeded the Norman, characterised by pointed arches and lancet windows.

However, the biggest attraction in the area is Chartwell, which is crammed with Churchill memorabilia including paintings, medals and cigars. It is now owned by the National Trust and open to visitors: so far so good, but, as Keith Spence points out, you can find it 'easily enough on summer weekends by following the nose-to-tail queue of cars and coaches through the back roads'. Hmm. Perhaps Bromley is the better bet after all.

Tyne & Wear

Currock Hill – 259 metres / 851 feet – NZ 107592

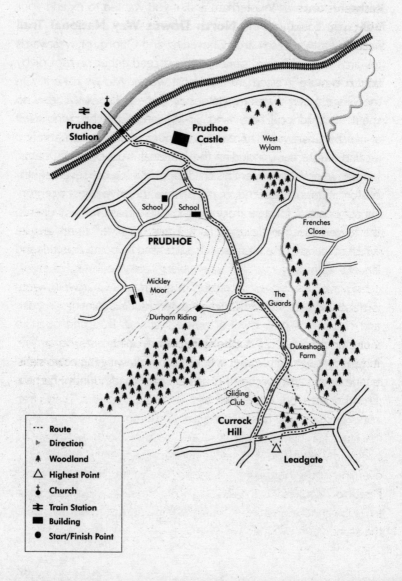

Prudhoe Station

Prudhoe Castle

West Wylam

School

School

Frenches Close

PRUDHOE

Mickley Moor

The Guards

Durham Riding

Dukeshagg Farm

Gliding Club

Currock Hill

Leadgate

- - - Route
▶ Direction
♠ Woodland
△ Highest Point
♱ Church
⇌ Train Station
■ Building
● Start/Finish Point

Length: 7 miles (6 miles if travelling by bus from Newcastle)
Start and finish: Prudhoe station/Prudhoe main street
Public transport: Regular trains serving Prudhoe on the Carlisle–Newcastle line; regular buses serving Prudhoe from Newcastle
Refreshments: Prudhoe (P, C, S)
Difficulty: Easy
Rating: **

I did it byway

There aren't many walks in this book that could be described as routine, but this is probably as routine as it gets. It's a straightforward easy walk, mostly on roads, in a metropolitan county whose name, like that of Merseyside, suggests heavy industry, and sweat and toil rather than rolling green pastures. (Like Merseyside, the county council has been abolished, but Tyne & Wear still exists both legally and ceremonially.) There are good transport connections, the views to the Tyne Valley are splendid as you gain height, there are ample refreshment opportunities at the start and end of proceedings, and the summit gives itself up without fuss. No rocky faces or steep banks, just a pleasant public byway, at the end of which you somehow feel the effort should have been a lot greater.

Your starting point is **Prudhoe station**. The man serving in the Pumpkin buffet at Carlisle, in return for my paying him for two slabs of Victoria sponge, gave me a lesson on how to pronounce Prudhoe so the ticket clerk knew where I wanted to go, but even after intensive rehearsal I decided it might just be easier to use the ticket machine. Having arrived at Prudhoe, exit the station on the south side, and walk the short distance to the roundabout; cross straight over and follow the road uphill, passing the English Heritage-owned **Prudhoe Castle** on the left. If you've time, it's worth stopping to look round the castle. It was built early in the twelfth century, the stone keep being added less than a century later, and passed to the Percy family in 1398; it has since been updated with a new great hall; it has in fact been continuously occupied throughout its existence. Continue on up the road to the top, reaching Prudhoe's main street (buses coming from Newcastle stop here), turning right and then shortly left into South Road. Follow the road until you reach a newsagents on the left and here turn right into Moor Road. This has a suburban feel to start with, then becomes more rural, descending gently past hospital buildings. Then, after a sharp left and sharp right bend, your road begins to climb, heading south-eastwards, with pleasant woodland to the left.

Having climbed steadily, you arrive at **Dukeshagg Farm** and the road becomes a public byway, veering south-westwards and continuing to ascend. The views are opening out very nicely behind you so it's worth pausing to look back every now and again. You arrive at a metalled road junction; turn left here, now on **Currock Hill**, and follow the ridge until just on the fringe of a clump of trees on the right, you turn right onto a signed path, crossing the border from Northumberland into Tyne & Wear. You pass through a gate beyond which the path follows the left-hand edge of a small wood, while to the left is a field, the highest point of which is the summit of Tyne & Wear. I was fortunate in that on the occasion of my visit the field had nothing growing in it and was easily walked over, but if you arrive at the wrong time, clearly you must avoid damaging crops, and technically you need permission to enter the field at any time. It's not the most stunning hill in the north of England and, at the time of writing, there wasn't even a Wikipedia entry for it, but it's still a very agreeable spot. The views are better to the south, towards the town of Consett, than to the north, the trees here rather getting in the way.

Now you need to head back, initially returning to the road. You could simply retrace your steps to Dukeshagg Farm the way you came or, for a bit of variety, you could turn right and follow the road eastwards to the hamlet of **Leadgate**. The OS map shows a pub here, but when I did this walk the pub in question, called the **Bairns**, looked sadly shut up. Just before the pub, you turn left to join another signed byway – you can do lots of walks in this book without ever meeting a byway, and suddenly here on this one you've two at once. Incidentally, a byway is legally a minor secondary or tertiary road open to all traffic, but usually unmetalled and used by the public mainly for walking and horse-riding. They account for less than 2 per cent of England's unsurfaced rights of way network. This one leads north-westwards back to Dukeshagg Farm and it's not too well defined in places, so follow the signposts as shown, but eventually you return to the farm and a T-junction with the path you followed as you ascended. Turn right here and simply retrace your steps to Prudhoe via Moor Road and then turn left into South Road to bring you to the main street. If you're on the bus, your walk ends here, as buses can whizz you to Newcastle from the bus stop on the north side of the road, but if you're on the train there's another half a mile to the station, reached by bearing right at the end of South Road, then shortly left and downhill past the castle and over the roundabout. Sadly no Victoria sponges available on the station platform.

Oxfordshire

Whitehorse Hill – 261 metres / 856 feet – SU 300863

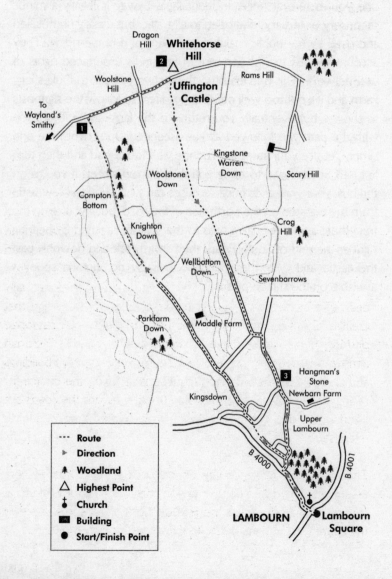

Length: 10 miles
Start and finish: Lambourn
Public transport: Regular buses serving Lambourn from Newbury and Swindon
Refreshments: Lambourn (P, C, S); none en route
Difficulty: Easy; one moderate climb
Rating: ****

Horse scents

The day hadn't got off to the best start. I'd missed my Newbury connection at Reading by no more than 30 seconds and, looking for solace in the Reading station branch of Burger King while I waited for the next train, found the aforementioned establishment unable to provide breakfast within the time available. And, on arrival at Newbury, the Pumpkin cafe on Platform 1 hadn't opened either. But fate had better things in store. A prompt bus from Newbury – a lovely village to begin my walk, with majestic autumn colours and a generous portion of glorious views mingled liberally with heaped tablespoonfuls of prehistory. This is a great walk.

It all starts – and finishes – in Lambourn, Berkshire, actually described in one of my guide books as a 'town', although that creates a misleading impression. No New Look, Accessorize or M&S here. It does have a twelfth-century church, Victorian almshouses, and a main street with a number of attractive buildings and shops, but its chief claim to fame is as being the centre for racing stables. Every day, my guide book goes on, the roads are 'filled with thoroughbreds walking in single file on their way to be exercised'.

Thankfully my bus encountered no such road blockages and, assuming yours doesn't either, it will drop you in Lambourn village square. From here, take the **B4000** north-westwards, keeping the church to the right, and follow this road, mostly paved, for just under half a mile, firstly past housing then keeping woodland to the right. Beyond the woodland turn right into Uplands Lane. Just beyond the Croft but before the No Through Road sign, with a gate on the corner, turn left along a narrow metalled lane, passing the **Malt Shovel pub**. At **Rhonehurst**, continue in the same direction along a mud track, although there is a parallel footpath. Go forward to reach a tarmac road and follow it, ignoring a road soon going off to the left. Shortly, at the thatched Lavender Cottage, turn right onto a road which very soon swings left and passes the **Kingsdown** complex, and you now keep on along the road for about a mile. It passes **Maddle Farm** and then becomes rough, firstly a dirt track then a grass track. Keep straight on in the same north-westerly direction, crossing over a footpath crossroads, and follow what is now a grassy track along a left-hand field edge, keeping a strip of woodland parallel with you to the left. I walked this at the end of October and the autumn colours were absolutely stunning, and I would certainly recommend that time of year to do this walk, if you have the choice that is. As you follow this path, you pass into Oxfordshire from Berkshire. Formerly the boundary was some way further north, placing Uffington Castle in Berkshire, and meaning that Oxfordshire's highest point was a rather anonymous spot further east in the Chiltern commuter belt, without the charisma or character of what follows below. So we do have something for which to thank the bureaucratic tinkerers.

Continue on along a clear track, the woodland to the left ending but a strip of woodland now parallel with you immediately to the right, then you walk alongside further woodland to the left. About 2 miles from where the tarmac ended, you reach **1 the Ridgeway** long-distance footpath and National Trail. This isn't the only county high point walk in this book which makes use of the Ridgeway; the walk from Milk Hill in Wiltshire back to Avebury does so, too, and there are notes about the trail in that walk description. Theoretically, therefore, you could 'link' the Milk Hill walk with this one, following the Ridgeway throughout – a distance of just over 20 miles. More legwork, but fewer waits for buses and less time at Reading station, which itself is probably reason enough for favourably considering it.

At the point ■ where you reach the Ridgeway coming from Lambourn, the direct route to the high point is by turning right. However, if you have even the slightest interest in prehistory you really should make the short detour to the Neolithic burial chamber known as Wayland's Smithy. To do this, turn left at ■ and follow the signed Ridgeway for just over a quarter of a mile, bearing right off the path as signposted to reach the chamber itself. It was used for burials over 5,500 years ago, the first structure being built around 3540 BC and consisting of a stone and timber box with fourteen people buried there. A further structure, in a long barrow edged with stones, was built in about 2800 BC, and the earlier structure was found with burials in wooden chambers. On each side of the Smithy is a ditch marked by lines of trees, and the principal entrance cairn is marked by four large stones. Wayland was the magical smith god of the Saxons and local legend says that if you leave your horse by the tomb with payment, the horse will have been reshod the next day.

Now retrace your steps to ■ and, whether you've detoured or not, proceed just north of east along the Ridgeway, going forward to a crossing track in just under half a mile, walking straight over the crossing and now climbing, soon passing **Uffington Castle**, which is to your left; it is an Iron Age construction, dating back to between 300 BC and AD 43. The trackside verge hereabouts enjoys a large variety of flowers including scabious, knapweed and vetch. As soon as the Ridgeway path levels out, just beyond the castle, turn left onto a signed bridleway which passes through a gate. Walk along a path which is effectively an outer bank of the castle, soon reaching the trig point, officially the highest point, although there are certain points on the inner perimeter of the plateau which might be said to compete for that honour.

Continue anticlockwise along the outer bank for about 50 yards to a gap **2** in the perimeter ridges, allowing you to cross the ditch; enter the plateau and also follow the inner bank back past the trig point, the ground here, as stated, possibly marginally higher. I do recommend you do a circle of the inner bank, in order to fully appreciate the north-facing views, including much unspoilt countryside as well as the less unspoilt office blocks of Swindon and the power stations of Didcot. Uffington Castle enjoys very rich and varied flora, with the ramparts supporting orchids, candytuft and field fleawort, as well as butterflies including chalkhill blue, small blue, gatekeeper and marbled white. However much of the inner bank you walk, retrace your steps to **2** but go straight on along a faint track towards the escarpment edge, taking Uffington church in the plain below as your marker then, as you approach the escarpment edge, use as a marker the straight road at the very foot of the hill going off slightly to the right of the church. You'll shortly arrive at the top of the **Uffington White Horse**, where a figure of that description has been carved out of the grassy slopes.

The White Horse obviously doesn't look as good from here as it would from further north, where its chalky outline is much clearer, and unless you undertake a substantial detour, requiring you to lose most of the height thus far gained, you will perhaps struggle to identify the various parts of the horse's anatomy. Signs request you refrain from walking on the chalk, so resist the temptation to stamp on the poor creature's eye. The White Horse sprawls 374 feet across the hillside; who cut it, and for what reason, will never be known for sure, but the most credible theory appears to be that it was a cult figure connected with Epona, the Celtic goddess of horses, cut in around 350 BC by the Iron Age Celts. Another more prosaic possibility is that it was cut in Saxon times to commemorate a ninth-century victory by King Alfred over the Danes. Standing on… whoops, beside the White Horse, there is a tremendous view to the village of Uffington which is built almost entirely of chalk, and the octagonal tower of its church of St Mary; it once had a spire but that blew down in 1740 and an extra storey was added to replace it. Between the White Horse and the village, on the right-hand side of the road that snakes down towards the houses of Uffington, stands Dragon Hill, said to be where St George slew the dragon – the bald patch on the hilltop was supposedly caused by the dragon's poisonous blood. Just across the road from Dragon Hill is the splendid natural feature known as the Manger, a dry valley formed by a melting glacier during the Ice Ages.

Now you need to retrace your steps to the Ridgeway via the trig point, turning right back onto the Ridgeway path. Almost immediately, however, turn left opposite the castle plateau onto a signed bridleway and follow it along a right-hand field edge; at the top corner of the field bear left, then very shortly right, keeping to the bridleway and aiming for the strip of woodland coming in from the right. Continuing on the path, pass the east end of the strip of woodland and just beyond it you reach a path junction. Don't fork right with the bridleway but keep on in the same direction along the signed footpath between posts, keeping the strip of woodland roughly parallel but some distance away to your right. You reach a post with (at the time of writing) two discs and direction arrows, both pointing the same way; continue along the path south-westwards, observing the direction of the arrows.

At this point, aim for a patch of woodland ahead. The path goes just to the left of it, following immediately alongside it in the same south-easterly direction. Continue on beyond the woodland, the bridleway coming in from the right, and, very shortly, a further bridleway goes off to the right; ignore this, continuing south-eastwards and going forward along a grassy track to join a wide dirt track, with gallops to the right. Follow this wide track south-eastwards for about a mile, reaching a major path junction where there's a post with an arrow pointing left. Turn left here, aiming for and passing immediately to the right of a barn with a corrugated-iron roof, crossing a gallop with care. You don't particularly want to be in the firing line of the next Red Rum.

Beyond the barn, go forward to meet a signed byway pointing left and right. Turn right onto the byway and follow it, soon being joined by a wide path coming in from the right. You now have a choice: you could stick to this wide path, part of the **Lambourn Valley Way**, which soon bends gently left and goes forward to a path crossroads **3** which you go straight over; or, you could shortly turn left onto what is a signed byway, a prettier route, which runs more or less parallel to the Lambourn Valley Way, in due course reaching a T-junction and turning right to soon reach the crossroads **3** and turn left. While you may be safe from galloping stallions, this path, as indeed are all bridleways hereabouts, is exceedingly popular with the riding fraternity, so be prepared to allow the room the horses need to pass you (in my case, not only horses but an assembly of bounding hounds as well).

From **3** follow a clear path south-eastwards in the shade of trees, shortly reaching a fork junction. Fork right along the signed footpath and continue downhill through the trees to a sharp left bend, now on a metalled road. Having swung left you swing shortly right, drop down quite steeply (now back on Uplands Lane), and walk on to the T-junction with the B4000, turning left to retrace your steps back to Lambourn. When I returned, the cafe had closed an irritating ten minutes before but I wasn't destined to go hungry, the village deli offering sausages coated not with pastry but with crispy mashed potato. Thus refreshed, and with the prospect of a Newbury-bound bus shortly thereafter, I thankfully felt no need to ascend back to the Smithy in the hope that by offering him my debit card details Mr Wayland might fix me a new pair of feet.

Warwickshire

Ebrington Hill – 261 metres / 856 feet – SP 187426

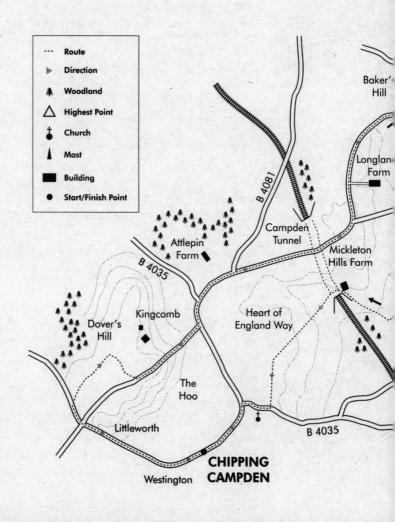

Key:
- - - - Route
- ▷ Direction
- ♠ Woodland
- △ Highest Point
- ☦ Church
- ▲ Mast
- ■ Building
- ● Start/Finish Point

Baker's Hill

Longland Farm

B 4081

Campden Tunnel

Mickleton Hills Farm

Attlepin Farm

B 4035

Heart of England Way

Kingcomb

Dover's Hill

The Hoo

Littleworth

B 4035

Westington

CHIPPING CAMPDEN

Length: 7 miles
Start and finish: Chipping Campden
Public transport: Regular buses serving Chipping Campden on the Stratford-Moreton-in-Marsh route
Refreshments: Chipping Campden (P, S, C); Hidcote (C)
Difficulty: Moderate
Rating: ***

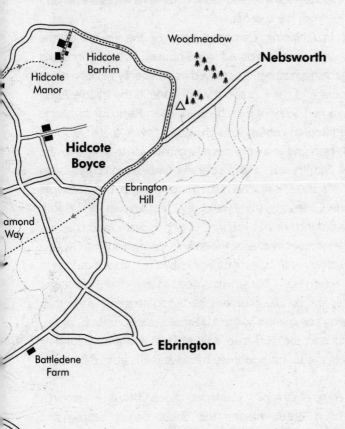

In many ways

Variety, they say, is the spice of life, and there's plenty on this walk: besides the view from the summit, there's a really beautiful Cotswold town, some splendid ridgetop walking, some quirky history, brushes with four 'named' long-distance footpaths, stunning gardens, and a very good en-route cafe. The walk has a distinctly Cotswold flavour and indeed most of it is in the traditional Cotswold county of Gloucestershire; you only enter Warwickshire a very short distance from the summit.

You start in Chipping Campden, one of the jewels of the Cotswolds, with honey-coloured stone houses, cottages, inns and shops lining the main street. It achieved its prosperity through being a principal centre of the Cotswold wool trade in the Middle Ages, and there is a rich array of merchants' houses. Particular highlights are the fine fifteenth-century church with a tower that's 120 feet (37 metres) high and is a very clear landmark for travellers in the surrounding countryside, and a splendid timber-roofed Jacobean market hall. It's also the northern start/finish point of the Cotswold Way (see the Gloucestershire walk), the best known of the four named long-distance routes you'll meet on this walk. In fact, as you sit taking refreshment in one of the town's tearooms or pubs, you may meet walkers with bulging rucksacks by their sides indulging in celebratory cream teas – but you may need to study the expressions on their faces and condition of their bodies to gauge whether they are celebrating completion of the 100-mile walk from Bath, or are just about to start the 100-mile walk to Bath and are celebrating completion of the six-hour journey by rail and bus from Billericay.

From the centre of Chipping Campden proceed south-westwards along the main street, passing the Sheep Street turning and **Volunteer pub**, both on your left-hand side. Continue straight along the street, making your way on into Dyers Lane, bearing right with the road and proceeding uphill, gently at first, then more steeply to reach a crossroads junction. Go straight over, and shortly on the right there is a gate and Cotswold Way signpost; pass through the gate and walk on to **Dovers Hill**, from which there are tremendous views across the Vale of Evesham. The hill is named after Robert Dover, who lived from 1582 to 1652 and founded the Cotswold Olympick Games that have been held on this hill since 1612, with sports ranging from sword play to tug of war and wrestling.

Continue to follow what is a splendid walk along the escarpment edge until you reach a trig point. Bear half-right here, soon reaching a gate and Cotswold Way signpost; turn right through the gate, and by following a clear footpath you will shortly reach the road again. Turn left and follow the road, Kingcombe Lane, enjoying tremendous views to Chipping Campden and the surrounding countryside, with the tower of the church at Chipping Campden very prominent to your right. You descend steeply to a T-junction with the **B4035** and here turn left; very soon, fork right into **Pike's Piece**, the **B4081** Mickleton road, and then take the first road turning to the right, Furze Lane, signposted for Hidcote Gardens. Follow Furze Lane for just under a mile, passing a strip of woodland where the Oxford–Worcester railway passes under the road by means of the **Campden Tunnel**, and take the next left road turn, signed **Heart of England Way**; this 101-mile route starts from Milford in Staffordshire and goes via Cannock Chase, Lichfield, the Arden countryside and the northern Cotswolds, ending in Bourton-on-the-Water. Follow the Heart of England Way along what is a very narrow road, offering beautiful views to the surrounding countryside as well as the splendid buildings of **Hidcote Boyce** to the right.

At the end, you reach a T-junction with a wider metalled road. Turn left onto it, then very shortly right over a stile onto the signed **Monarch's Way** footpath, entering a field. (See the Dorset high point chapter for more information about the Monarch's Way.) Cross the field diagonally to the far top-left corner, then go forward as signed on a straight line initially. However, you need to follow the path, which is fairly obvious on the ground, round to the right, following the right-hand edge of the area of grass; you then need to bear round to the left and go forward, slightly uphill, to a kissing gate, keeping to the Monarch's Way as signed. Beyond the gate, walk along the left-hand field edge and arrive at the top end of a lane. Turn left to follow the lane, which passes the beautiful buildings of **Hidcote Bartrim** and the late seventeenth-century Hidcote Manor, with its fine Georgian frontage, reaching the entrance to the landscaped Hidcote Gardens.

These gardens are magnificent and well worth a visit. They were created by the American-born horticulturalist Major Lawrence Johnston over a period of forty years during the past century and acquired by the National Trust in 1947; they're particularly noteworthy for their 'outdoor rooms', each with their own individual colours and planting schemes (the 'rooms' created by the use of box hedges, hornbeam, yew and stone walls), as well as vast herbaceous borders and very artistic topiary. If the gardens are open you really should stop off and enjoy them, as well as the adjoining tearoom which offers delicious scones, cakes and sandwiches.

Beyond the entrance to the gardens, go forward to a T-junction with lanes going to the left – effectively the approach road to the gardens for vehicles – and right. Turn right at this T-junction and go forward on what is marked as a 'restricted byway' consisting of a clear wide track going uphill. Follow the track, veering sharply right then sharply left, and reach a mast which marks the summit of **Ebrington Hill**, the highest point in Warwickshire. You only actually cross into Warwickshire from Gloucestershire a few yards short of the summit! By turning left along a field boundary just before the mast, and following the boundary, you'll come to a trig point, but you'll quickly see that this isn't quite the highest ground and that to find the topmost terrain it is necessary to get up close to the mast. To get the best views to the west, it's worth going to a point immediately in front of the perimeter of the mast area. On my first visit the question was academic, as all the views were blotted out by a pea-souper of a fog. (Note that you should also technically seek permission to roam from the track here, as none of this is on designated rights of way.) Although on a clear day the view is pretty good, with the Vale of Evesham stretching out ahead of you, there are much better panoramas in the nearby Cotswolds, so don't agonise too much if you find you've left your binoculars behind or the batteries you bought yesterday for your digital camera conk out after only four shots.

Return to the track, and follow it past the mast to a junction with a narrow road. Turn right onto the road and follow it down to a junction with a wider road, bearing right to follow this to a sharp left bend, with a road going off to the right here. It's worth pausing here to enjoy the view, because you will shortly lose most of the height gained since Hidcote. Turn left with the bend but almost immediately bear right over a stile onto a signed path; the path isn't very clear but simply walk over the field in a straight line from the stile. Cross over a further stile into another field and then go forward, downhill, to cross over a couple more stiles and reach Hidcote Road. Turn right, then immediately left, along a path which follows the right-hand field edge then drifts slightly away from it, crossing a small footbridge and continuing clearly downhill through a cornfield. You're now on the **Diamond Way**, the fourth named footpath that you will meet on this walk: the Diamond Way, named for its rough diamond shape, starts and finishes at Moreton-in-Marsh, taking in lots of lovely Cotswold villages and countryside in between.

At the bottom of the field, bear left then shortly right over another footbridge. Bear left beyond the footbridge on a left-hand field edge beside a stream, keeping close to the field edge and veering round to the right with the field edge to reach a gate and footpath junction. Here you bear right and follow a really lovely clear path on a left-hand field edge, then on across fields aiming for the obvious **Mickleton Hills Farm**. Immediately before the farm buildings, turn left and aim just to the left of the earthwork ahead, joining an obvious path which passes over the railway, which you can see below you to the left going into Campden Tunnel. You drop downhill to arrive at a track.

Turn left onto the track but then immediately right onto a signed path. It looks unpromising at first but then becomes obvious, following the right-hand field edge on what is another snippet of the Heart of England Way. Ignoring a path which goes away to the right, you go past the east side of a large school and, just beyond it, you reach a field corner. Bear right here to pass to the left of the school buildings, then left to follow a path running parallel to the school approach road, and arrive at the road leading to Chipping Campden. Turn right to follow this road, which immediately bends sharply left to pass the splendid church and soon reaches a T-junction with the main street, and at this T-junction you bear left to arrive back in the centre of Chipping Campden. I was lucky enough to be staying in the area so, after experiencing zero views from the summit of Ebrington Hill, I was able, after a day's unashamed Cotswold trippery, to revisit the hilltop in much clearer conditions. The fog-bound walker just here for the day will face the choice of investing in a return trip in hopefully better weather, or spending the long homeward journey hoping friends and relatives will be able to tell that the photo of the whitey-grey haze is Ebrington Hill and not the southern approach road to Luton Airport car park.

Buckinghamshire and Hertfordshire

Haddington Hill – 267 metres / 876 feet – SP 890090
Hastoe Hill – 244 metres / 800 feet – SP 914091

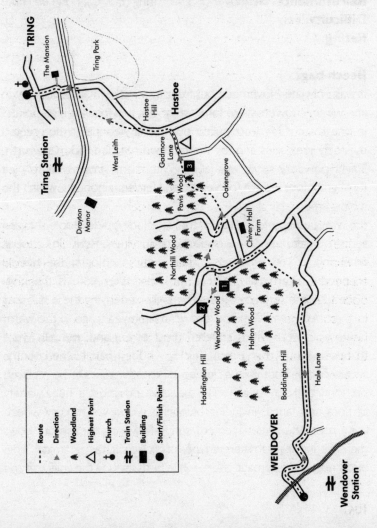

Length: 6 miles
Start: Wendover station
Finish: Tring High Street
Public transport: Regular trains serving Wendover and Aylesbury on the London–Aylesbury line; regular buses serving Tring on the Luton–Aylesbury route; regular trains serving Tring on the London–Milton Keynes route
Refreshments: Wendover (P, S, C); Tring (P, S, C); none en route
Difficulty: Easy
Rating: **

Beech bag

It was only late November, but freezing weather had already set in and wintry showers were forecast for this two-county-high-points-in-one march. My train pulled out of Marylebone to be greeted by steely grey skies and, by the time we reached Rickmansworth, a light powdery snow was falling. With many stations still to pass through before we got to Wendover, I fervently hoped it wasn't the wrong type.

I was perhaps four weeks too late; my guide book showed seductive pictures of the woodlands of Buckinghamshire in October time and, if you want spectacular autumn colours, the heavily wooded Chiltern Hills, where this walk takes you, is the ideal place to come to enjoy them. The chalk underlying these hills was formed between 70 million and 95 million years ago in the warm Cretaceous seas which covered most of England; the hills were to become one of the most thickly wooded part of the country, initially of oak, but this was cleared in Neolithic times to be replaced predominantly by beech. The beechwoods host a huge variety of flora and fauna, including bluebells, wood vetch, cow-wheat, coral root, the sweet-scented, spring-flowering mezereon, dog's mercury and several different types of orchid such as pyramidal, frog, bird's nest and enigmatic ghost, while birds include the chiffchaff and willow warbler. You may also find the edible dormouse, which was considered a delicacy in Roman times and introduced into Britain in 1902. But I still recommend you bring sandwiches.

From **Wendover station**, make your way up the station approach road; turn left at the end onto the main village street, but then bear shortly right into South Street, which you follow for just over a quarter of a mile. Bear left into Chapel Lane and continue to its end (the lane narrows into a path but simply keep to that path). Turn right at the end, onto a road, then bear shortly left along Hale Lane, which you follow for about 1 mile, although there is a parallel path to the left for part of the way which will make a change from tarmac crunching. There is then quite a sharp bend of the road to the right and, on this bend, there are two signed footpaths to the left almost adjacent. Ignore the first but take the second, signed as the **Icknield Way** path; you need the path immediately before the signpost, not the driveway beyond. The Icknield Way, whose name is thought to derive from the Iceni tribe, who may have used it as a warpath, was historically a trading route linking Norfolk with south-west England, although it's not as old as the Ridgeway. Where possible, it followed ridges and the lower chalk shelf, which was found to provide easier going than the Chiltern woods.

Follow the sunken path through the woods, ignoring any forking paths, and you are soon joined by the **Ridgeway path**, continuing uphill; this isn't the only county high point walk which meets the Ridgeway path – so do the Wiltshire and Oxfordshire walks. The path widens and arrives at a minor road. Turn left to follow it, and in just under half a mile you pass a reservoir to your left; go on past a couple of houses immediately beyond the reservoir and you'll notice the road bending right. Look out at this point for a gate ■ in the hedge to your left, with a signed footpath. Pass through the gate and follow the signed path to the far end, at the edge of woodland. On a clear day this will be straightforward and easy, but when I walked it the powdery snow, which had created the daintiest of dustings on Hale Lane, had stopped and freezing fog had set in, completely blotting the way ahead, there was suddenly a surreal calm across the Chiltern landscape. I now guessed how the enigmatic ghost orchid might have got its name.

As soon as you enter the wood, now officially on **Haddington Hill** (although in reality it's just part of a broad plateau), you reach a fork junction and you need to take the left fork path through woods. This path could be very muddy and it most definitely was for me. You reach a thin clearing and line of telegraph wires coming in from the right **2**, with prominent telegraph poles to the left, and go forward to a forest road. Turn right and follow the forest road very briefly, then, ignoring the path going off immediately to the right, continue on to the next path going away to the right, signed for walkers only, and join it. It passes through the woods, bending left, and then bending left again; at the second sharp bend, bear right along a path which takes you to the Chiltern Summit cairn. The view is obscured by surrounding woodland, part of **Wendover Wood**, but with so much fog about there wasn't much for me to see anyway, which is why it was nice that I at least had the cairn to admire. There is a plaque on the cairn telling you it was erected to commemorate the Queen's Silver Jubilee in 1977, by the Forestry Commission, RAF, and Aston Clinton and Halton Parish Councils. There must be a pub quiz question there somewhere.

Retrace your steps to the road at the point shown at **1** above, remembering to bear right as marked by a tree arrow at point **2** above – don't follow the telegraph wires! On reaching the point at **1**, turn left onto the road, then in a couple of hundred yards turn right onto the Icknield Way trail, as signed, just before a big house, passing through a gate to join the path. Follow the path through the woods, continuing to a road and a junction with the Ridgeway path; ignore the Ridgeway path sign pointing to the right, but cross over the road to join the Ridgeway path signed beyond. Now follow the

Ridgeway path through **Northill Wood** and **Pavis Wood**, arriving at another road ■, Gadmore Lane.

Turn right here and follow the road. As you continue along the level road, the land immediately to the left of you, officially **Hastoe Hill**, is in fact on the highest ground in Hertfordshire – the road is the border between Buckinghamshire and Hertfordshire. You soon reach a slight right-hand bend and there's a gate to the left which you could pass through to say you are officially in Hertfordshire. Trevor Montague's otherwise impeccable listing of county high points in his A to Z of Britain and Ireland is marginally misleading, as he says this high point is Pavis Wood but, while you can see the wood, you are not in it. This, in fact, has to be one of the most desperately disappointing high points described in this book, as there is no view, no satisfying summit plateau, still less a triangulation point, still even less a cairn with plaque provided by the Forestry Commission, RAF, and Aston Clinton and Halton Parish Councils.

Return to the point ■ above and now continue along Gadmore Lane, which bends to the right and continues to the hamlet of **Hastoe**. The road bends left at Hastoe and you follow it round, then in a quarter of a mile or so you reach a signed footpath going off to the left at Grove Wood – signed 'Tring via the Downs'. There's a barn here, and you need to take the footpath which goes to the left of the barn and then alongside the edge of the wood, along a left-hand field edge. The path is signed actually into the wood but continues close to the edge in the same general direction. You reach a path junction and take the signed path which resumes its course along the field edge, then goes forward through fields with good views to Tring. I know – I got my first decent view of my walk during this section, the fog having lifted and a watery sunshine trying to pierce through the wintry cloud cover. Continue downhill, bearing right at the path junction at the top of the A41 cutting, then turn right to continue beside the cutting to Hastoe Lane.

Turn left at the end into Hastoe Lane, passing under the A41, and walk on along the lane, soon kinking right then immediately left to reach **Tring High Street** and journey's end (although a shortish bus ride will get you to the Bedfordshire county high point walk). The town has an excellent range of amenities and eateries but is best known for the Natural History Museum at Tring, which was founded by Lionel Walter Rothschild in the late nineteenth century and which houses the world's largest collection of fleas. And this may explain why, having avoided any thorns or stinging nettles throughout your walk, you're still scratching the back of your legs as you sit down for your celebratory Costa coffee.

West Midlands

Turner's Hill – 271 metres / 886 feet – SO 967887

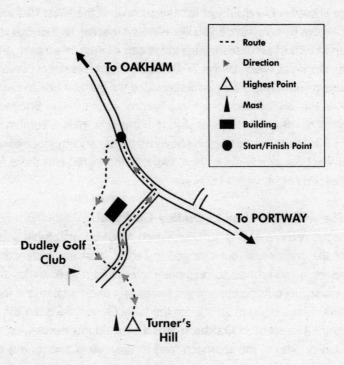

Length: 1 mile
Start and finish: Dudley Golf Club
Public transport: Regular buses serving Dudley Golf Club on the Dudley–Birmingham route (service 120 at the time of writing)
Refreshments: None. NOTE: Ample refreshments are available in Dudley, a short bus ride away
Difficulty: Easy
Rating: *

Hum Brum

The omens for this weren't great. On my mini-break in the Midlands I'd enjoyed a sensational ascent of the Kinder Scout plateau in Derbyshire; a triumphant march to Shining Tor, which made a superb summit for Cheshire; and a fabulous climb to the heights of Shropshire. Which just left the summit of the West Midlands – Greater Birmingham, if you like – involving some serious bus travel and a hazardous dash through the streets of Wolverhampton, trying to work out which of the 26,000 buses plying its streets on a hot airless Tuesday morning in July provided the quickest ride to Dudley. And this on the back of a most uncomfortable stay in Bridgnorth. With a rather lumpy bed, slightly burnt skin, plus a combination of the sounds of the rushing Severn and the church clock chiming every hour of the night, there were all the ingredients there for a sleepless night, which I duly got.

The walk starts close to **Dudley Golf Club**. Initially I'd thought about recommending a route which followed a sizeable section of the golf course but changed my mind, perhaps influenced by having a fortnight or so previously attempted a walk across a golf course just outside Epsom, got hopelessly disorientated and found myself on a collision course for the Gobi Desert. So catch the bus to the bus stop on **Oakham Road** situated just north-west (the Dudley side) of the approach road to the club. If that sounds a bit convoluted, just ask to be dropped by the approach road to the club and walk on to the bus stop.

Immediately beyond the bus stop turn left off Oakham Road to follow a rough grassy path, very shortly arriving beside the fairway of the first hole of the golf course. Bear left to follow the fairway, then walk in front of the first tee and go forward to pass immediately in front of the clubhouse, aiming for a clear dirt track just beyond it. Now, maintaining the same direction, walk along the left-hand side of the fairway of the third hole, towards the tee of the fourth hole. But just before you reach it, bear left by a public footpath sign to arrive at a metalled lane, in fact a continuation of the golf club approach road, and go straight over it onto a crude path that goes over rough grass, aiming for what looks like a golf club practice fairway. To your right are the twin masts – actually BT radio towers – of **Turner's Hill** and separating you from it is a sloping field fenced off by barbed wire. So, two issues: one, it's private, so you should seek permission before ascending further (if you proceed without permission, you do so at your own risk) and two, if you're not careful, your treasured knickerbockers will be torn to ribbons. However, if you look carefully, you will see a point in the fencing where the barbed wire has been raised, enabling you to pass underneath without too much difficulty.

Now, pleased that you've been able to make some use of all those winter evenings at the local adult education college perfecting the art of limbo dancing, make your way up to the stout metalled fencing protecting the masts. By standing hard up against the fence at the nearest point to the masts, you are in fact on the highest ground in the West Midlands. The views from this spot aren't fantastic, but there are none better from this elevation; this is the only accessible point on the summit plateau (if you can call it that), other hilltop or hillside wanderings precluded by fencing going all the way round the masts, and a large working quarry on the south side. It is true that on a clear day you should, both from up top and on your way back down, be able to see the hills of Shropshire as well as Kinver Edge, the Clent Hills and possibly even the Malverns. But it's not a classic panorama – sorry.

The simplest way back to the bus stop is to return to the metalled lane, turn right and follow it back to Oakham Road, turning left to return to the bus stop; although note that for a bus back to Birmingham you'll need to cross the road from the bus stop on the golf course side, turn right along Oakham Road, then turn shortly left. However, for more exercise and better scenery, you could create your own route around the golf course – the hole numbers are given on each teeing area, so you shouldn't get lost – but as far as possible avoid walking along or across fairway; and keep a watchful eye for maverick balls.

Leicestershire

Bardon Hill – 278 metres / 912 feet – SK 459131

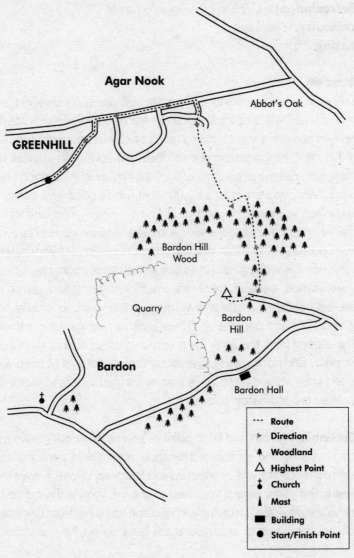

Agar Nook

Abbot's Oak

GREENHILL

Bardon Hill
Wood

Quarry

Bardon
Hill

Bardon

Bardon Hall

`- - -`	**Route**
▶	**Direction**
♠	**Woodland**
△	**Highest Point**
♁	**Church**
▮	**Mast**
■	**Building**
●	**Start/Finish Point**

Length: 4½ miles
Start and finish: Greenhill, near Coalville
Public transport: Regular buses serving Greenhill on the Leicester–Markfield–Whitwick–Coalville route
Refreshments: Greenhill (S); none en route
Difficulty: Moderate
Rating: **

Blast off

This is, in a sense, a 'textbook' county high point. An excellent bus service obligingly drops you not so far from your objective that you have to raid every store within a radius of 15 miles for extra supplies of Kendal Mint Cake, but not so close that you'll find yourself up there with half the population of the East Midlands. It is a good brisk climb, taking you to not far off 1,000 feet, with a good view awaiting you when you get there, and you'll know exactly where and when you've reached your objective. A bit like a space rocket: take off from obscurity and shoot straight up to the heights. Unfortunately, however, this won't go down as one of the classic county high point walks, simply because there are insufficient paths and places of interest nearby to create a rewarding circular walk, so it really has to be an out-and-back march. There is also a practical issue, namely that blasting from the adjoining quarry may affect access, chiefly on weekday afternoons, and I have to say there's not a lot to keep you entertained at base camp while waiting for the blasters to knock off for their tea and bacon butties.

Greenhill, the start and finish point of your walk, struck me on my visit as untidy and sprawling; teenagers hung about aimlessly, the community centre was boarded up and litter was strewn all over the greens and parks. Unless you need to use the shop in the centre of the village, I suggest, assuming you've come up by bus from Leicester, you ask the driver to drop you at the last stop on the main street,

Cropston Drive, before its junction with Greenhill Road. Go forward to the junction and turn right up Greenhill Road, heading just north of east; follow it for just under half a mile, then just beyond Stamford Drive, which is on the left, look out for and join the signed **Ivanhoe Way** path going off to the right. The sign announces that **Bardon Hill**, your objective, is 1½ miles from here. Bardon Hill is part of the area known as Charnwood Forest, and is one of a number of rocky outcrops for which the 'forest' is noteworthy; the 1819 novel *Ivanhoe*, written by Sir Walter Scott, was set in Charnwood Forest in the twelfth century, and the 35-mile Ivanhoe Way, which starts and finishes at Ashby-de-la-Zouch, follows the countryside which was the setting for the novel. Although much of the area is no longer covered by trees, there are some large areas of woodland, while a former coalfield lies on its western edge.

Follow the path forward into Vercor Close, aiming for the top left-hand end of the close, where you'll find the path continues on in a south-easterly direction.

Leaving the houses behind, continue along this path, which follows left-hand field edges, proceeding clearly and obviously, and going up to reach a wood. Turn sharp left onto the path which follows the edge of this wood, but shortly look out for and take a gated path going off to the right, leaving the Ivanhoe Way. The path goes uphill quite steeply through the wood, then emerges into a grassier area with much younger trees. Looking half-right you should be able to see the trig point, your ultimate objective, on a cliff edge just to the right of the mast. Keep on along the obvious path to the top, passing a bench, then drop down very slightly to reach a metalled kissing gate. Go through it, bearing right with the path, then turn right again onto a metalled driveway that soon becomes a rougher track leading to the mast.

Pass round to the right of the mast and then take your pick between the rocky paths which go through an area of thick vegetation to the base of the cliff on which the triangulation point is built. Now climb to the trig point, the highest ground in Leicestershire. Immediately below you is the **quarry**; in fact, it provides a supply of granite that is extremely valuable for road construction, formed from volcanic activity millions of years ago, but isn't terribly scenic. The view just beyond isn't that great either, consisting of the houses and factories of Coalville. Yes, the name says it all – it was a mining town serving the coalfield that once existed here. But the views beyond Coalville to the west are extensive and very rewarding, as they are to the higher-lying Charnwood Forest to the north and east. They are obscured to the south by the vegetation immediately nearby, so don't bother trying to train your binoculars on the Leicester bus station cafe which served you that rather good chocolate flapjack you enjoyed while waiting for the 29A.

It now simply remains for you to retrace your steps, scrambling down from the trig point onto the rocky ground immediately beneath, following one of the narrow rocky paths through the trees to the mast, then passing to the left of it and veering left to the metalled kissing gate. Just before you do, enjoy the view to Leicester which is now available. Beyond the kissing gate, it's downhill all the way; first through the plantation, then the wood, remembering to turn left onto the path at the bottom, then shortly right, out of the wood. You then follow what is, on your return walk, the right-hand field edge, and go on past the houses along the Ivanhoe Way to reach Greenhill Road, bearing left to return to the junction with Cropston Drive. Turn left into this drive and make for the first bus stop on the left; if you're in need of chocolate therapy you'll need to plough on that bit further to reach the shops, but I have to say that you would need to be fairly desperate for a choccy fix to want to risk missing a bus to get you away from here – begging Greenhill's Bardon.

Dorset

Lewesdon Hill – 279 metres / 915 feet – ST 437011

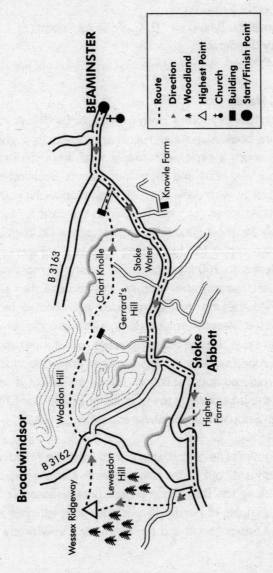

Length: 6 miles
Start and finish: Beaminster
Public transport: Regular buses serving Beaminster from Bridport (in turn served by buses on the Dorchester–Axminster route) and, less frequently, Crewkerne
Refreshments: Beaminster (P, C, S); Stoke Abbott (P)
Difficulty: Moderate
Rating: ****

Bus me, Hardy

You couldn't ask for more: a lovely town to start and finish your walk, two picture-book villages and magnificent scenery throughout. And it's pretty much a circle, with only a small amount of repetition just at the very start and end. Your start is Beaminster, which Thomas Hardy, who drew so much inspiration for his novels from the beautiful Dorset countryside, used as the basis for Emminster in arguably his most famous novel, *Tess of the D'Urbervilles*. The whole town centre has been designated as a conservation area, with no less than 200 listed buildings. Among its most interesting features are seventeenth-century almshouses, the sixteenth-century Pickwick's Inn, the market square and stone-roofed market cross, and the fifteenth-century church with a splendid tower of old tinted Hamstone. It once boasted a variety of industries and trades, including rope, sailcloth, shoes, wrought ironwork, clockmaking and embroidered buttons. It's not served by rail but is served by bus from the larger nearby towns of either Bridport or Crewkerne – although Bridport has no railway line either.

From the town's fine central square, follow the main road (**A3066**) north-westwards out of the town towards Crewkerne, but then bear left along the **B3163** signposted Broadwindsor. Follow this road for a couple of hundred yards, then turn left onto the road signposted Stoke Abbott and New Inn. It's a very pretty country road which you follow for the mile and a half to **Stoke Abbott**, a delightful village with thatched cottages, pretty gardens and a stream running beside the village street. Its church of St Mary the Virgin is of Norman origin and boasts an Early English chancel and Jacobean pulpit; it was struck by lightning in 1828 and wasn't restored for another fifty years. Some Norman features remain, including a window on the north side and carved stone font. Stoke Abbott does have one dark memory: in 1858 a cottage in the village caught fire and the body of a twenty-three-year-old woman was found in the wreckage with her throat cut. A relative was subsequently found guilty of her murder and was hanged... Let's move on.

At the far (southern) end of the village street at **Higher Farm** the road bends to the right, but you go straight on along a lane, very shortly turning right onto a signed path, actually a dirt track. This shortly peters out so you need to join the grass to your right and follow a narrow but clear path downhill, aiming for a gate; go through the gate and carry on down to the next gate, going through it, and forward to a metalled lane and a third gate. Pass through it and now walk very steeply downhill through the field, as shown on the footpath (**Jubilee Trail**) signpost, keeping to the right of a very large tree in the middle of the field, and aiming for a gate at the bottom right-hand corner. (Just in case you're curious, the Jubilee Trail is an 88-mile walk between Forde Abbey and Bokerley Dyke, crossing Dorset from border to border, created to celebrate the Diamond Jubilee of the Ramblers'.) Go through the gate and onto a boardwalk then, observing the footpath sign, climb steeply uphill on the other side; at the top bear right to follow a left-hand field edge to a gate at the top left-hand corner of the field. Continue along the path, which is rather overgrown, keeping buildings to the right, then veering right just beyond the buildings to reach a road.

Turn left and follow the road, shortly reaching a crossroads with the **B3162** Bridport–Broadwindsor road; the views from here are magnificent and just get better as you continue. Go straight over onto a lane but in about 20 yards leave the road by turning right into a field. There was no footpath sign here at the time of writing but this is a right of way; it is undefined through the field and you need to aim for the trees uphill ahead (the ones on which you can see the tall barks, rather than the mass of woodland just to the right of them). Soon you'll see a gate which you pass through, and beyond the gate there is a clear path bringing you to a metalled farm lane. Turn left and in just a few yards turn sharply right up a signed bridlepath. Look shortly, very carefully, for two paths going off to the left in close succession, with a bridleway sign between the two. You need to take the second of these two paths, just beyond the sign, and this now takes you decisively and quite steeply uphill through the woods, rich in beech and oak. Do pause from time to time to enjoy the views through the trees southwards across rolling Dorset hill country.

Keep walking, and in due course you will pass an information board telling you that you are now on the National Trust-owned **Lewesdon Hill**, the site of an Iron Age settlement, and formed from greensand, a kind of sandstone consisting largely of grains of quartz and glauconite. Continuing to gain height you keep to your path until you finally reach the narrow plateau marking the summit of Lewesdon Hill. You are now on the highest ground in Dorset, although previously it was believed that Pilsdon Pen, 2 miles or so to the west, may be the county's highest ground; there was the geographer's equivalent of a stewards' enquiry on the matter, until it was established that Lewesdon had it – by just 2 metres. The two summits are so close and so lofty that it's natural to think of them as twin peaks and understandable that Dorset folk speak of things 'as much alike as Lewesdon Hill and Pilsdon Pen'.

The highest point on the Lewesdon Hill plateau is a small green elevation (precise grid reference, if you want to prime your GPS toy, ST 43778 01171) at the start of the plateau as you reach it, where green paths fork right and left. Note how steeply the ground drops away from the plateau on all sides. There are sufficient gaps through the trees to get some tremendous views, particularly to the south where, beyond a rolling patchwork of fields and hedgerows, you can clearly see the sea. It is a wonderfully unspoilt and peaceful spot, the solitude and the silence quite magical; even on the fine Saturday in late July when I visited, I had the plateau to myself. But all good things must come to an end and you will need to move on, taking the right-hand fork of the green paths at the start of the plateau. Follow it initially along the edge of the plateau then steeply downhill through beautiful woodland, enjoying views through the trees to the north this time. At the bottom of the hill you reach a crossroads of paths; don't go straight over through the gate, but turn right onto a stony track skirting the northern edge of the woods and offering fine views to the left, including the pretty village of **Broadwindsor**. This track is part of the **Wessex Ridgeway**, which runs for 137 miles from Marlborough to Lyme Regis via Avebury, and its prehistoric standing stones, the Vale of Pewsey, Salisbury Plain, Cranborne Chase and Cerne Abbas.

The track, continuing along the Wessex Ridgeway, loses more height, going quite steeply downhill in places to reach the B3162. Your way is straight across, but you could, and if you have time certainly should, detour left for the walk of just over half a mile to Broadwindsor. A full forty houses in the village are listed as being of historic interest by the Royal Commission on the Historical Monuments of England, while the church boasts a fifteenth-century tower and a seven-sided Jacobean pulpit. One cottage in the centre of the village bears a plaque stating that Charles II stayed the night there (at that time the cottage was part of the Castle Inn) on the night of 23 September 1651, on his way to France after his defeat at the Battle of Worcester. There is another long-distance footpath, based on the route he took in fleeing from the parliamentary forces, called the Monarch's Way, which goes right through Broadwindsor. This monster path starts from Powick Bridge in Worcestershire and runs via Boscobel (site of *that* oak tree), Stratford, the Cotswolds, the Mendips and a section of the south coast between Charmouth and Shoreham-by-Sea in West Sussex. It does tend to go the pretty way and, incredibly, covers 615 miles, making it the longest named inland route in England. Weary walkers for whom the novelty of following in regal footsteps wore off after the first 100 miles might be forgiven for wishing the Merry Monarch had, after leaving Worcester, made a beeline for the sea at once and engaged a willing boatman in Weston-super-Mare.

Having crossed the **B3162**, walk between farm buildings where you will see a choice of paths; you need to take the right-hand one, along a clear track which soon passes through two adjacent gates and goes uphill to gates side by side. You go through the right-hand one and now follow a much less distinct path, sharing your route not only with the Wessex Ridgeway but the Beaminster Ramblers Millennium Walk. Which, bless the Beaminster Ramblers, doesn't measure quite as long as 615 miles. The waymarks of the named paths guide you as, keeping **Waddon Hill** with its ancient fort to your right, you continue along left-hand field edges following in the same direction. You get within sight of the pretty buildings of **Chart Knolle** and here you have to be careful not to get sucked away into one of the steeply sloping fields to the left. You are, in fact, signposted immediately to the left of the path, which goes in front of the house, but having got past the house you need to veer right, over two stiles in quick succession, then uphill, enjoying splendid views back to Lewesdon Hill as you proceed.

Near the top of the hill, known as **Gerrard's Hill**, the path veers to the left, moving from south-eastwards to eastwards, but you should detour to the triangulation point on the hilltop and enjoy gorgeous views, including those to Stoke Abbott which you passed through earlier on. Return to the path and now drop down steeply, the buildings of Beaminster visible ahead. Now you need to be careful; as you progress, you'll see to your half-right some buildings on the hillside, while ahead of you, but between you and Beaminster, is an area of woodland. From where you stand you should be able to see what is your path emerging from the woodland towards its top left-hand corner. The path signs rather confusingly seem now to lead you alongside an electric fence going towards the buildings, but you need to keep left of that and walk very steeply downhill, aiming for a stile roughly on the line of the top left-hand corner of the woods.

Cross the stile and drop down to the start of the woodland, reassured by a Wessex Ridgeway waymark, and now it's plain sailing, a clear path through the woods taking you uphill, out of the woods, and then briefly downhill. You reach a farm building and here it's important to bear round to the right with the path, soon reaching a stile and entering a field. Follow the clear path through the field to another stile, going forward along an obvious track through the trees to reach a minor road. Turn right onto that road, then at its end turn left onto what is the Beaminster–Stoke Abbott road. You've come full circle! It just remains for you to follow this to a T-junction with the B3163 and turn right to follow this road back to the A3066, turning right to arrive back in the centre of Beaminster.

There are plenty of shops and eateries in the town but, if you have a list of buses and trains to get you back to your Saturday evening date with Harry Hill or Gary Lineker, you may not feel disposed to hanging around. That said, the bus services hereabouts are pretty good and the service from Bridport to Dorchester, the nearest railhead, has improved greatly in recent years. Nonetheless, my bus was very late into Bridport and I spent a nail-biting thirty minutes fearful of missing out… not on Messrs Hill and Lineker but on my keenly anticipated poached eggs on toast in the Horse with the Red Umbrella in Dorchester.

West Sussex

Black Down – 280 metres / 919 feet – SU 919296

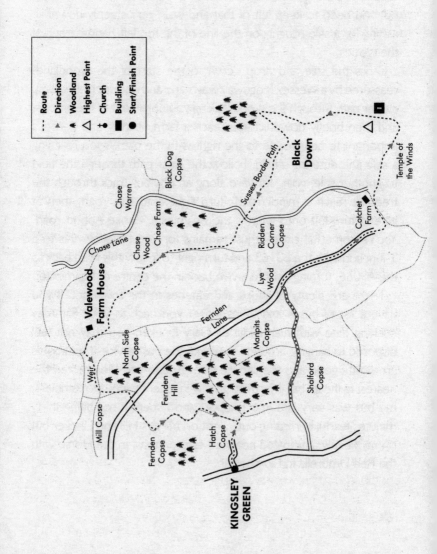

Length: 5½ miles
Start and finish: Kingsley Green, A286 just north of junction with Hatch Lane
Public transport: Regular buses serving Kingsley Green on the Haslemere–Midhurst route
Refreshments: None
Difficulty: Moderate
Rating: ***

Could do verse

Whereas other beauty spots in England, such as the Lake District and the Malverns, have associations with a number of writers, poets and composers, Black Down enjoys a link with just one poet – but what a poet. 'The Lady of Shalott', 'The Charge of the Light Brigade', 'In Memoriam A. H. H.', 'The Revenge, Come into the Garden', 'Maud' ... Yes, who else but Alfred, Lord Tennyson, for whom Aldworth House, high up on the east side of the hill, was built in 1868–69 as a summer retreat when Farringford, his home on the Isle of Wight became 'too well known', as Nikolaus Pevsner, author of *The Buildings of England* series, quaintly put it. Pevsner was no great lover of Tennyson's new Sussex bolt-hole, calling it a 'fussy small hotel halfway between French and English sixteenth-century style'. Keith Spence is more complimentary, describing it as 'unpretentious', commenting favourably on its stone carvings and the breathtaking view from the garden terrace. Tennyson, who died in 1892, spent the last twenty years of his life here, and wrote much of 'Idylls of the King', based on Arthurian legend, in the garden. There's now a lane named after him, linking the hillside with the nearby town of Haslemere.

Aldworth House isn't the only building of note on its slopes: on the south face is Blackdown House, described by Pevsner as a 'handsome, plain stone manor house', which dates back to 1640, although it was significantly altered 200 years later. Neither

Aldworth House nor Blackdown House are open to the public, nor are they on your route. But at least if it does start to rain there are enough trees up there to shelter you from the worst of it.

Anyway, back to business. From the bus stop on the north (Haslemere) side of Hatch Lane, Kingsley Green, walk back to Hatch Lane and turn left along it. It shortly swings right, and very soon after it does so you bear left along a clear path which proceeds south-eastwards through woods, veering south to a T-junction with another bridleway. Turn left along it, following a generally easterly direction, avoiding being sidetracked, being careful not to take the signed footpath going off hard left. At length you reach a metalled lane. Go straight over it onto a path the other side, the path veers left then round to the right and downhill; keep rolling fields to your left and arrive at Fernden Lane.

Turn right to follow the lane, passing lakes which are to your left, then in roughly half a mile turn left opposite the **Cotchet Farm** sign onto a signed path going left. Take the path, which goes up to some houses where there's a footpath junction and National Trust sign for Black Down, and at this junction you turn right and follow the path uphill. As you reach the heights of Black Down, you arrive at a path junction with a sign for Temple of the Winds. Go straight on (that said, you should detour to the Temple of the Winds for the best views) but very shortly bear left along a clear path heading north through the woods. Continue along this path until, in a hundred yards or so, you reach a fingerpost ◼ with the bridleway signed forward and backward, and after wet weather there may be a little pond just to the right. Bear left here onto a signed National Trust path which rises gently, then just beyond the top of the rise, as it starts to drop, turn right onto a narrow path which keeps to the topmost ground and arrives at the **Black Down** trig point, which is the highest point in West Sussex.

It's described by Pevsner as a 'great whale-backed sandstone hill'; Peter Brandon, author of numerous books about the Sussex landscape, refers to the 'riotous heather blossom' which annually decorates the hillside; and Keith Spence calls it the 'nearest approach to a mountain in these parts… shaggily coated in trees like one of the foothills of the Jura'; and Tennyson once wrote: 'When I came back this summer and looked from the terrace at Black Down I thought it was exactly like Italy.' It is the profusion of trees which deprives Black Down of any real photogenic quality and can often restrict the views. Even from the best viewpoint, in the vicinity of the **Temple of the Winds** (see the detour above) the vista is not panoramic; but, despite that, and the fact that there's no temple here – although there could well be a lot of wind – the construction does still provide a splendid vantage point to enjoy miles of beautiful Sussex countryside towards the South Downs. The trig point itself, and the highest point in the whole of Sussex, East Sussex included, is accessed only by a rather thin path, contrasting with the wide tracks decorating the slopes of Black Down at many points. Moreover, it is shrouded in woodland, but it is still a lovely, quiet, totally unspoilt spot, and there are fine views through the trees.

Now retrace your steps to the fingerpost at ◼ above and turn left to continue along the bridleway. You shortly have a choice between taking a left-hand bridleway, which veers gently north-westwards then north-eastwards, or a right-hand bridleway, which veers gently north-eastwards then north-westwards. Shortly beyond the point where these bridleways reunite – the signposting makes it clear when they do – take the next signed path to the left which almost immediately brings you to a junction with another bridlepath, the **Sussex Border Path**. This route starts near Emsworth and works its way round to Rye, aiming to follow the Sussex border throughout. It doesn't quite do what it says on the tin – although in fairness if it did, you'd need your bathing costume as there'd be a good bit of river swimming and ditch hopping involved. It was opened in 1989, as the signposts often tell you, although one might complain that there aren't enough signposts around; you certainly couldn't do it without a map, as I found out the hard way when walking it myself.

As you descend from Black Down, you'll also meet the **Serpent Trail**, a 64-mile walk along the hills of the Sussex greensand, linking Haslemere with Petersfield. Residents of the Surrey/Sussex/Hampshire border or commuters on the Portsmouth–London Waterloo line may wonder how it takes 64 miles to walk between two towns which aren't more than a few minutes apart by road and rail, but like a serpent, the trail is a slithery beast and actually follows an 'S' shape around West Sussex, going via Petworth and Midhurst on its journey. The trail is part of the Sussex Wealden Greensand Heaths Project which aims to restore heathland in West Sussex; over three-quarters of it has been lost in the past 200 years. In contrast to the Sussex Border Path, signposting is very generous, so much so that there are places where it seems to be indicating two routes at the same time. Nothing like going round in circles to please a tired walker at the end of a long day.

Now on the Sussex Border Path, turn left to follow it briefly south-westwards, then at the next multi-path direction turn right as signed, *not* hard right down the path through the gully. You head north-westwards along the Sussex Border Path and come to a crossroads of paths, going straight over through the gate and forward through the woods to a T-junction of paths. Turn right here, still on the Sussex Border Path, with a fence to your left. Bear left shortly, as signed, to drop down through the woods, turning sharp left and arriving at the edge of a lovely piece of parkland with splendid views to Valewood Farm House and beyond; go right to follow a clear path across the field, dropping down at the far end of the field. The Sussex Border Path then describes a large horseshoe through the pasture ahead, but a signed path pointing left here gives you a much shorter, steeper descent to a track by a gate.

Turn left to pass through the gate and follow the track round to the right to arrive at a metalled drive; bear right onto the drive which veers left, heading for a road, but just before the road turn left to proceed along the Sussex Border Path over a footbridge by a weir. Veer sharp right to continue along the path, using a boardwalk through the marsh, and then up steps to a T-junction with a lane. Turn right onto the lane, going forward to a T-junction with another lane, here turning left to walk up to **Fernden Lane**; bear right here then, very shortly, as the road bends to the left, turn left onto a signed footpath, which is in fact a metalled driveway. Go straight along it, south-westwards, then veer left, just east of south, arriving at a junction of driveways with signs to private houses. Turn right here as signed and shortly left, downhill on a clear path, keeping houses to your left.

At the bottom of the hill turn right onto a path with woodland to your left and a field to your right, going forward through woods to arrive at a T-junction with the bridlepath you followed soon after you began your walk. Turn right onto it, going forward into Hatch Lane and shortly arriving back at the start. Buses are available to the historic towns of Haslemere and Midhurst, which offer plenty of good coffee shops and pubs.

Having been introduced to the Sussex Border Path you may want to walk more of it, but when walking it myself I met very few other walkers and there is indeed very little literature available on walking the route. Although if that means fewer visitors to Black Down… well, maybe that's the way Alfred would have wanted it.

Surrey

Leith Hill – 295 metres / 965 feet – TQ 139431

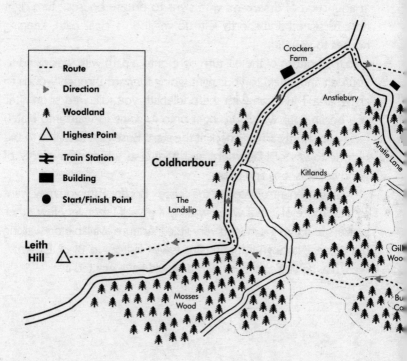

Length: 5½ miles
Start and finish: Holmwood station
Public transport: Regular trains serving Holmwood (not Sun) on the Horsham-Dorking line
Refreshments: Coldharbour (P)
Difficulty: Moderate
Rating: ***

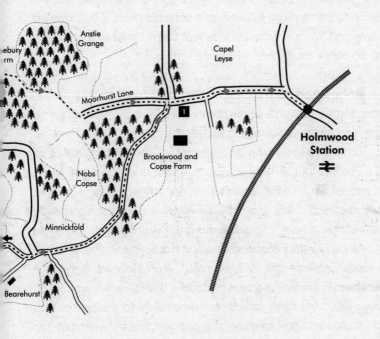

Hunting tower

Despite its proximity to London, Surrey boasts some fine countryside, hilltops and viewpoints. Box Hill is a particular favourite with visitors, being close to the centre of Dorking and very accessible by road. But, contrary to what the swarms round this particular honeypot might believe, it isn't the summit of Surrey; that particular honour goes to Leith Hill, just a few miles to the west of Box Hill and posing a few more logistical problems to the car-less traveller. To start with, if you are relying on public transport, you can't realistically do this walk on Sunday as your base station, Holmwood, is one of very few on the Southern Railway network which goes to sleep on the Sabbath. It lies off the fast Horsham–Crawley–Gatwick line into London on a more leisurely and certainly more scenic one via Dorking and Epsom, with less frequent trains than many Southern lines. So check times carefully before setting out.

From **Holmwood station**, follow the road immediately above the station north-westwards briefly, bearing left by a 30 mph sign onto a signed footpath, which soon reaches a T-junction with a metalled lane. Turn left to follow this lane, passing a signed path going off to the left, before long arriving at a junction with lanes forking off to the right and left ∎. Take the left fork here and follow a clearly defined, initially metalled, track which heads south-westwards, first beside fields and then through pleasant woodland. Veering right, you arrive at a T-junction with a metalled lane and follow this to shortly arrive at a road. Cross straight over the road onto a driveway signed for **Bearehurst**; follow this drive very briefly, then take the signed path heading off to the right, with trees immediately to the right as you follow it. You go uphill to arrive at a path junction between patches of woodland, and here you bear left, *not* hard left. Now, keeping the woodland to your left, follow the left-hand field edge on a reasonably clear path, heading in a westerly direction and ascending.

Now simply continue along the path through the area of pasture between woodland to the left and right, climbing steadily and eventually arriving at a T-junction with a metalled road. Turn right and almost immediately left onto a signed path which heads very pleasantly uphill through woodland to arrive at another metalled road. Turn left here, then bear right into the so-called **Landslip car park**; walk all the way through the car park running roughly parallel to the road, passing an information board, which is to your right, and then exit the car park by joining a path signed for **Leith Hill** summit. It's then simply a case of following the tower symbols on the signposts which take you clearly through the woods, heading predominantly south-westwards. There is one last quite gruelling climb to the summit and its Gothic-style tower.

We'll come to the tower in a minute, but this hilltop is of interest in a number of ways. Firstly, and most obviously, are the superb views which extend to London one way and to the South Downs escarpment the other. Secondly, it is suggested that it was here, in 851, that Æthelwulf of Wessex, father of Alfred the Great, defeated the Danes who were heading for Winchester, having sacked Canterbury and London. Thirdly, it's the highest point on the Greensand Ridge (and the Greensand Way long-distance footpath, a 107-mile walk between Haslemere in Surrey and Ham Street in Kent), and the second-highest point in south-east England, dwarfed only by Walbury Hill, the highest point in Berkshire. It's claimed that looking east, the next ground of equal height is the Ural Mountains in Russia. You'd need a reasonably good telescope to confirm that though.

If possible, you should try and ensure you do the walk when the tower is open, which it is at weekends for most of the year and on some weekdays in the summer. It was built in 1766 by Richard Hull who lived at nearby Leith Hill Place, later the home of the composer Ralph Vaughan Williams. His aim was to 'raise' Leith Hill to above 1,000 feet (305 metres) and in fact he comfortably succeeded, the 64 feet (20 metres) tower taking the summit of Surrey, very artificially, to 1,029 feet (314 metres). Originally the tower consisted of two rooms and there was a Latin inscription to the effect that it was intended not only for Hull's enjoyment but the enjoyment of others. He gave visitors 'prospect glasses' similar to a small telescope which, it was claimed, enabled thirteen counties to be seen on a good day. Hull died in 1772 and was buried beneath the tower; following his death the tower fell into ruin, but almost a hundred years after its construction, it was reopened by a William Evelyn of the nearby Wotton House. Then in 1984 it was fully restored by the National Trust, which installed a shop and even a handrail for those climbing the steps to the top.

Return to the Landslip car park, following the car symbols with an 'L', and then turn left onto the road. Follow the road into the village of **Coldharbour**, past the very attractive little church and on to (and possibly into!) the welcome **Plough Inn**. Continue along the road beyond the pub, a tremendous view opening up to the left, and arrive at a road junction; bear hard right onto the road then almost immediately left onto a metalled farm lane, from which the prospect is again quite delightful. You drop gently to pass between farm buildings, immediately beyond which is a path junction, and here you fork right onto the clear path and head diagonally along it through the field. This is still really beautiful walking and will certainly dispel any feelings of anticlimax after leaving the summit of Leith Hill behind.

Having reached the bottom-right corner of the field, cross over a stile to continue along the path through woodland, emerging onto a path that heads clearly eastwards across pasture, arriving at a thin line of trees. At this point you veer gently right, more steeply downhill, keeping another line of trees to the left, to arrive at a T-junction with a metalled lane. Turn left and follow this lane and you'll arrive back at the junction at **1** above. Now simply retrace your steps to Holmwood, following the lane just north of east and turning right onto the footpath just beyond the **Capel Leyse** turning (on the left), bearing right at the end of the footpath to shortly arrive back at the station.

If you fancy another walk, easily reachable by rail from here, hop onto the train and in a few minutes you'll be at Box Hill & Westhumble. But if you've misread the train times or lingered too long at the Plough Inn and it's late on Saturday evening, let's just hope you're equipped with a good book and two nights' worth of Snickers bars.

Wiltshire

Milk Hill – 295 metres / 968 feet – SU 104643

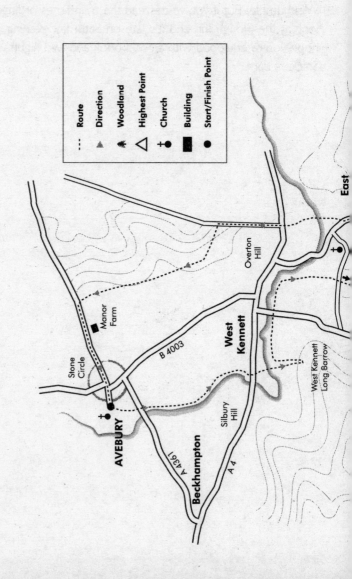

Length: 10 miles
Start and Finish: Red Lion, Avebury
Public transport: Regular buses serving Avebury on the Swindon–Trowbridge route
Refreshments: Avebury (P, C, S); none en route
Difficulty: Moderate
Rating: ****

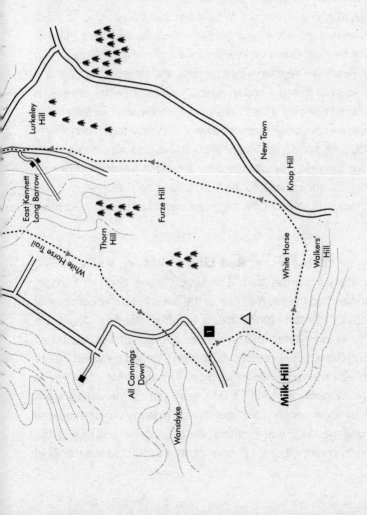

Tomb with a view

This is, like the walk to the summit of the East Riding of Yorkshire, a classic example of a 'better to travel hopefully' walk. While the roof of Wiltshire could be seen as an anticlimax, the tramp there and back, in terms of the wealth of interesting features on the way, is as rewarding as any walk in this book. Avebury and its surroundings provide a fascinating glimpse into our prehistoric past, so much so that you may never actually start the walk to the top of Milk Hill.

So get studying those rail timetables. It's always nice to have choice, and you have the luxury of two ways of approaching Milk Hill if coming by train: one is via Pewsey, where there is a railway station on the Reading–Westbury–Taunton line, the other is via Swindon where you can board a bus to Avebury. In practice, there really is no contest. Pewsey is a very ordinary little town and, despite being on the main London–Penzance railway, very few trains stop there, so if you miss your train you're likely to have to wait about three hours for the next. My train sociably arrived at Swindon in perfect time to allow me to walk to the bus station and patronise its buffet with copious supplies of the biggest Belgian buns known to man. Go via Swindon.

Getting off the bus by the **Red Lion** at Avebury, you're basking in prehistory from the start. The largest stone circle in Europe, Avebury formed the heart of one of the finest Neolithic ceremonial landscapes in Britain. More than a hundred standing stones are arranged in one outer and two inner circles, surrounded by an enormous bank, 13–17 feet (4–5 metres) high and between 70–95 feet (21–29 metres) wide at its base, forming what is known as a henge monument, 4,500–5,000 years old. Some stones were buried by local people for superstitious reasons during medieval times and beyond, while others were used for building in the eighteenth century, but they were partly restored to their original position by Alexander Keiller in the 1930s. The stones, called sarsens (boulders composed of sand bound by silica cement), came from the nearby Marlborough Downs; it is believed they may represent human figures, the tall narrow stones males and the rough diamond shapes females. The village itself is a cluster of thatched cottages and farms, including a fine aisled thatched threshing barn of the late seventeenth century, and the church of St James combines Saxon masonry with broken fragments of stone from the prehistoric circle. There's the Alexander Keiller Museum, pub, shop, cafe and two visitor information centres.

But Milk Hill beckons. From the Red Lion walk down Avebury's main street, turning left along a path just to the left of the Old Vicarage beyond the church. It shortly reaches a T-junction; turn right and then veer left, along the left side of the car park, to reach the **A4361** crossing. Turn right then almost at once bear left through a gate with a blue bridleway arrow, going forward to a second gate and following the path on. Always keeping **Silbury Hill** to your right, continue in the same direction, going forward as directed by the yellow arrow when the bridleway goes off to the right; keeping the River Kennet to your right, kink slightly to follow a right-hand field edge and reach the **A4**. A detour to Silbury Hill is possible here, and definitely recommended.

Silbury Hill, which, with its distinctive conical shape, is the tallest prehistoric construction in Europe, is thought to date back to 2780 BC, the late Neolithic period. It has a base diameter of 551 feet (168 metres) and is 131 feet (40 metres) high. Material for the mound was quarried from the massive ditch that encircled it, although this ditch has now silted up. From as early as 1776 a number of excavations took place on the mound and ditch but no burials came to light, so nobody was any the wiser as to why it was built. Just under 200 years later further excavations revealed that the mound was created as a group of 'drums' built on top of each other, divided by chalk blocks to make the mound stable. Turf from within the mound enabled the hill to be dated, but still nobody knew why it had been built! It appears to be a round barrow and, although no burials have been found there, its purpose may have been a ritual one; and much later in the eleventh century AD, the mound was used as a medieval fort.

Cross the very non-prehistoric A4 with care, turning left then almost immediately right along a track signed West Kennet Long Barrow. The track veers sharply left and shortly the fencing on the right ends to allow a right-turn detour uphill to view the **Long Barrow**. (If you make this detour, which I would highly recommend for its historic interest and spectacular views across Wiltshire, return to the track the same way.)

The Long Barrow is a Neolithic burial mound, which dates back 5,500 years and is one of the largest preserved chambered tombs in southern England. It consists of a long green mound, guarded by stones of local sarsen stone and limestone, and is topped by chalk dug from side ditches which are now silted. It was a communal tomb, and over 1,000 years at least forty-six people were buried there, ranging from very young folk to elderly people. During excavations few complete skeletons were found intact, the suggestion being that the bones may have been rearranged or removed, probably as ritual practices. It is believed that the tomb was filled in about 4,000 years ago. An analysis of the bones shows that arthritis and toothache were common complaints in Neolithic times!

Whether you detour or not, continue on beyond, eastwards, to a narrow lane, crossing straight over and following a right-hand field edge. Walk on to very nearly the top-right corner of the field, but just before the corner turn right to follow the narrow but clear **White Horse Trail** disc-signed path veering southwards to a T-junction of paths. Turn left then immediately right, up to a further T-junction of paths, keeping the village of **East Kennett** to your left. At this next T-junction, turn right then immediately left along a clear track, gradually gaining height; you reach a metalled gate which you simply pass through to continue, keeping a fence to the left, and climbing to a T-junction of paths immediately beyond a fence. Turn right and shortly drop sharply downhill, veering left at the bottom of this short sharp incline to continue along a path with the fence to the left, now heading resolutely south-westwards. Ignoring the crossing track, go on, dropping down and switching to the adjacent field to the left, following the right-hand field edge and, at the top end, veering slightly left to pass through a gap, with **Wansdyke** ridge immediately ahead. Descend very briefly to the ditch, then climb steeply up onto the ridge and turn left to follow the ridgetop eastwards, soon having to leave it by means of a stile at a break in the ridge, but able to pick up the ridgetop again using another stile.

This part of the walk is pleasant rather than spectacular, with Silbury Hill the one obvious landmark that leaps out at you whenever you look round to admire the view. Wansdyke is no Striding Edge and is hardly a challenge to vertigo sufferers, but the ridge, which was built to repel invaders from the north and thought to date probably from the fifth or sixth century AD, provides the best walking of the journey so far. There's a great view westwards along the ridge, and after a climb where all the good views have been achieved by craning your neck behind you or to your right, you get a tantalising glimpse ahead to the Vale of Pewsey and a sneak preview of joys to come a little later on.

Your arrival on the ridge brings you onto the **Mid-Wilts Way**, an east-to-south-west traverse of Wiltshire providing a mixture of open downland walking, strolling beside the Kennet and Avon Canal, and pleasant valley rambling below the western edges of Salisbury Plain. It is 68 miles long, starting at Ham on the border with Berkshire. As well as being on this long-distance footpath, you're now in the heart of the **Pewsey Downs National Nature Reserve**. The thin, dry, lime-rich soil is poor in nutrients, preventing vigorous plants and grasses from taking over, so there are wild flowers in abundance, including many orchids such as the burnt-tip and pyramidal orchid, and other plants to be seen include small scabious, autumn lady's tresses, wild thyme, round-headed rampion, gentian, rock rose and saw-wort; there is a profusion of butterflies including marsh fritillary, chalkhill blue and Adonis blue; and among birds you may see the skylark, grey partridge and kestrel.

Continuing along the ridge you shortly reach a double stile and, observing the Mid-Wilts Way signage, you cross both stiles and turn right, going over the track running parallel to Wansdyke to reach a gate **1** with a Pewsey Downs information board. To detour to Milk Hill, bear left into the field adjacent to the gate on the other side of the fence to the left. Now follow the left-hand field edge running parallel to the track and Wansdyke till you are level with a cylindrical tank next to a brick construction on the right (actually a reservoir). Just above this construction is the highest point of the Milk Hill plateau.

It has to be said that **Milk Hill** itself is a slight anticlimax, and one of those occasions when you wish that one of the shapelier hills nearby was the highest point, perhaps topped by a triangulation point. On entering the field you'll pass a sign you need to follow to reach the hilltop, which indicates there is a permissive route enabling you to cross the highest ground in Wiltshire, but this field-edge route skirts the highest ground rather than going over it. The plateau itself is disappointing; when I explored it there was no difficulty in walking right across it, but you may not be so lucky if crops are being grown hereabouts. Frustratingly, wherever on the plateau you happen to be, the ground immediately around you always looks higher than the ground you're standing on, so it is physically impossible to identify one particular 'high point'. It doesn't help that the contour drawn on Milk Hill on the OS Explorer map makes the plateau look much smaller than it is. So don't lose any sleep over it (well, I didn't); just content yourself with the knowledge that in roaming the plateau you'll have explored the highest ground in Wiltshire, then move on.

Black Hill, the highest point of West Yorkshire.

The splendid aqueduct on the descent from Whernside, North Yorkshire.

The memorial on the roof of Nottinghamshire.

Silbury Hill, one of the highlights on the way up to the summit of Wiltshire.

The frost-bound top of Bedfordshire.

South Yorkshire at its finest and rawest – the ridge walk near its summit at High Stones.

Glorious Derbyshire scenery on the descent from Kinder Scout.

The plaque on top of Somerset.

Bardon Hill, the roof of Leicestershire.

A magnificent Shropshire panorama atop Brown Clee Hill.

The cairn atop the highest ground of Greater Manchester at Black Chew Head.

Field edge walking is necessary to reach the top of Lincolnshire.

The shapely summit of Shutlingsloe from the approach to Shining Tor, the roof of Cheshire.

Approaching Green Hill, the summit of Lancashire.

Delightful Berkshire downland scenery on the walk between the tops of Berkshire and Hampshire.

'Jill' windmill on the way up to Ditchling Beacon, the highest point in East Sussex.

Return the same way to the gate next to the Pewsey Downs information board at ◼ above and now pass through the gate, walking along the turf and keeping the fence to the left. The ground suddenly falls away ahead of you, and you can now enjoy superb views across the Vale of Pewsey, veterans of the Pennine Way perhaps recalling a similar sensation on reaching High Cup above Dufton. Now veer left and contour the steep hillside near to the top of it, keeping Milk Hill to the left, then veering right as instructed by Mid-Wilts Way signs (don't go forward to the gate to the left). Now moving away from the plateau south-westwards, walk along the obvious path downhill, but be sure to veer left at the cattle trough, veering sharply eastwards and now contouring the hillside some way down the slope, aiming for and going forward to a gate in the fence ahead. Go through the gate and walk on along the path immediately above **Alton Barnes White Horse**.

This is a journey of pure joy, with lovely views down to the church at Alton Priors; you may well feel tempted to detour from the path to the burial mounds sitting on the hillsides, providing even more extensive views, although Milk Hill looks as undistinguished from a distance as it did when you were on it. The White Horse itself, measuring 160 feet (49 metres) from nose to tail, and 180 feet (55 metres) from ear to hoof, is visible for 22 miles on a good day. It dates back to 1812 and the cutting was paid for by one Robert Pile; he asked a travelling sign-painter to design and cut it, and gave him £20 as payment. But the sign-painter disappeared without doing the work, so Pile had to pay again to get it done. Moral: don't trust travelling sign-painters.

Continue on the path, veering right through the gorse then left over **Walker's Hill** with the big mound of **Adam's Grave Long Barrow** to the right, your path now on a mini-ridge. As you pass below Adam's Grave, look to the half-left for a car park and, taking that line, head for a stile in the fence to the half-left with a Mid-Wilts Way disc on it. Cross the stile and, still aiming north-eastwards for the car park, arrive at another stile; cross over it, and go forward to just short of the gate and broken stile separating you from the road. Turn left to walk parallel with the road, reaching another stile, which you cross, and beyond which you take the path going half-left (*not* hard left) away from the road. Heading just east of north on what is a byway, go through two gates in close succession, and rise, the path quite wide and chalky; continuing gently uphill, go through a further gate, cross back over Wansdyke and pass through the trees. You emerge from them and, keeping to the obvious track, pass **Cow Down**. Its steep grassy banks are decorated with patches of mixed woodland which are at their best in the autumn, the rich green of the firs blending harmoniously with the sparkling gold of the birches. Immediately beyond, the views to the north open out again, Silbury Hill making a reappearance, diminutive, set among the patchwork of rolling Wiltshire hills, yet instantly recognisable.

Descend to arrive at a farm track, turning right to follow it to a T-junction with a road; turn left here to follow the road past houses of **East Kennett**, then, in a couple of hundred yards, take the first road turning right signed 'West Overton 1 (mile)'. Just beyond Ridgeway House go straight on northwards, not veering right. Cross the Kennet by a bridge, the road petering out and becoming a byway which you continue to follow, veering left and shortly right, then going uphill to arrive at the A4. At **Overton Hill** your walk offers another history lesson – not that you needed any more – as you find yourself on the **Ridgeway path National Trail**.

The Ridgeway path as we know it today follows parts of an old road with Bronze Age origins, known as the Great Ridgeway, which linked Lyme Regis in Dorset with Hunstanton in Norfolk, the route serving as a drove road, trading route and convenient track for invaders. Parts of the Great Ridgeway were absorbed into routes such as the Wessex Ridgeway, the Icknield Way and the Peddars Way. The light soils of the chalk were workable by primitive implements; this encouraged settlers and traders, and explains the large number of burial mounds and forts on the route – and indeed there is one very impressive tumulus, or burial mound, just before the A4 crossing at Overton Hill. The Ridgeway path itself is now designated as a National Trail, stretching for 85 miles via the Berkshire Downs and the Chilterns to Ivinghoe Beacon. A signpost at the A4 crossing reminds walkers how many miles separate them from this distant objective, but comfortingly announces that Avebury is just 2 miles away.

Cross straight over onto the Ridgeway path at Overton Hill, following it until the next path junction indicating Overton Hill as 0.4 miles back; turn left along the byway, taking care to keep to the right of the clump of trees you shortly reach, and continue north-westwards along the byway until you reach a T-junction at **Manor Farm**. Turn left along the signed road to Avebury, passing Manor Farm and soon arriving back at the Red Lion. I'd arrived at Avebury first thing in the morning, found the place deserted, and spent much of the ensuing five hours on tracks where the peace and solitude could almost be touched, so it was certainly a shock for me to return to Avebury and find the pub garden crammed and noisy, with hordes of people grouped around the standing stones. As I walked along the village street, I was passed by a number of appropriately clad Druidic followers who, for obvious reasons, see Avebury as a place of pilgrimage, and who exuded a relaxed and unhurried demeanour, no doubt borne of their one-ness with the mysterious spirituality of prehistory. Which I could only envy as I waited an hour and a half for the delayed bus back to Swindon.

Berkshire and Hampshire

Walbury Hill – 297 metres / 974 feet – SU 373616
Pilot Hill – 286 metres / 938 feet – SU 397601

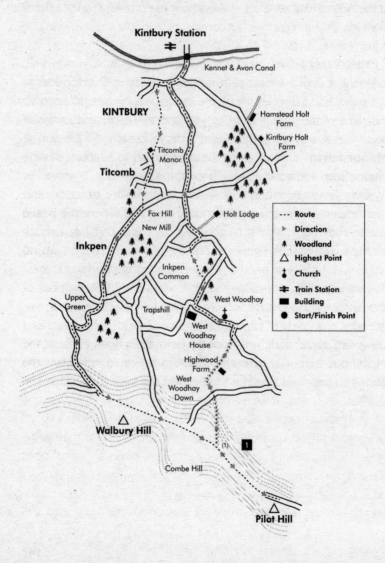

Length: 8 miles
Start and finish: Kintbury station
Public transport: Regular trains serving Kintbury on the London–Reading–Newbury–Bedwyn line
Refreshments: Kintbury (P, S); none en route
Difficulty: Moderate
Rating: ****

Corn hill test

First let's deal with the spoilsports. Yes, we know, Berkshire doesn't actually officially exist anymore. It's been split up into lots of unitary authorities during the massive local government reorganisations of recent years so, yes, we should say that Walbury Hill is really the high point of… a lot of unitary authorities all lumped together, so what's the point of including it? But let's rise above the bureaucratic meddlers and say that historically this was all Berkshire and many people, perhaps most people, living within its historic borders would say they still live in Berkshire today. And it's a good, high, high point. Nothing beats it any further east across southern England. So no excuses. Set the alarm, as I did, for 4 a.m., and get out there.

Anyway, this is a 'two-for-the-price-of-one' walk, as it includes the summit of Hampshire, which undoubtedly is still alive and well; the two county high points are less than 2 miles apart, and it's a delightful circular walk with superb views from what is part of the North Hampshire Downs chalk ridge. It's best done out of the corn-growing season – you'll see why when you get to the top of Pilot Hill – but whatever time of year you decide to do it, you need a good clear day. Assuming you're relying on public transport, I do recommend you start from Kintbury, which has a reasonably good rail service from and back to London, via Reading; looking at the map, you'll see the village of Ashmansworth, between Andover and Newbury, appears to be marginally closer to the hilltops you're aiming for, but a quick Google of public transport provision will confirm that one missed bus to or from that village may mean a wait of several decades for the next.

One word of advice: cut some sandwiches for the journey to Kintbury from London or Reading, as there'll be no refreshment trolley and, if you're like me and think a break of journey at a busy town like Newbury will yield a breakfast bap in the station buffet, think again. Even at 7.45 a.m., hardly the middle of the night, I found the buffet closed and had to dash into the town for a hasty takeaway snack, the sprint tiring me out before I'd even got going.

Kintbury isn't quite the archetypal picture-postcard village but it's certainly very pleasant; perhaps the most agreeable part of it is what you see almost straightaway as, having left the station and made your way south-westwards towards the village centre, you go over the **Kennet & Avon Canal**. This is a delightful stretch of water, and an undoubted visitor attraction, but it was once of vital commercial importance, being part of a canal system that linked Reading with Bristol. The Kennet & Avon Canal section ran from Newbury to Bath and was opened in about 1810. Keeping on the road, you arrive at the village centre with its well-stocked shop, and as there are no further refreshment opportunities on the circular walk, you're advised to take advantage of this opportunity to top up your supplies of Curly Wurlys.

Continue on past the village store and the road leading to the church, and go on briefly westwards, turning left into Titcomb Way where there's a footpath signpost. Follow Titcomb Way briefly, going forward very shortly onto a really charming footpath in the shade of woodland, heading southwards. You cross a stream and, sticking to the obvious path, veer west of south, climbing gently to pass to the left of the impressive **Titcomb Manor**. Go forward to the road, joining it and proceeding in the same direction (south-westwards). You reach a T-junction of lanes but go straight over on a signed path and follow it southwards, going up to another road.

Turn right to follow the road past the village of **Inkpen**, walking along the road for about a mile; it's not the most enjoyable part of the day, but the road isn't that busy and you can look on it as a warm-up for what's to come. At the end you reach a T-junction, and ahead you can now see clearly, for the first time, the escarpment on which Walbury Hill is situated. Turn right and then almost immediately left onto a road which passes a farm. Beyond the farm buildings the road bends sharp right and then left, but you can cut the corner by bearing left onto a signed footpath over the field. Having rejoined the road you follow it briefly, the views both to your left and ahead now really inviting, but soon look out for and follow another footpath going off to the left, which cuts another corner, crossing a field, to arrive at a road which provides access to the top of the escarpment. Turn left to follow this road steeply uphill, reaching a road junction at the top with a road going off to the left. Bear left onto it but then almost immediately right onto a track, actually the beginning of the **Wayfarer's Walk** which you will now be following. The Wayfarer's Walk, in case you were curious, is a trek from the very north-west corner of Hampshire to its very south-east corner at Emsworth.

Proceed along the track gently uphill, enjoying superb views across miles of countryside to the left. In a little over a quarter of a mile you reach the top of the rise, and you'll see a trig point over a field to the right, separated from you by a gated track. There is a wooden fence you can climb over, leaving the Wayfarer's Walk, to access the track and it's then a short walk to the trig point; note that this isn't a public right of way, so technically you should seek permission for this last bit.

You're now on **Walbury Hill**, the highest point not only in Berkshire but in south-east England, at a fraction under 985 feet (300 metres) above sea level. (There is an argument that Berkshire should properly be regarded as part of south-west England, but since Berkshire doesn't officially exist any more, perhaps the debate is futile anyway.) The hilltop is the site of an Iron Age hillfort known as **Walbury Camp**. Just a short way beyond the trig point is a low-level circular red-brick construction, probably a disused reservoir; I couldn't resist hauling myself up onto it and enjoying the splendid views from there, most extensive to the north but still impressive to the south, too. But it is quite a long way up, with no real chance of gaining a foothold, you climb at your own risk (and obviously you should on no account cause any damage to it), and you need to be careful lowering yourself down as well – there aren't too many specialist ankle fracture units up here.

Return to the Wayfarer's Walk and turn right, continuing along the track and going forward to a road. Carry on along the road in the same direction (south-eastwards) to the point where it veers sharply off to the right, with another going to the left. Turn left here but then almost immediately right onto the path which continues along the top of the escarpment, and the views across the Berkshire countryside to the north remain magnificent as you drop gently downhill, after about a quarter of a mile passing a signed bridleway **1** going off to the left across the field, and dropping to a crossroads of paths. Go straight over and now walk uphill, still enjoying stunning views to the left and arriving in a charming area of woodland. Here the path veers very decisively left and emerges from the woodland, with high fencing alongside the path on the right.

When the fencing ends, there's then immediately a gate going into the field to the right, and you need to go through it. You're now on **Pilot Hill**. By turning half-left and walking up into the centre of the field, you'll arrive at what is Hampshire's highest point; there is a conspicuous trig point further on, but slightly below the highest point. It's all a bit of an anticlimax after Walbury Hill, as the views even from the top of the field are nowhere near as good. In any event, the field is not a public right of way so you should technically seek permission to access it. And to make matters worse, when corn is growing, you will actually have trouble accessing the highest point in the field anyway, because clearly you should avoid damaging crops. By following the field edge round, at right-angles away from the Wayfarer's Walk, you should be able to identify crude 'paths' through the corn, but it's a bit like one of those infuriating mazes in children's puzzle books where every way forward you try is obstructed. And children's puzzle books tend not to come complete with an angry farmer asking what the hell you think you're playing at.

Return to the Wayfarer's Walk and, enjoying what are rather better views than from the 'summit', retrace your steps to the signed bridleway marked ■ above. Turn right to follow this bridleway over the field along the hillside, and you can now look back and enjoy tremendous views to Pilot Hill, which looks much more impressive from here than it did when you were on the top of it! You drop down quite steeply to a road, going straight over onto a farm track, which shortly turns sharp right and drops down to **Highwood Farm**. Go straight past the farm buildings and continue as signed along the farm track north-eastwards to reach a T-junction with a road. Turn left here to shortly arrive at a road junction, where you turn left again. You soon pass the very attractive church of St Laurence, **West Woodhay**, with roses growing beside the church path in early summer, and go on past the grounds of **West Woodhay House**, certainly the most memorable feature of your return journey from the heights back to Kintbury. The house was built in 1635 by the poet, writer, lawyer and MP Sir Benjamin Rudyard, and, yes, it was him from whom the later writer Kipling derived his first name. The house was sold in 1710 to a William Sloper, who rebuilt the parish church, replacing the church that had been on the site since the beginning of the fourteenth century; the replacement is believed to have been designed by Sir John Vanbrugh. However, this church was destined not to survive – in fact all that is left now are the foundations and some tombstones – and a third church was built in 1883 (and extended in 1894) which is the one that survives today. The house, meanwhile, was acquired by Henry

Henderson in 1920 and it was he who developed the magnificent gardens with their very colourful herbaceous borders; arboretum with unusual species, including snake-bark and paper-bark maples, yellow-berried hollies and several varieties of birch; and series of pools which cascade from one into the next.

Beyond the grounds you shortly reach another road junction where you bear round to the right, and follow the road as signed towards Kintbury. Having followed the road for just over a quarter of a mile beyond West Woodhay House, you reach a signed footpath going off to the left in the shade of trees. You could simply ignore this, carry on along the road and then, at the next road junction, turn left and just follow the tarmac for 2 miles into Kintbury. However, if you wanted a brief break from road walking, you could turn left onto the signed footpath and follow it in the shade of trees. Very shortly the path emerges from the trees and bears right across open grassland; a sign directs you to veer gently left, following the left-hand edge of the grassland along a reasonably clear path, which then drops down to a footbridge over a stream. Beyond the stream the most recent OS mapping suggests you should go straight on, but the path sign directs you sharp right, along a right-hand field edge. At the far corner of the field, don't continue to follow the field edge round but go straight ahead to immediately reach the Kintbury road. Turn left to follow the road back to Kintbury.

As stated, Kintbury has a fairly good rail service, although don't be misled by the fact that it's on the London–Penzance main railway line, as none of the Devon and Cornwall-bound services stop there. And do accept that as you sit on Kintbury station platform in the pouring rain waiting the forty-five minutes until your all-stations-to-London train arrives, you'll witness any number of sleek, comfortable expresses tearing through the station at a 100 mph – and they will probably pass you again coming the other way before you've even hit the outskirts of Reading.

Gloucestershire

Cleeve Hill – 330 metres / 1,083 feet – SO 996245

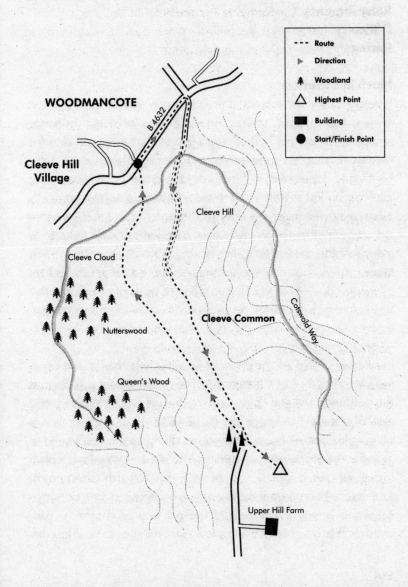

Legend:
- - - - Route
- ▷ Direction
- ♣ Woodland
- △ Highest Point
- ■ Building
- ● Start/Finish Point

WOODMANCOTE

B 4632

Cleeve Hill Village

Cleeve Hill

Cleeve Cloud

Nutterswood

Cleeve Common

Cotswold Way

Queen's Wood

Upper Hill Farm

Length: 3 miles
Start and finish: Cleeve Hill village
Public transport: Regular buses serving Cleeve Hill on the Cheltenham–Winchcombe route
Refreshments: Cleeve Hill (P); none en route
Difficulty: Moderate
Rating: ****

Much in common

Breaking news for anoraks: this is the only county high point in England that tops 300 metres. Breaking news for sluggards: having arrived at Cleeve Hill by bus, you'll find that pretty much all of the hard work has been done for you and, although there will be a little climbing to do, there is, in the words of a certain TV magician, not a lot. Probably just as well, as the towns lying either side offer hospitality which may well make any upward movement thereafter feel, shall we say, something of an imposition. I tackled this walk twice in as many months, the first time after tackling a cricket-pitch-sized treacle flapjack in Winchcombe; the second after a breakfast in Cheltenham offering a choice of at least fifteen different types of cereal, and that was before tucking into an interesting combination of scrambled eggs, smoked salmon – and, er, bacon. Well, it worked for me…

Ideally you should ask the driver of your bus, whether you've come from Winchcombe or Cheltenham, if he or she will set you down at the bottom of the golf course approach road on the Winchcombe side of Cleeve Hill village on the **B4632**. If your driver is not obliging, or doesn't know what you're talking about, you'll need to get off at the Stockwell Lane turning. This is a designated bus stop in the village itself, but further down the B4362 towards Cheltenham, so if you've been dropped off here you'll then need to walk north-eastwards beside the B4632 to the golf course approach road, which is clearly signed. It'll add a few extra minutes to your journey but it's the rush of traffic, rather than the amount of additional legwork, that you'll probably regard as more irksome.

Much of your walk will overlap with the Cotswold Way. The Cotswold Way, which runs for 102 miles from Bath to Chipping Campden, is one of the more recent additions to the family of National Trails, although it has been around as a 'named' path for years. It follows, as the name suggests, the range of limestone hills known as the Cotswolds, averaging at 600 feet in height and peaking in the Cleeve Hill area. With excellent signposting, the Way is a really rewarding trek, although it tends to skirt the Cotswolds rather than enter their heart, so the seeker of chocolate-box honey-coloured stone villages may be disappointed. Nonetheless, there are some splendid highlights, among them Stinchcombe Hill, Painswick Beacon, Birdlip Hill and Cleeve Hill, the subject of this walk. I thoroughly commend it to any walker, but suggest you go in the summer. I attempted the first leg of it one Sunday in January 1982, about twenty-five years before it achieved National Trail status, only to be beaten back by mud, snow, poor signposting, gathering darkness... oh, and wanting to get back in time for *That's Life!* with Esther Rantzen.

Walk up the golf course approach road from the B4632, passing the golf clubhouse, and arrive at a fork junction with the Cotswold Way. It's at this point that the Way does a hairpin bend, forking off to the left towards Winchcombe, and going in a straighter direction towards Cheltenham. Keep going straight ahead along the clear track, but don't veer away to the right with the signed Cotswold Way; rather, carry straight on, aiming for the three tall transmitter masts which are clearly visible. For now, don't be tempted to the higher ground to the right, but keep on along an excellent clear track towards the towers, enjoying really lovely views to Winchcombe on the left, surrounded by miles of beautiful countryside. You're now in the heart of **Cleeve Common**, an area of about 3 square miles, designated a Grade 1 Site of Special Scientific Interest with a variety of orchids, glow-worms and butterflies. There are also a number of Iron Age earthworks.

Now just keep on towards the masts, leaving the track to walk right up to them by a more direct route. The masts themselves are fenced and, when you reach the fence, bear left to walk alongside it, keeping along the right-hand edge of the grass, almost immediately passing a sign to a footpath which is on the right. Then keep straight on, gently uphill, aiming for the trig point at the top of the rise, with a fence and a rather disjointed stone wall to your right, still keeping along the right-hand edge of the grass. The trig point which you come to is the highest point not only of Cleeve Common and the Cotswolds, but of Gloucestershire. Yes, it really was that simple. You can see the Malvern Hills poking up in the distance, but the wider views are lost, and you'll need to wait till you reach Cleeve Cloud (see below) to get them.

Return to the masts, but this time continue in the same direction and aim for the isolated tree on the highest ground immediately ahead; your reward for reaching it is an opportunity to sit down on the bench there and enjoy the stunning surroundings. There is a thin path which leads you to this spot, but the grass is so pleasant to walk on, with no restrictions on access in this part of the common, that you almost don't need a path. The views on your left to Cheltenham are particularly fine here on a good day. On the day I walked it, I was able to see a large belt of rain closing in from the south-west, slowly enveloping and blotting out the town and the surrounding countryside, and it was with a sense of inevitability that I saw the deluge sweep onto the common and, in turn, sweep me off it as quickly as I could force my soaking limbs to do the job. The common is very exposed, with little or no chance of shelter, so if it does rain expect to get wet – and muddy.

Anyway, let's hope you're luckier than I was. Using the line you have followed to the tree, look half-left to the high ground at what is effectively the top corner of the plateau and you will identify another trig point, which, it has to be said, enjoys a more exciting setting than the actual county high point and, at 1,040 feet (317 metres) it is just 43 feet (13 metres) less high. If you want another marker, which may prove handy if the mist comes down, there is a small clump of conspicuous gorse bushes on the same line just a 100 yards or so ahead of you. Now proceed to the trig point, dropping gently downhill, then climbing again, taking care to dodge any golf balls from the adjoining golf course. From the trig point you can enjoy the views that were denied you at the county high point, and you may well wish this was the county high point, particularly as that would have meant an easier and shorter walk generally. Although the map suggests a 360-degree viewpoint here, the most interesting and varied views are to the west, across to the Malvern Hills, Bredon Hill and the Welsh mountains, including the Brecon Beacons. Just north-west of the trig point there is the Ring, an Iron Age settlement covering about half an acre.

Your arrival at the trig point brings you to the Cotswold Way again. This part of the plateau edge is known as **Cleeve Cloud**, and if you were to detour southwards along the Cotswold Way you would be able to follow the plateau edge and enjoy the splendid sight of the steep crags of Castle Rock. It's certainly worth doing if you have the time. But to complete your walk back to **Cleeve Hill**, you need to follow the Cotswold Way northwards from the trig point so, heading for the road and spectacular views below you, follow the path indicated by the Cotswold Way marker very steeply downhill and then, again as signed by the Cotswold Way, turn right along the line of the slope.

As you walk along this path, look carefully half-left and you'll see an imposing stone ivy-clad house, with a tarmac drive snaking round the front of it. When a further Cotswold Way signpost points half-right, away from the line of the house, leave the Cotswold Way and walk directly towards the tarmac drive and house; you could drop down to follow a clear path that heads that way, or you could simply walk through the rough grass in a straight line. As you reach the drive, look left and, below you, you'll see a gate and stile with the B4632 immediately beyond. Make your way down to the gate and stile, going forward to the main road, and you'll see the bus shelter by the Stockwell Lane turning immediately adjacent. And if it's the same driver who steadfastly refused to drop you off by the golf course approach road in the first place, having completed your walk in a Cleeve Cloud-burst you won't feel too bad about bringing half of the common onto the bus with you.

Cornwall

Brown Willy – 420 metres / 1,375 feet – SX 159800

Length: 8 miles. NOTE: It could be shortened to 4 miles if you get a lift or taxi to the National Trust car park at the foot of Rough Tor
Start and finish: Camelford
Public transport: Regular buses serving Camelford on the Bude-Wadebridge route
Refreshments: Camelford (P, C, S); none en route
Difficulty: Strenuous. NOTE: Bodmin Moor is very prone to mist and you would be well advised to take a compass or GPS device on this walk in such conditions
Rating: ****

Not to be mist

Cornwall has some of the most romantic, intriguing and bizarre place names in England: Jamaica Inn, Goonhavern, Minions, Trelights and London Apprentice to name just a few. So it is ironic that its summit should boast such an undignified name, which has even made its way into a book of rude place names. It's perhaps inevitable that respect for the summit may be diminished as a result. And walkers arriving by wheeled transport at the car park at the end of Roughtor Road, finding themselves blessed with a fine, sunny day, may wonder why respect is required: a gentle climb, a rocky but not overlong descent, another stiffer climb on a good path, job done. It didn't quite work out that way for me. Arriving at the car park at 5.45 a.m. (you may not be surprised to know there weren't too many buses about at that time of day, hence my resorting to private transport for this adventure), I walked the first couple of hundred yards in the clear before entering a pall of

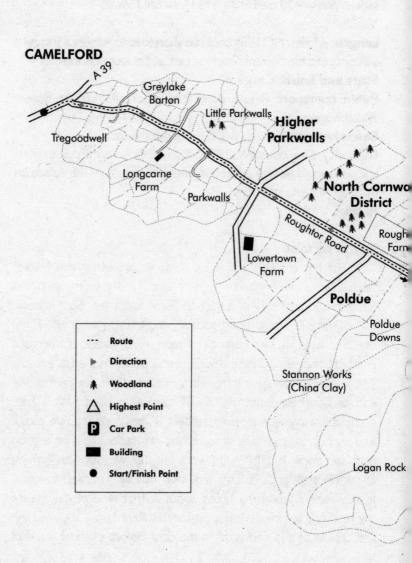

mist, which without the aid of a GPS device could have been fatally disorientating. Brown Willy (right, one last snigger and then let's get serious) demands respect. It is situated on Bodmin Moor which has certain similarities with Dartmoor: tracts of bog, heather, rocks and boulder-strewn hillsides known as 'tors', the weird granite stone shapes formed by thousands of years of weathering, a wilderness in a county better known for cosy coves and clotted cream.

Logistically, this isn't one of the easiest high points to access, even though the moorland walking isn't that lengthy. You somehow need to find your way to Camelford – hardly a seething metropolis but still a busy little community that clearly thrives from its position on the

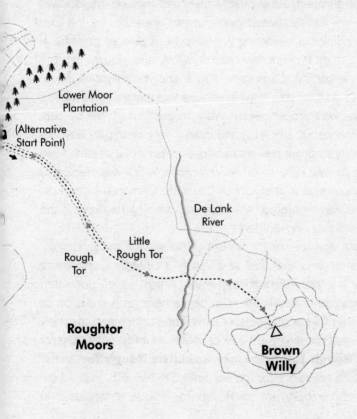

Lower Moor
Plantation

(Alternative
Start Point)

De Lank
River

Little
Rough Tor

Rough
Tor

**Roughtor
Moors**

**Brown
Willy**

A39, the so-called 'Atlantic Highway' conveying holidaymakers to destinations along the north Cornwall coast. The nearest rail link is Bodmin Parkway and at least two buses will be required from there, via Wadebridge, although there are direct buses from Exeter as well.

From the centre of Camelford, head north-eastwards up the **A39** past a little church on the left, look out carefully for **Roughtor Road** leading away to the right, and walk up this road towards the village of **Tregoodwell**. The sign is half-hidden so you may miss it; if you do, there's another right turn a bit further up the road, signed Tregoodwell, and that'll bring you back to Roughtor Road, onto which you turn left. Simply follow the road through Tregoodwell village centre and south-eastwards out into open country, the road initially winding but becoming very straight. It plunges downhill at one point, then immediately rises up again, and ploughs on to a spacious car park. It is a slog, no doubt, and you may well decide on a taxi to do it for you; don't even think that there might be a bus.

Now the walk proper begins. Walk straight through the car park (GPS reference SX 139 818) and onto a very clear path beyond, which promptly drops down to a bridge crossing of a stream; if you look here to your right you'll see a memorial which was erected by public subscription in memory of Charlotte Dymond, a domestic maid, who was murdered by a fellow servant while walking on the moor one Sunday in April 1844.

The path now begins the ascent of Rough Tor straight ahead, but becomes very indistinct and frankly it's hardly worth trying to follow it exactly through the grass, which is well populated with sheep and cattle. There is evidence here, as there is on or around other tors hereabouts, of early stone settlements, possibly Bronze Age. Proceeding just east of south, your first goal is the col between **Rough Tor**, to the right, and **Little Rough Tor**, to the left, the GPS reference for the col being SX 147 808. In practice, the impressive rocky pile on Rough Tor will be conspicuous in all except the real pea-soupers, and providing you have the col clearly in view (either actual view or on your GPS device) and can therefore re-orientate, it's worth detouring up Rough Tor. When I walked it, I was able to climb out of the mist and enjoy an extensive view towards the north Cornwall coast, while the mist hung about like a tower of grey cotton wool immediately below. One particularly prominent feature is the lake that's part of the now closed **Stannon China Clay works**, which at one time produced 50,000 tons of china clay slurry a year. At the top of Rough Tor is Logan Rock, which is actually said to rock, rather like the more famous Logan Rock on the south Cornwall coast between Land's End and Penzance – a granite block which 'logs' or rocks at the slightest touch. Now make your way back to the col, taking care to watch where you're putting your feet as you scramble back through the rocks; Bodmin Moor is no respecter of delicate ankles.

From the col, your next aim is the **De Lank River crossing** (GPS reference SX 153 805), reached by veering gently left and proceeding south-eastwards. The path is pretty much invisible for the most part; occasionally you may see something vaguely path-like amid the rocks and the grass, but there are no restrictions on access so simply choose a descent which involves the least wear and tear on the joints, and be patient. However, as you continue downhill, the going does become easier and, assuming you're on course, you should see a wall coming in from the right and then veering sharp right to run in the same direction as you're heading. As you join the wall, and walk parallel with and immediately to the left of it, you'll find yourself on a clear path which takes you down to the crossing of the De Lank River.

Before crossing the river you pass the **Fernacre Stone Circle**, a collection of fifty-six stone megaliths, although some are partly buried. 'River' is a rather flattering name for the comparatively narrow and modest moorland channel that is the De Lank, but you'll be glad you don't have to ford it; there is a bridge and beyond it a welcome sign indicating that you're on the permissive path to **Brown Willy**. You can relax in the sense that there's no more navigational skill required – although the GPS reference for the summit of Brown Willy is SX 159 800 if there's a ring of 'famous last words' to that observation!

The path south-eastwards uphill to the top of Brown Willy is very clear, even in the mist. However, it can be boggy, so be careful. You reach a stile where an arrow sign points the way forward, and beyond the stile the going becomes steeper and the surroundings feel more remote. The path veers more round to the right to head just east of south and, finally, you reach the trig point and cairn which confirms your arrival at the summit. Be sure you mark the direction in which you have come, especially if it's misty. I am reliably informed that on a good day you can see all the way across Cornwall, from Fowey in the south to Tintagel in the north, but I'll have to defer to those who've been luckier with the weather than I was. And for others who because of the lack of views have to do the same, it is vitally important to come off the hilltop by the right route, using the marker you carefully took on the way up.

It's now simply a case of retracing your steps: first north-westwards to the De Lank River, then beside the wall and on in the same direction, again north-westwards, to the col between Little Rough Tor and Rough Tor, and from then on downhill, just west of north, to the car park. In mist don't hesitate to use the GPS references above. If you've enough energy when you reach the bridge just before the car park, you might want to detour along the stream-side path to view the memorial more closely. Then, given the prospect of a long road walk back to Camelford, you could be forgiven for calling for a taxi to get you back there again – subject of course to your still having enough money to splash on the beer and Cornish-pasty-the-size-of-Reading you promised yourself if ever you found your way out of the mist.

Worcestershire

Worcestershire Beacon – 425 metres / 1,395 feet – SO 768452

Length: 2 miles minimum, but theoretically could be up to 18 miles
Start and finish: Great Malvern
Public transport: Regular trains serving Great Malvern on the
Worcester–Hereford line
Refreshments: Great Malvern (P, C, S)
Difficulty: Strenuous in places
Rating: *****

Slope and glory

Anyone undertaking this walk must pray for a fine clear day and, if
their prayers are not answered, should consider postponing… and
then pray again. These are some of the best views you'll find in this
book – or should be. The Malvern Hills, while not exceptionally
high, give the impression of great loftiness because of the way they
rise out of the surrounding plain, providing what the diarist John
Evelyn described as 'one of the goodliest vistas in England'. Once
part of the royal forest of Malvern Chase and now designated as an
Area of Outstanding Natural Beauty, they have inspired many other
writers and poets, most notably the composer Edward Elgar, who
was born in nearby Worcester and spent much time in the hills,
walking, cycling and reputedly kite-flying; J. R. R. Tolkien, whose
fictional Misty Mountains in his books were inspired by the hills;
W. H. Auden, who wrote a poem entitled 'The Malverns'; and
William Langland, who took the hills as the setting for his poem
'The Vision of William Concerning Piers the Plowman'. Part of the
appeal of the Malverns is the fact that so much of the area consists
of open common land, meaning that the visitor is not necessarily
restricted to the marked paths and may wander at will among

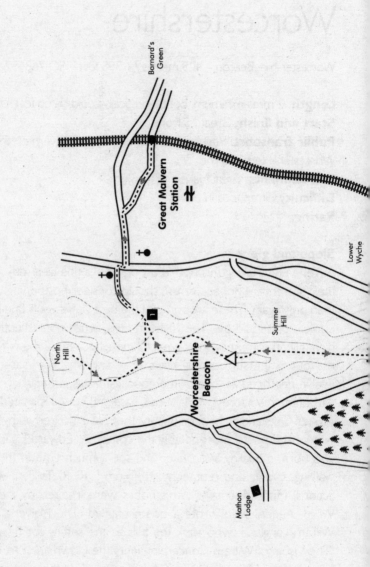

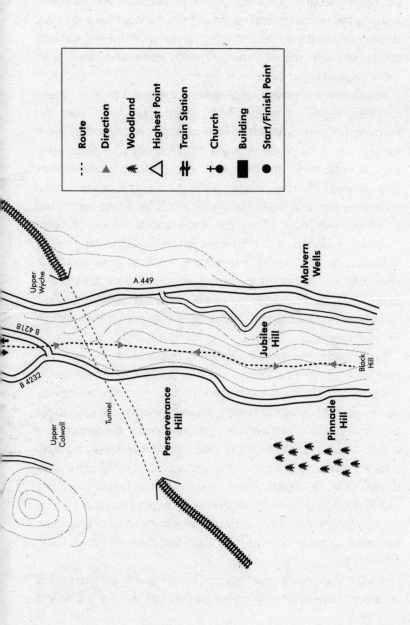

Route · · · · ·

Direction ▲

Woodland ✦

Highest Point △

Train Station ⇶

Church †

Building ■

Start/Finish Point ●

Upper Wyche

A 449

B 4218

B 4232

Malvern Wells

Jubilee Hill

Black Hill

Tunnel

Upper Colwall

Perserverance Hill

Pinnacle Hill

the open grassland, scattered with heath bedstraw and harebells, enjoying the seemingly endless views from the ridgetop and peaks, or venture into the woodlands which at the southern end is chiefly sessile oak, with yellow archangel, wood sorrel and ramsons on show, depending on the time of the year.

The Malverns are made up of some of the oldest rocks in Britain, consisting largely of igneous and metamorphic rocks from the Precambrian period, which contain no fossils because they were formed before life on earth. It was the Victorians who popularised the hills not only for the fresh air, exercise and spectacular views they offered, but the waters gushing from the many natural mineral springs and wells, such as St Ann's Well that were used to effect water cures. Thus the resort and spa town of Great Malvern developed, which *Brewer's Britain & Ireland* describes as 'a cornucopia of Victorian architecture, much of it therapeutic in origin'. As well as being superbly placed to give very quick access to the ridge, the main street of Great Malvern provides a splendid springboard for a walk in the Malvern Hills and is really an ideal base for your expedition.

If you need some divine inspiration to help you on your way you could visit the splendid Priory church of St Mary and St Michael, a combination of Norman and Perpendicular Gothic architecture with stained glass dating back 600 years; a baker's shop on the main street provides well-filled sausage rolls as sustenance for the forthcoming ascent; the tourist information office is positively bursting with booklets of described walks on the hills, and boasts a freezer of tasty locally made ice cream, with a range of exotic flavours including such delights as lemon curd or strawberry and champagne; and, on return from the hills, there is a wide range of restaurants and hotels waiting to welcome both you and your debit card.

To do the walk, make your way up Church Street, the main street in Great Malvern, bearing round to the right to pass the tourist information centre and reach a T-junction with Bellevue Terrace as it goes forward into Worcester Road. Cross this road and turn right, then almost immediately bear left into St Ann's Road and begin to climb. When St Ann's Road turns left, effectively a right-angled turn, go straight on up the hill through the woods, leaving the buildings of Great Malvern behind but remaining on what is a metalled lane. As you gain height, with the ground rising steeply to your right, the lane bends sharply left and goes forward to reach an open area which is a popular viewpoint, the metal surface giving way to a rougher but quite wide track. Now turn hard right to proceed uphill along the track, through woodland, and emerge from the woods to reach a T-junction **1**. To reach **Worcestershire Beacon**, turn left and simply keep walking uphill on a very obvious path, aiming for the left (higher) of the two peaks you can see ahead, the lower peak being **Table Hill**.

The summit of Worcestershire is reached almost too easily and quickly from the centre of Great Malvern. You somehow think it ought to involve a longer walk. You can artificially delay your scaling of the big one by detouring to Table Hill but you may decide to attack the summit direct, as I did. As you climb, the going becomes rather steeper and stonier, but it is still hardly mountaineering. Despite the comparative straightforwardness of the ascent, it's a great thrill to reach the top, marked by a trig point and topograph (erected in 1897 to commemorate Queen Victoria's Diamond Jubilee), and boasting views which extend to the Cotswolds, the Welsh borders and mountains, Cannock Chase in Staffordshire, and the Wrekin and Clee Hills in Shropshire. The views down to Great Malvern aren't too bad either, while the sight of the rest of the Malverns to the south provides a study in shades of green, from the dark patches of woodland to the light, well-trodden grassland of the upper slopes. Around you there may be butterflies including pearl-bordered fritillaries, while above you there may be skylarks and tree pipits. You may find yourself in the company of other walkers, too, especially during holiday periods and at weekends, and satisfaction at reaching the peak of Worcestershire may be tempered by sharing your topograph experience with families whose flip-flops and Crocs make you with your Brasher boots seem spectacularly overdressed.

Once you're up there, you won't want to come straight back, even if you've left your long-suffering partner/children/sisters/cousins/aunts browsing in the Oxfam bookshop on the main street of the town below. Looking southwards from the summit, you'll see what is a clear path along the ridgetop, and each peak seems to be decorated with a path gracefully sweeping over each summit, effectively saying to the walker: 'Come to me; I'm all yours.' But there's a certain devilishness in the invitation; it looks no distance at all to Pinnacle Hill, and it's only after the ridgetop path has seduced you along for a few hundred yards, providing magnificent views in all directions, that you find yourself sucked inexorably downhill to the road crossing at **Wyche Cutting**, losing much of the height gained in the conquest of Worcestershire Beacon, and forcing more hard work out of you as you toil on. Just on the nearside of the bus shelter at the road crossing there are steps available which bring you back onto the ridge, and in close succession you can continue to **Perseverance Hill**, **Jubilee Hill** and **Pinnacle Hill**. Perseverance is certainly rewarded, as the views back to the Beacon from the top of Pinnacle Hill are magnificent.

Beyond Pinnacle Hill you could forge on to the distinctive Herefordshire Beacon, although you would need to negotiate another descent to a road crossing at **Wynds Point**. The top of this hill forms part of a large Iron Age fort known as **British Camp**, and although it's around 300 feet (85 metres) lower than Worcestershire Beacon, its distinctive shape adds to its charm. Elgar based his 1898 cantata 'Caractacus' on the British chieftain's last stand at British Camp, but it's not one of his best-known works.

Now, however far you've come, simply retrace your steps along the ridge back via Worcestershire Beacon to the point ■ above. You may care to walk on past point ■ to view North Hill, walking along the ridge, then taking the obvious path up to the summit; it's the northernmost of the Malvern Hills, the summit only actually barely 100 feet (28 metres) lower than that of Worcestershire Beacon. From here there is an uninterrupted view northwards and, because it is set slightly back from the Worcestershire Beacon–Pinnacle Hill ridgetop walk, it seems more tranquil. The quickest way back to Great Malvern is to return to point ■ above and, following the indication given by the impressive sign, descend steeply through the woodland via the track you used to ascend from St Ann's Road. Turn hard left at the lower viewpoint to pick up the metalled road which shortly swings sharply right and drops back down to Great Malvern. After this, Worcestershire's other big hilltop, **Broadway Tower** at a piffling 965 feet (294 metres), may seem a bit of an anticlimax. Especially when you find you've got to pay nearly a fiver for the privilege of climbing it. If Elgar had had to pay to climb Worcestershire Beacon, there might never have been a 'Pomp and Circumstance March'. There's a thought…

Somerset

Dunkery Beacon – 519 metres / 1,705 feet – SS 891415

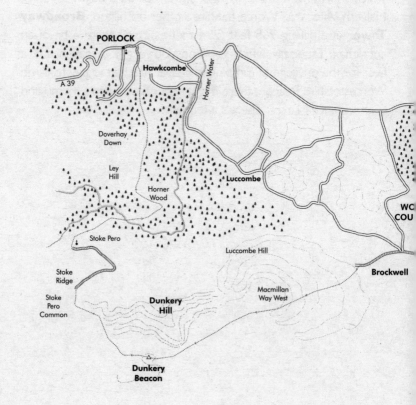

PORLOCK

Hawkcombe

A 39

Horner Water

Doverhay
Down

Ley
Hill

Luccombe

Horner
Wood

Stoke Pero

WC
COU

Luccombe Hill

Stoke
Ridge

Brockwell

Macmillan
Way West

Stoke
Pero
Common

Dunkery
Hill

Dunkery
Beacon

Length: 13 miles
Start: Dunster
Finish: Porlock
Public transport: Regular buses serving Dunster on the Taunton–Minehead route; regular buses linking Porlock with Minehead
Refreshments: Dunster (P, C, S); Wootton Courtenay (P, S); Porlock (P, C, S)
Difficulty: Strenuous
Rating: *****

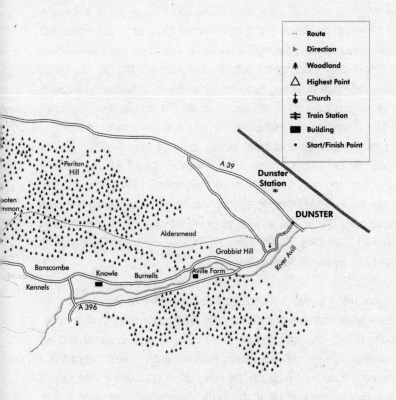

Up and doone

This is a cracker. Not only is your objective for this walk, Dunkery Beacon, one of the best county high points in England, but Exmoor, on which the Beacon is situated, has something for everyone. The nature lover will appreciate the contrasts between the heather moorland and large expanses of woodland, with its ash, rowan, hazel, mosses, bracken, ferns, lichens and liverworts. The countryside lover will marvel at the deep, steep-sided valleys and bracing ridges, offering views across miles of countryside and coastline. The book lover will think of the literary associations and particularly *Lorna Doone*, and its reference to Dunkery Beacon as the 'haighest place of Hexmoor'. The architecture lover will enjoy the contrast between the splendour of Dunster Castle and the remoteness of the church at Stoke Pero. And if you're a steam buff, you can easily incorporate into your itinerary a trip on the West Somerset Railway which runs from Minehead to Bishop's Lydeard.

I've suggested a linear route rather than a circular one, as you'll be able to appreciate more fully the tremendous variety of scenery, and both the start and finish points are not only well served by public transport but very attractive. Dunster is such a lovely starting place that you may find it hard to tear yourself away and actually do the walk, while Porlock, although less obviously photogenic, has lots to offer the visitor, as well as being famous for its treacherous Porlock Hill and the 'Person from Porlock' who caused Coleridge to forget his dream of 'Kubla Khan'.

The bus from Taunton doesn't go into the centre of Dunster, but it's a short walk from the bus stop by the **A39** to Dunster's main street via the A396. Dunster is dominated by its castle, which originated in Norman times and was rebuilt in stone in the twelfth century; a fortified manor was built on the site 200 years later. It was rebuilt again, by George Luttrell, in the early seventeenth century but after the English Civil War its defences were dismantled; remodelled with turrets and towers in Gothic style in the nineteenth century, it was given to the National Trust in 1976, and is surrounded by sub-tropical gardens containing a fine collection of strawberry trees. The other very distinctive feature of the village is the seventeenth-century octagonal yarn market; at that time a type of woollen cloth was made locally, known as 'Dunster'. The main street veers sharply right to pass the church, and just beyond the church, turn right into a twitten which quickly brings you to St George's Street. Turn right into the street and follow it uphill to just opposite Rockfort, number 34, here turning left onto a signed bridleway for **Grabbist Hill**. Please note that this could be very soggy underfoot.

Go uphill to the edge of the wood and turn left at the path junction then immediately right as signed for Wootton Courtenay, but before you press on, look back for a splendid view to Dunster and the sea behind. It's now a very straightforward 2-mile walk along the ridgetop, going steadily uphill on a good clear path; at one point you're signed right then almost immediately left to continue in the same direction. This is quite superb walking, with magnificent views to Minehead and the very conspicuous Butlins holiday camp, and you should also look back for increasingly extensive views to the Bristol Channel coast.

Having followed the ridgetop for 2 miles you reach a signed path junction, and you need to turn left as signed for Wootton Courtenay, not carrying on as signed for Tivington. You're 984 feet (just under 300 metres) above sea level and seem very elevated, the bad news is you're going to have to lose most of this height in the next mile, and then climb to well over 1,640 feet (500 metres)! After turning left, you soon reach a path fork and will need to take the left one, following the narrow path very steeply downhill; take care not to be sucked away to the right and always observe the yellow footpath signs. Continuing through the woods, you drop down to a T-junction with a wider track, turning right to follow it and emerging from the woods to follow a field path steeply down to the road. As you emerge from the woods, there's a great view ahead to the moors you'll be tackling shortly, and in the circumstances it seems a shame to be losing all the height you've gained so far.

Turn right to follow the road through the centre of **Wootton Courtenay**, which has a good range of amenities for a small village, and reach a three-pronged fork junction. You take the left prong, signed Brockwell, and follow the road uphill, crossing a cattle grid with an adjacent gate and its rather touching sign: 'PLEASE SHUT THE GATE, KEEP THE PONIES ON DUNKERY'. At **Brockwell** the road swings very sharply left; you go straight over onto a signed path, with a sign saying Dunkery Beacon is 2½ miles away. Follow this path, initially through a gully, ignoring the fork left at the first junction but going forward to a T-junction of paths where you turn right onto a clearer path. You pass south-westwards through some woodland and reach another path fork; the signage wasn't clear here at the time of writing, but you need to take the right fork. Suddenly the whole landscape changes and you now find yourself striking out across the moors, climbing with no obvious alternatives on a stony path. The loose stones can be awkward and slow progress, so just be patient.

As you rise, you bend slightly left and reach a road. Cross straight over and continue south-westwards then westwards. Now you can see the monument marking **Dunkery Beacon**, the summit of this route, and the summit of Exmoor and Somerset, and it's exciting to be getting closer and closer to your goal. It's so much more satisfying to know exactly what you're heading for, which isn't always the case with county high points. As you arrive at the monument, you'll also see a topograph, at a slightly lower level, and this will help you to pinpoint where particular locations should be even if it may not be clear enough to see them. But you'll want to advance the few steps to the monument, with its plaque commemorating the gift of Dunkery Beacon to the National Trust in 1935. Despite the fact that it was blowing a gale, I couldn't resist climbing to the top of the monument and sitting on it to enjoy the views; on a clear day you may see the Brecon Beacons, Dartmoor, Bodmin Moor, the Severn River Crossings and Cleeve Hill, but even on days of lesser visibility there is still a colossal variety of landscapes and seascapes on show. The summit, composed of Devonian sedimentary rock and the site of a number of Bronze Age burial mounds, is covered in ling and bell heather which gives it a deep-purple colour in the summer.

Immediately behind the monument is a green mound, and you need to join the path which hugs the left side of the mound, then carry on along it heading westwards. Shortly you reach a path crossroads with a cairn, and here you turn right to follow an obvious stony path which drops down the hillside. Ignoring the green-depicted path which OS Explorer maps show leaving this one, and which is not properly signed or defined, simply continue down the hillside on the obvious path, and arrive at a T-junction with a wider track. Turn left and drop down to **Bagley Combe**, fording a stream; when I walked this, it was one of the highlights of the whole journey, with flowering hawthorn bushes adding to the beauty of the surroundings.

At the stream your path turns sharp right, climbing to reach a road. Turn right to follow the road; although road walking is generally less inspiring than path walking, it's a narrow road with very little traffic, and the views from the road along this section are exceptional. You reach a junction where you turn left, signed Stoke Pero, and follow the road round to the right to reach **Stoke Pero Church**. (If you're curious about the name, 'stoke' means 'outlying farmstead', while 'pero' denotes manorial ownership in the Middle Ages by the Pyrhou family.) Unless you are in a great hurry, you should go into the church, magnificent in its simplicity; it dates back to the thirteenth century, although it was extensively restored in the nineteenth century. The road beyond the church plunges into a deep valley and the local people were said to have loud voices from having to shout from one side to the other.

Don't actually follow the road down into the valley, but just beyond the church turn right through a gate along a signed bridleway through the farm, going forward on a clear path with woodland to the left. Look out for and follow a path going off to the left which then enters the wood – it is an obvious path into the wood – and then continue along the clear path, going steeply downhill north-eastwards then south-eastwards to reach a footbridge over a stream. Cross the bridge; don't join the riverside path but go straight over onto a path going uphill, crossing Lord Edbrington's Path, sticking to what signposts call **Granny's Ride**. Enjoying lovely views through the trees back to Dunkery Beacon, you go over another path crossroads, swinging left and rising, heading just north of west and reaching two junctions in quick succession. Follow the signed route for Ley Hill, bearing right to emerge from the woods, and enter open country with views towards Porlock and the sea, now having graduated from Granny's Ride to **Flora's Ride**. It's worth looking back, up to Dunkery Beacon, and thinking what a long way back it suddenly seems.

Don't be sucked down to the right but continue at the same level, going forward onto a wider track and reaching a crossroads where the best-defined track turns left. You need to take this track which reaches a road; turn right onto the road and shortly left, as signed, along a bridleway which soon veers right and drops very steeply downhill through closely packed trees to reach a T-junction of paths. Turn left then shortly right onto a much nicer woodland path through the **Doverhay Plantation**, soon reaching a gate just beyond a footpath sign for Cawter Hill. Go through the gate then immediately left steeply downhill to the road, turning left and walking down the road to the A39 and **Porlock**'s main street. Your entrance to the village is likely to be less taxing than that of motorists coming from the west, who have to negotiate a 1 in 4 gradient hill with hairpin bends.

The village boasts a fine range of amenities with which you can celebrate completion of your walk. The **Ship Inn** in the High

Street, which featured significantly in *Lorna Doone*, may act as a draw to many, while those seeking tea and cakes will have at least three cafes to choose from. This includes the Whortleberry Tearoom, where one can enjoy whortleberry preserve with scones and cream. On the occasion of my visit, the doors were locked to would-be whortleberry hunters, but I saw at least two other tearooms open and, although I had contented myself with a slice of Victoria sponge, I've no doubt that had I looked closely enough I'd have found a *Lorna Doone* Special Set Tea. If not a Person From Porlock Platter.

Shropshire

Brown Clee Hill (Abdon Burf) – 540 metres / 1,772 feet – SO 593865

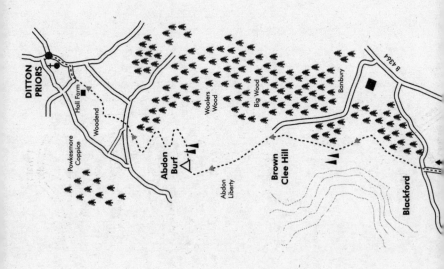

Length: Minimum 11 miles, maximum 18 miles
Start: Cleehill village
Finish: Ditton Priors or Bridgnorth
Public transport: Regular trains serving Ludlow on the Shrewsbury–Hereford line; regular trains between Wolverhampton and Shrewsbury; regular buses serving Cleehill on the Ludlow–Kidderminster route; regular buses from Bridgnorth to Shrewsbury, Kidderminster and Wolverhampton
Refreshments: Bridgnorth (P, C, S); none en route
Difficulty: Strenuous
Rating: ****

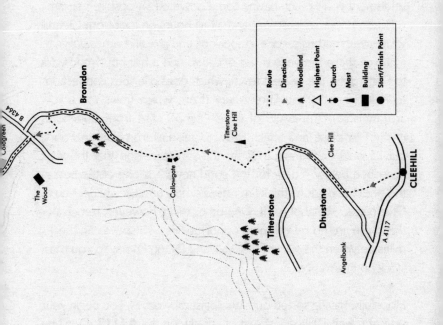

Happy Burfday

It's all very straightforward: you start in Cleehill which isn't a hill but a village, soon reach a Clee Hill which isn't actually Brown Clee Hill, and forge on to Brown Clee Hill which is actually not one but two hills.

Let's start again – with bad news. This isn't an easy assignment. Not only is it a long and tiring walk, but logistically it is a real headache, assuming you're relying on public transport. There are a number of options available, none very satisfactory, so I've suggested a fairly adventurous and hugely scenic walk which starts at a place well served by public transport, and will leave you to decide the best option at the other end. I'm assuming that you're starting from Ludlow – as I did – or Kidderminster, both having railway stations, and from both there's a good bus service to the start of my suggested route at Cleehill village. Using my route, the first settlement you'll reach having come down off Shropshire's summit is Ditton Priors, at least four and a half hours on foot from Cleehill village, with no bus service to speak of, and it really comes down to a choice there between a taxi or a two and a half hour road walk to Bridgnorth, the nearest town, which does offer bus connections to Kidderminster and Shrewsbury (from which trains to Ludlow are available). You could of course simply start from Bridgnorth in the first place and attack Brown Clee Hill from Ditton Priors, but I would discourage that, for the simple reason that the walk described below – now for the good news – is one of the best in this book. And I don't think I'm biased simply because I happened to have perfect weather for it. One other thing, however: remember that there are no refreshment opportunities whatsoever on the 11 miles between the start of this walk and Ditton Priors, so you must stock up in advance.

Hopefully, having sorted out your logistical worries, you begin your walk at Cleehill village just east of Ludlow on the **A4117**. Don't be misled by the fact that you're starting at a village called Cleehill – you've a long old walk ahead of you, with your principal objective still many miles away. Leave the village by taking the road heading northwards immediately opposite the B4214 turning, the road soon petering out and reaching an open area; aim for the gate at the top right-hand corner of this area and go through it. Walk up to the wooden fence at the end, and climb over to turn left onto a track which you follow. Alternatively, just before the fence, turn left to contour the hillside keeping the track above you and to your right, veering slightly left to pass through a gate, then continuing parallel with the track before shortly joining the track via a gate. The track, providing magnificent views, veers right as the houses of **Dhustone** are approached. Cross the stile, then veer left to go forward to the road, onto which you turn right.

Follow the road north-eastwards, veering more northwards, climbing and reaching a very sharp right-hand bend which you round. Here you join the **Shropshire Way**, which you will stay with all the way to Brown Clee Hill and beyond, and it is very well signposted. The Shropshire Way is a 139-mile circular route starting and finishing in Wem and passing through Shrewsbury, Clun, Ludlow, Wenlock Edge, Ironbridge and the Wrekin. Once you've negotiated the bend, bear left very shortly to leave the road, as signposted by the Shropshire Way, heading initially north-eastwards then veering north-westwards to reach the trig point on the hilltop. This isn't Brown Clee Hill, so don't unscrew the celebratory bottle of Co-op freshly squeezed lemonade yet; it's actually **Titterstone Clee Hill**, a piffling 23 feet (7 metres) shorter. The views, as might be expected from this 1,749 feet (533 metres) summit, are absolutely stupendous, with particularly good views to the masts of Brown Clee Hill to the north, which look deceptively close from here. Indeed, the AA's *50 Walks in Shropshire* states that notwithstanding the scarring of the hillside by quarrying (see below) and radar installations, 'Its massive presence and charisma remain undimmed, and the view from its southern flank is claimed to be the finest in England.'

As you look to Brown Clee Hill, this is a good time to call to mind the industrial importance of both Brown Clee Hill and Titterstone Clee Hill. Iron ore, clay, lime, stone and coal have been extracted from these hills since the Middle Ages. In the nineteenth century, it was coal that was the most significant output and, indeed, Brown Clee Hill could boast the highest coalfield in England. Subsequently, the hard stone of the hills, a black basalt known as dolerite or dhustone – hence the name of the village passed by a short while back – was commissioned for the construction of Cardiff Docks. It was also found to be of use for cobbled roads and, as a result, three quarries opened on Titterstone Clee Hill to meet demand. Although quarrying ceased on Brown Clee Hill in 1936, one operational quarry on Titterstone Clee Hill was to continue into the present century, generating stone used for building roads.

From the trig point, heading in the direction of the masts of **Brown Clee Hill**, follow the path aiming for the stone outcrop; pass to the right of it and, following the Shropshire Way signs, veer a little left following a narrow path downhill. The path does widen and, although it becomes indistinct in parts, you need to aim for the buildings of **Callowgate** directly ahead, with a more clearly defined section of path just in front of it. Continue along the signed Shropshire Way path in the same direction along a lovely shady path, going forward to a wider track and veering north-eastwards to arrive at a road near **Bromdon**.

Turn left onto the road and follow it for about half a mile, then look carefully for and follow a signed Shropshire Way path to the left along a track leading to buildings. However, before reaching the buildings turn right across a field, as signed. The course across the field is indistinct but aim for a new bridge over a stream; cross it and turn right in the direction shown by a Shropshire Way arrow, aiming for the right-hand corner of the field, and reaching a drive. Turn left to follow the drive to the **B4364** Ludlow–Bridgnorth road, turning right then immediately left. You begin your walk along a clear farm lane, veering from north-west to north-eastwards at the buildings of **Newton**. The lane becomes very narrow and overgrown in places, and if you're wearing shorts you may wish you weren't, as the nettles do their worst on your exposed legs. It's also a very steep climb, but in due course you reach a road.

Cross straight over the road, only to find yourself on an equally narrow path – don't be tempted onto the wider lane immediately running parallel with it to the left – and continue uphill, being sure to observe the Shropshire Way signs as the path veers north-eastwards. You reach a gate which you pass through, and this is the cue for things to improve greatly, as you continue along a really beautiful path in the shade of trees on the north-western fringe of a wood. You're then signed left to proceed more gently uphill on a clear path across rough grass, aiming for the masts, enjoying superb views all the while. However, on reaching the top, do not be misled – this is still not the highest point in Shropshire! It is in fact the first of the two Brown Clee Hill tops, this one known as **Clee Burf**, and it is not the higher of the two. Nobody knows when people began to make use of the Clee Hills, but forts were constructed on Brown Clee during the Iron Age, and Iron Age people hunted there. As stated above, quarrying started to take place here in the Middle Ages and there are numerous shafts on the hillside with ironstone being dug from the coal measures and feeding a number of forges around the hill. Later, wagons transported stone down a steep incline to the railway at Ditton Priors.

It's only when you reach the top of Clee Burf that you see, for the first time, the second and slightly higher summit, known as **Abdon Burf**, again furnished with masts. Permit yourself a rest on the top of Clee Burf, then forge on. The path beyond Clee Burf, heading north-eastwards towards Abdon Burf, is not always well defined.

The best plan is to keep the woodland and fence immediately to your right, following the right-hand edge of the rough grassland. You should shortly see a path slightly further away from the fence but remain parallel with it, maintain height and don't allow yourself to be sucked away into a gully down to the left coming up from Cockshutford. You need to aim for a seat and gate at the very top of the gully; if you have followed the fence edge, you'll reach a Shropshire Way signpost at the entrance to a small patch of woodland, pointing you towards the seat. In conditions of poor visibility you may not be able to see the seat, and you may wish to set your GPS navigator to reach it safely, the full grid reference for the seat being SO 59616 85404.

On reaching the seat, there's a choice of paths forward. Don't take what appears to be the main path going hard left here, but take the higher one to the right of it. Now follow a very good path, soon seeing the mast marking the summit of Abdon Burf to the right; as you get level with the 'summit furniture', you reach a Shropshire Way signpost pointing along a path leading directly to the summit. Note that some older maps show the Shropshire Way taking a different route here, but you do need to take the new, signed Shropshire Way path, leading you shortly to the summit of Abdon Burf. This really is the highest point in Shropshire and a magnificent spot. The summit is marked by a topograph providing mileage indicators to various landmarks, some visible, some not. There is a stunning variety of scenery on show including, of course, Titterstone Clee Hill and Clee Burf, the deliciously verdant Corve Dale to the west, Ludlow visible to the south-west and, rather further afield, the distinctive escarpments of Wenlock Edge, the Wrekin and the Malverns, as well as beautifully shaped hilltops with a distinctly volcanic look dotted all around. The only pity is the immediately adjacent masts which do obstruct the view to the north.

Beyond the topograph, observe the Shropshire Way signposts taking you to a narrow metalled road a little way beyond. Turn right to follow the road which swings left then goes downhill, keeping a pond to the right. Carry on along the road which veers from north-east to north-west, then swings sharply right (north-eastwards) to reach the top end of thick woodland. Following the Shropshire Way signpost, turn left to walk north-westwards along a lovely path in the shade of trees. As the Shropshire Way veers left, turn hard right onto a signed footpath, actually a track; the track, emerging from the trees, provides a glorious view eastwards, particularly to the Wrekin. The Wrekin is arguably Shropshire's best-known summit, and while just 1,335 feet (407 metres) high, considerably lower than that of Brown Clee Hill, its isolation from other hills makes it stand out in spectacular fashion. The prosaic explanation for its origin is that it was formed through volcanic activity some 600 million years ago. Legend, however, says that a giant was on his way to Shrewsbury to flood the town, carrying a shovelful of earth, and asked a cobbler how far he had to go; he was so disgusted by his response that he threw down his bundle of earth, thus creating the Wrekin!

Now I'm afraid it gets messy – and I don't just mean the Clee Hill mud on your boots. Having emerged from the trees, watch very carefully to the left for a gate and signed footpath leading hard left away from it; go through the gate, join this footpath and drop downhill steeply, taking a hairpin bend to arrive at a road. Turn right onto the road, soon passing a road going off to the left and, just beyond this junction, turn left onto a signed footpath going downhill along a left-hand field edge. Go forward into the trees, turn immediately left as signed, then, emerging from the trees beyond a gate, turn right to walk as signed along a right-hand field edge.

Enter the next field and keep along the right-hand field edge to a stile; turn right to cross the stile and enter another field, following the left-hand field edge to shortly reach a signed path going left into an adjacent field. Walk north-eastwards through this field, aiming for a stile and, beyond it, going forward in the same direction along a much clearer path leading to **Hall Farm**. Pass just to the left of the farm and go forward to a lane, which leads to a road. Turn right onto the road, then very shortly left onto a signed footpath across fields to the trees beyond. Continue through the trees just to the right of a little stream, then emerging at a junction of paths turn half-left (not hard left) along a path which takes you to a metalled road. Join it, proceeding in the same direction, to arrive at the church at **Ditton Priors**. Turn right onto the road here, almost immediately bearing left to reach a road junction, with Bridgnorth stated to be 9 miles ahead (don't worry, to you it's 7 miles) and a minor road going off to the right towards Middleton Priors.

Ideally, you would find here, the first settlement of any significance since you left Cleehill, a bus stop with regular services to Bridgnorth or Ludlow. Sadly the reality is very different. If you are reliant on public transport and have no car or lift available to you from here, you essentially have two options: one is a taxi to Bridgnorth (so make sure you have the numbers of local taxi firms and a mobile phone handy) and the other is a 7-mile road walk from Ditton Priors to Bridgnorth. The quickest route is to turn right along the minor road referred to at the end of the paragraph above, and follow it via Middleton Priors, Middleton Baggot, Lightwood and Harpswood to reach the B4364, turning left along what is a busy road (with no pavement) to a roundabout with the A458 bypass. Beyond the bypass the road at least has a pavement and soon leads to the centre of Bridgnorth, one of the most beautiful towns in the Midlands. Apart from the section from Harpswood to the A458 roundabout, it's not unpleasant walking, but it's hardly scenic either. Yes, I decided that the money a taxi ride would have cost me was more pleasantly spent on funding a better B & B in the town – only to find that it failed to offer coffee-making facilities and 9 p.m. found me, following my long pilgrimage from the various Clee Hills, not lazing in a cosy lounge with an improving book, but wandering the streets in search of a heated beverage, after Subway, for reasons best known to themselves, had decided to shut down their hot drinks machine an hour before closing. But I loved this walk all the same, with its majestic views across the heart of Shropshire, and if you're lucky with the weather I know you will, too.

South Yorkshire

High Stones – 548 metres / 1,798 feet – SK 188943

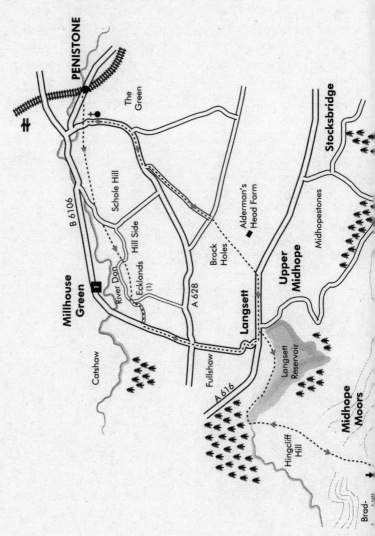

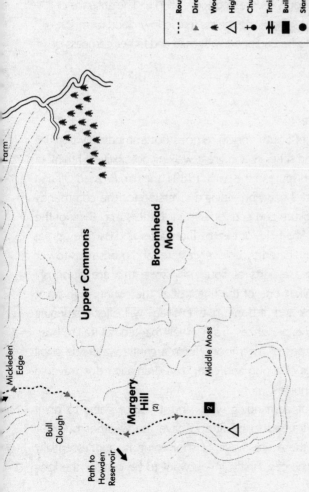

Key

- ••• Route
- ▲ Direction
- ← Woodland
- △ Highest Point
- ✝ Church
- ⇌ Train Station
- ■ Building
- ● Start/Finish Point

Farm

Mickleden
Edge

Bull Clough

Path to Howden Reservoir

Upper Commons

Margery
Hill
(2)

Broomhead Moor

Middle Moss

2

Length: Minimum 11 miles, maximum 18 miles
Start and finish: Penistone, Millhouse Green or Langsett (see below)
Public transport: Regular trains serving Penistone on the
Huddersfield–Barnsley line; regular buses serving Millhouse Green
from Penistone
Refreshments: Penistone (P, C, S); Millhouse Green (P, S);
Langsett (P, C)
Difficulty: Strenuous, severe in places. NOTE: The absence of
clear landmarks or signposting means that in low cloud or mist it is
essential for you to be equipped with map and either compass or
GPS device
Rating: ****

Moor and more

To me, mention of South Yorkshire does not immediately conjure
up visions of grand scenery and great walking possibilities. I think of
the bitter mining dispute in the early 1980s, the film *Brassed Off* and
Pete Postlethwaite's band providing a diversion for the community
threatened by closure and economic ruin. Others may think of the
great steel city of Sheffield, or nearby Doncaster and Barnsley, great
urban sprawls dominated by unlovely estates and monstrous tower
blocks. Yet there are parts of South Yorkshire that are gloriously
unspoilt. This walk is one of the finest of all the county high point
walks in this book and, if done in its entirety, will offer a stunning
variety of walking experiences: from a well-marked rail trail to bog-
hopping on the tops of the moors, from a gentle waterside stroll
within easy radius of a pub and cafe, to a dramatic ridge traverse
high up in the Pennines.

It's a terrific but demanding walk, and if you're going to do it
all in a day, you'll need to be fit and have the weather on your
side. However, there are ways of shortening it, and essentially
you have three choices. Firstly, if you want to be in it for the long

haul, you could begin at Penistone, a most attractive town with good amenities and rail links. Secondly, you could catch one of the many advertised buses from Penistone to Millhouse Green, saving you some 4 miles altogether, and start from there; or thirdly you could take your chances with a bus to Langsett, although the posted timetable I saw in September 2011 showed that virtually all bus services to Langsett had been withdrawn despite indications on the Internet to the contrary. I do recommend that if you can, you start from Penistone but in the description that follows I indicate how it could be modified if you prefer.

Having left the train at Penistone, make your way to the crossing point between the two platforms, facing eastwards (towards Barnsley). By bearing right here you almost immediately arrive at the **Trans Pennine Trail**. This trail runs for 350 miles and is a coast-to-coast walk, starting at Hornsea on the North Sea coast and finishing at Southport on Merseyside, making use of old railway lines, canal towpaths and other waterside routes. The particular section you'll be following is part of an old railway linking Manchester and Sheffield, via Glossop and Crowden, that's been converted into what you will find is an excellent footpath. Turn right to follow the Trans Pennine Trail westwards, initially past the houses of Penistone then out into open countryside. It's lovely peaceful walking, but don't expect to be on your own, especially at weekends. After two miles or so, you cross a road, with the village of Millhouse Green signposted to the right; a couple of hundred yards beyond this crossing (precise grid reference SE 21924 02589), you will see a little flight of steps to your right, leading to a path that runs parallel to but above the old railway line, rising to reach a road onto which you turn left, immediately crossing over the old line **1**. If you're starting your walk from **Millhouse Green**, having come from Penistone by bus, turn off the main A628 road down Birks Lane in the centre of the village, descending to a bridge and then a junction, turning right to follow the road signed Ecklands and arriving at point **1** above. Now united with the route from Penistone, follow the road past the Ecklands farm building and go forward to reach the **A628**. Turn left to follow it for just over half a mile to the point where the A628 veers sharply right, but rather than veering right with it, walk straight on along a minor road which goes forward to meet the A616 at Langsett. This village boasts a pub and cafe, at the time of writing, which is impressive for such a modest place.

On reaching the **A616**, turn left and walk beside the road to Bank View Café (if you've come by bus, ask to be dropped here), leaving the A616 opposite the cafe by following the road signposted Strines and Derwent Valley. Very soon you'll reach the **Langsett Reservoir**, and immediately before the reservoir begins, turn right onto a path which hugs the reservoir edge. There are numerous paths hereabouts – this is extremely popular walking country for locals – but just stick to the one going closest to the reservoir itself and you won't go wrong. The views across the reservoir to the moors provide a foretaste of what you'll be enjoying soon, and there are benches available for you to sit and enjoy the scenery. Eventually you leave the reservoir behind but stick to the path in the woodland nearest the stream that feeds into the reservoir, arriving at a T-junction with a stony path. Turn left to follow the stony path downhill and cross a bridge; bear left again immediately beyond the bridge to join the path signposted Cut Gate and Slippery Stones, passing a number of information boards. The path soon bends very sharply right and rises steeply, then veers sharp left and now proceeds in a more sedate and less dramatic fashion south-westwards. You're now properly on your way into the moors.

The next 4 miles or so present no navigational or real technical difficulties, as you follow a path which is always very well defined, particularly early on where it is reassuringly wide. The surroundings become more and more remote and wild as you proceed away from the gentle reservoir-side woodland, and march higher and higher into the heather moors, one of the most unsung parts of the Pennines and largely ignored by the guidebooks – well, certainly the many guidebooks provided at my Glossop B & B the previous night. At weekends, however, don't expect to be on your own, as this path is very popular with cyclists and you may be asked to get out of the way to let them pass – only for them to have to return the compliment, as I had to, when the path is obstructed by hapless riders grappling with buckled wheels and/or gashed inner tubes. The climbing is never severe, but at times seems relentless as you venture further and further into the moors, initially over **Hingcliff Common** (ignoring a left fork) and then along **Mickleden Edge**, the ground falling steeply away to Mickleden Beck to the right. A signed path comes in from the left, but there are no other landmarks to speak of as you keep climbing, sharing your route for a time with the course of a stream, although there are plenty of options to prevent your feet getting wet. Alongside Mickleden Edge you'll have been heading southwards, but then veer gradually south-westwards, the path remaining easy to trace on the ground – just look for the cycle tyre marks.

The time to sit up and take notice is when the gradient eases and you find yourself on level ground, the sense of remoteness now quite palpable. It's a land of heather, of tufty grass, of streams and pools, and more streams and more pools. Christopher Somerville, author of *Britain & Ireland's Best Wild Places*, describes the scene thus: 'Here are cloughs, groughs, gutters, and dikes, and springs, all names for innumerable threads of water.' There are one or two small cairns but the one to look out for is a large cairn of substantial stones set in the centre of the path, just as the ground in front begins to fall away downhill (grid reference SK 18579 96061), the steep drop ahead of you known as **Howden Edge**. Look to your left by the cairn and you should be able to make out a thin path through the peat. In wet conditions this could be very juicy indeed, so be patient as you head along the path, aiming for a large fenced enclosure up ahead. This enclosure has been set up to protect Margery Hill, a Bronze Age burial mound. As you reach the enclosure, aim for the information board towards its near right-hand end, bear right beside the board and pass round the right-hand edge, effectively the nearside corner, of the enclosure, remaining parallel with the fence. Veering left with the fence, you should see the path striking out to the right, away from the fence, along a ridge edge.

You're now less than a mile from your objective and in mist this is a good time to set your GPS (grid reference SK 188 943), although hopefully you'll have had the luxury of choosing a clear day for the walk, as the final three-quarters of a mile of this walk is quite magnificent. You now continue forward along a clear though narrow path which, having crossed a stile **2**, proceeds unerringly southwards along the top of the ridge, **Wilfrey Edge**, with quite astonishing views to the west and south-west. Most of the hard work was done much earlier, but the ground does rise perceptibly to reach the summit of **High Stones**, marked by a small cairn. The views to the south-west are particularly good here, the Howden Dam on the Howden Reservoir clearly visible below, and an assortment of shapely hills, one or two of which bear a more than passing resemblance to Great Gable in the Lake District, rising up behind. In the foreground is the open moorland of Upper Hey and in the late summer the purple heather presents a breathtaking sight. You have to remind yourself you're in South Yorkshire and not North Yorkshire or Northumberland, the surroundings being so spectacularly unspoilt and almost frighteningly remote. It would be tempting to plough on southwards to Howden Moors, the path proceeding invitingly on in that direction, but this will take you further and further away from civilisation, and if you're to be back in time for *Coronation Street*, you need to turn round.

You will simply be returning to Langsett the same way. However, although you could retrace your steps initially along the ridge edge, you may want to mix things a little as you come to the stile at

■ above; it's possible to detour beside the fence, and climb to the bizarre rocky outcrops known as the Margery Stones and the nearby bright white triangulation point. This is in many ways a more satisfying summit than High Stones, commanding views which are every bit as good, but it is built on ground that is an infuriating 6 feet 6 inches (2 metres) shy of the 1,798-foot (548-metre) summit of South Yorkshire. Return to the stile at ■ and cross it, then on arriving at the **Margery Hill** enclosure work your way round the fence to the left, veering right with the fence to find yourself by the information board again. From here you should, in clear conditions, easily identify the path heading off to the left, back to the large cairn at SK 18579 96061, but in mist it's essential to reprogramme your GPS to get back to it. Once you're back at the cairn, the pressure is off, as you simply bear right to retrace your steps along the path all the way to Langsett Reservoir. There is the option of a signed path going off to the right at Mickleden Edge, tempting you to Langsett, but I suggest you stick to the path you followed on the way up, enjoying superb views towards Bleaklow in the heart of the Peak District National Park. (In case the name seems familiar, it's on the Pennine Way between Snake Road and Crowden, part of the traditionally infamous first day on the trail.) Gradually the surroundings become more hospitable, the path widens, cyclists having patched up their tubing can shoot past you with ease, and you find yourself back at the bridge over the stream feeding Langsett Reservoir. Cross back over the bridge and climb up the stone path, bearing first right along the reservoir-side path, sticking to the paths closest to the reservoir and, in due course, arriving at the road. Turn left to follow the road back up to the A616.

If you're planning on calling it a day here, either with the help of an unadvertised bus or a taxi, goodbye and, to quote Lord Sugar, see you on the next task. If you're returning to Millhouse Green, turn left to follow the A616 briefly, then bear right as signed up the road which takes you to the A628 Manchester Road. You could simply follow this road back to Millhouse Green, or retrace your steps by turning right along the Ecklands road, bearing left into Birks Lane and arriving back in the village. However, if you're walking back to Penistone from Langsett, there is an alternative way of getting there, which I would recommend for variety as well as good views. To follow this alternative route, turn right, not left, onto the A616 and follow it in a dead straight line for just about half a mile to the point where the road veers slightly right. Here you bear left onto a signed bridleway heading north-eastwards, soon crossing a section of old railway and continuing north-eastwards across pasture aiming for just short of a pylon and arriving at a farm track. Turn left onto the track, passing under the pylon lines immediately to the left of the pylon, then as the track veers left, bear right as signposted and go forward uphill, initially along a left-hand field edge. You reach another arrow sign which points you diagonally uphill, following a clear dirt track just north of east over grass, aiming for a stone wall. The hill climbing will seem incongruous after all the downhill walking you've had to do, but it's not much really, and once you've made the top of this one, it really is all downhill after that. Just short of the stone wall veer gently left, north-eastwards again, along a farm lane, soon being reassured by a sign, going forward to reach a road junction.

Look back to enjoy your final view of the moors you've been following, then go straight ahead along **Brock Holes Lane** downhill, following it all the way to its end where you turn right into Chapel Lane. Continue downhill to another T-junction and turn left, soon arriving in the centre of Penistone. If you've the time and the energy after your walk, it's worth spending a while pottering in the town which has traditionally divided its interests between agriculture and the steel industry; its very prominent church dates from the thirteenth century, while there's a former cloth hall and a shambles dating back to 1768. To reach the station, bear right as signed into Shrewsbury Road, passing another interesting building, the splendid Paramount

Cinema, as you follow it. It is the epitome of old-fashioned cinemas and is still thriving in the modern age. Shortly beyond the cinema you pass under the bridge carrying the Trans Pennine Trail. Remember that all those hours ago? Once under the bridge, turn shortly right as signed to walk up to Penistone station, where regular trains can convey you to Huddersfield or Barnsley, to link with services to Manchester and Leeds. So it's back into South Yorkshire business as usual. Following the tranquillity and remoteness of the 18 miles I had just completed it was quite a contrast for me to be crowded into a two-coach Barnsley-bound train listening to a beer-bellied, curly haired, earringed man opposite boast to the attractive woman sitting next to him about the number of tattoos decorating his body. Thankfully he stopped short of providing a free exhibition.

Cheshire and Staffordshire

Shining Tor – 559 metres / 1,834 feet – SJ 994737
Cheeks Hill – 520 metres / 1,706 feet – SK 026699

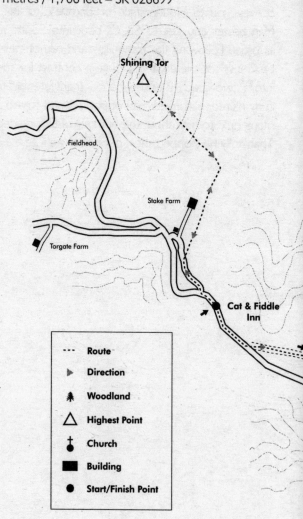

- - -	**Route**
▶	**Direction**
♠	**Woodland**
△	**Highest Point**
✝	**Church**
■	**Building**
●	**Start/Finish Point**

Length: 7 miles. NOTE: The walk could be increased to 8 miles if you continue to Buxton rather than Burbage

Start: Cat & Fiddle Inn

Finish: Burbage or Buxton

Public transport: Regular buses serving the Cat & Fiddle and Burbage on the Macclesfield–Buxton route

Refreshments: Cat & Fiddle (P), Buxton (P, C, S)

Difficulty: Moderate, strenuous in places

Rating: ****

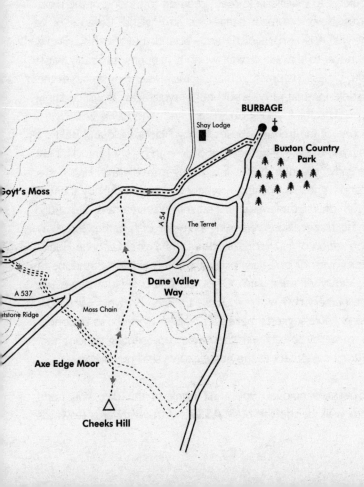

Over the Moon

It doesn't get much better than this. A walk that starts at a pub, could actually finish there if you wished and goes past it in the middle. For not a great deal of physical effort you get, in terms of scenery and views, one of the best county high points in England. And if that isn't enough to satisfy you, there's a town nearby that offers excellent public transport links, superb hospitality, great architecture and exceptional fish and chips. So… what's stopping you?

Well, if you're reading this in December or January, possibly snow. Your walk starts at the Cat & Fiddle Inn on the notorious A537 Buxton to Macclesfield road, reputed to be one of the most dangerous, if not *the* most dangerous, in England. Because of its great height, it is also regularly snowbound, but the BBC Radio 2 travel news to that effect will, when it happens, probably wash over you. Unless, naturally, you are actually intending to target the Cat & Fiddle Inn that same weekend, in which case it will certainly cause you to rethink your plans. But if and when all is well, you'll hop on one of the frequent buses linking Macclesfield and Buxton, dropping you obligingly outside the pub, with most of the climbing done already. The pub itself is interesting in two ways. Firstly, it is the second highest in England, exceeded in height only by the Tan Hill Inn which will be familiar to Pennine Way veterans. Secondly, there is much speculation regarding the origin of its name. Some say it is a corruption of *'le chat fidele'* (the faithful cat), 'Caton le Fidele' (a former governor of Calais) or 'Catherine la Fidele' (Catherine of Aragon, Henry VIII's first wife). Or of course it could just have come from the nursery rhyme 'Hey Diddle Diddle'. Brewers' *Dictionary of Phrase & Fable* suggests there's a possible reference to the once-popular game of tip-cat, with the fiddle representing dancing that might attract customers to the hostelry. We shall never know.

Having perhaps enjoyed your first drink of the day, you need initially to walk beside the busy **A537** north-westwards (towards

Macclesfield) away from the pub; there is, fortunately, a crude roadside path on the pub side of the A537, as this road is extremely busy. As the road bends to the left, bear right to leave the roadside along a clear path on the hillside, enjoying excellent views to your left. In just a couple of hundred yards you reach a path junction, where you turn right to follow a very clear path just east of north. You pass above and to the right of the buildings of **Stake Farm**, then in roughly half a mile from the path junction referred to above you reach another, signed, path junction, with a signed path to Shining Tor heading off to the left. Turn left here and walk uphill, north-westwards, keeping the dry stone wall to your left, to reach the trig point marking the summit of **Shining Tor** – the highest point of Cheshire, albeit just a couple of steps from its border with Derbyshire.

The views are fantastic, particularly ahead to the west, and you can contrast the great scenic variety westwards, including the townscape of Macclesfield, the radio telescopes of Jodrell Bank and the sprawl of Manchester, with the wilder Peak District scenery behind you. Perhaps the most pleasing prospect is southwards to the distinctive, elegant and beguiling summit of Shutlingsloe, which will have been in your sights for most of this walk. Known as Cheshire's Matterhorn, its unusual name is thought to derive from 'Scyttel's hlaw', meaning 'the hill of Scyttel'. While the conquest of Shutlingsloe is outside the scope of this book, you may be tempted to scale it during your stay in the area.

Now retrace your steps back to the Cat & Fiddle Inn, by descending to the signed path junction, turning right to walk above and to the left of Stake Farm, and at the T-junction at the end turning left to arrive at the A537 and following beside it back to the pub. Well, you've earned a drink now so, having enjoyed it, walk on alongside the A537 briefly, then turn left to follow a minor road downhill. In just under a mile, but crucially before the road peters out into a rough track, turn right onto another metalled road, taking care to veer right with it to arrive back at the A537. Cross straight over onto another minor road, which you follow briefly to reach a T-junction with the **A54**; turn left onto the road and then almost immediately right onto a further minor road, following it south-eastwards and gaining height gradually. In just over half a mile you reach a signed footpath going off to the right (just beyond it, there's a signed path off the road to the left, so if you reach that, you've gone too far).

Turn right onto the signed footpath, which heads southwards across the moor, soon descending to cross over the **River Dane** then rising and going forward to a dry stone enclosure, and veering hard left to attain slightly higher ground just a few yards away. You're now on **Cheeks Hill**, the highest ground in Staffordshire, although ironically the ground rises to **Axe Edge** to the east. You're actually at the very north tip of Staffordshire at this point; the view southwards across this county is lovely, and although it lacks the drama of Shining Tor, it is still very beautiful. But still you have to, in this respect anyway, feel rather sorry for poor Staffordshire – a county with some great scenery and in Flash boasting the highest village in England, but the highest ground in the county is cruelly dwarfed by uncaring Derbyshire hills immediately adjacent; and with a name more synonymous with bottoms than tops.

Retrace your steps via the Dane crossing to the road, turning right onto it then immediately left onto another signed path, now following the course of the **Dane Valley Way**, initially northwards then just east of north. This is a superb path across **Axe Edge Moor**, with magnificent views particularly ahead and to the left. You drop down gently to reach the A537; although you could turn left onto the A537 and retrace your steps for a third visit to the Cat & Fiddle Inn, the recommended route crosses straight over, the Dane Valley Way going off to the right. Continue northwards along a clear path offering magnificent views to Buxton and its surrounding hills, again to your right. You reach a T-junction with a stony path, turning right to follow it downhill, going forward to a metalled road and a more suburban landscape with houses on both sides. At the end of the road you arrive back at the A537 at the village of **Burbage**, close to the village church. There are buses available from here into Buxton, but if you don't want to wait, it's a brisk walk of about a mile beside the A537 beyond the church into Buxton.

Buxton, at 1,007 feet (307 metres) one of the highest towns of England, is a beautiful place, and you would need to be in a tearing hurry not to linger here awhile and celebrate the conclusion of your lovely walk. A spa town, it owes its fame to the fifth Duke of Devonshire who, at the end of the eighteenth century, built the town's splendid crescent, to compete with the beauties of Bath. Its warm springs have been utilised continuously since at least Roman times and, to this day, Buxton is a well-known and successful brand of bottled water. Among many other superb buildings in the town are the Devonshire Royal Hospital, with its huge dome, which dates back to 1859, and also the excellent Edwardian Buxton Opera House. There are numerous pubs, restaurants, cafes and B & Bs, a takeaway on the main street offered me certainly the best cod and chips I'd ever had, and there's a very popular and successful arts festival every summer. There is also a good train service back to Stockport and Manchester, with connections there for all parts of the country, to enable you to get home. Secure in the knowledge that the next time the A537 and Cat & Fiddle Inn are mentioned on the BBC Radio 2 travel bulletin as cut off from the outside world, you can slump deeper into your armchair with nothing more awkward to exercise your mind than the crossword in your *Country Walking* magazine.

Greater Manchester and West Yorkshire

Black Chew Head – 542 metres / 1,778 feet – SE 056019
Black Hill – 582 metres / 1,908 feet – SE 078046

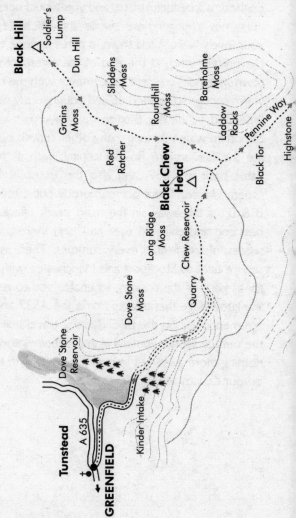

Length: 17 miles

Start: Greenfield station

Finish: Glossop station

Public transport: Regular trains serving Greenfield on the Manchester–Huddersfield line; regular trains between Glossop and Manchester

Refreshments: Greenfield (P, S); Glossop (P, C, S); none en route

Difficulty: Severe. NOTE: There is one section of this walk that is particularly dangerous in bad weather. Please read the walk description carefully before setting out. You should equip yourself with a map, plus compass or GPS device. In an emergency there may be accommodation available at Crowden Youth Hostel towards the end of the walk

Rating: ****

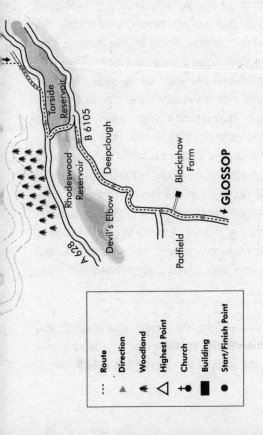

Wain wrong

'I have always thought any mountain or hill worth climbing, the only exception being Black Hill,' so wrote the great Alfred Wainwright, in days when, admittedly, conditions for the ascent of Black Hill, which is on the Pennine Way, were a great deal tougher than they are now. Even so, it hardly encourages you to tackle the roof of West Yorkshire. In fact, this walk, which provides two county high points for the price of one, is a superb march, with scenery as spectacular and truly awe-inspiring as you will find in any of the walks in this book.

Before you make a dash for your walking boots and your laptop to book your cheap rail tickets online, though, a word of warning. While there is only one climb of any significance, along a metalled road, you will certainly cover much of the ground very quickly, the section of this walk around the Laddow Rocks on the Pennine Way could be exceedingly dangerous in the wrong conditions. The path, often rocky and involving several awkward steps, goes perilously close to the edge of a ridge with a virtually sheer drop of several hundred feet. Just one slip or stumble on a piece of wet rock could be fatal. As you head back towards Longdendale, there is then a very steep rocky descent where, if daylight is fading, you are tired and start getting careless, a false move could result in very serious injury. Moreover, the walk from Chew Reservoir to Black Chew Head can navigationally be quite awkward even in clear conditions, and potentially very confusing in mist. Unless you are properly equipped with suitably stout footwear and navigational aid, and have time on your side, you should not contemplate this walk, especially in bad weather.

But if neither the great Wainwright nor I have put you off, you will report for duty at **Greenfield station** on the Manchester–Huddersfield line, exiting the station and joining the **A669**, which promptly executes a hairpin bend and drops steeply down south-eastwards into and through the village of Greenfield itself. As you pass through the village you'll cross the Pennine Bridleway, a National Trail which provides a journey up the Pennines that is rather gentler than its big brother the Pennine Way, but when complete will be considerably longer. Continue to the very end of the village street and turn left to follow the **A635 Holmfirth road**, a classic trans-Pennine route; there's even a sign indicating that the road may be closed in bad weather. There is a pavement, rendering the road walk not too unpleasant, and in just a few hundred yards you leave this road, forking right along Bank Lane, signposted **Dove Stone Reservoir**. There's no pavement along this road and it can be busy, so be careful. The road reaches the bank of the reservoir, and clearly you'll want to get to the top of the bank to walk beside the water rather than trudge along the road. The signage isn't very clear and although there appeared to be a path, I simply shinned up the bank; think of it as a dress rehearsal for stiff climbs ahead. Once you've made the top of the bank, turn right to enjoy a delightful walk southwards alongside the reservoir, a relaxing interlude ahead before the much harder work to come.

At the south-west corner of the reservoir, the waterside path veers left, south-eastwards, still following the reservoir but a little further away from it. You pass a sailing club building and continue along an excellent track in the shade of woodland, to arrive at the south-east corner of the reservoir and a path junction. Do not veer left to continue beside the reservoir, but simply continue on south-eastwards along what is a metalled track which you can see heading uphill. This track is part of the **Oldham Way** and is known as Chew Road, serving, as it does, Chew Reservoir. Now the serious legwork really begins. You can at least console yourself that this is the longest climb you'll have to do all day, but a climb it certainly is. The views are particularly good to begin with, the valley scenery around Greenfield and Uppermill contrasting with the steep rocky hillsides of Alderman's Hill and Dick Hill; the obelisk on the latter will need no introduction to northbound Pennine Bridleway veterans, who will remember it from their descent to Uppermill, an obvious staging post on the journey.

Keep climbing, not being discouraged by the fact that what looks like the summit of the climb is in fact just the prelude to the next bit of climbing. The views become more restricted and suddenly the Sunday afternoon strollers round Dove Stone Reservoir, whose longest planned walk of the day is to the pay machine in the car park, seem a very long way back. Do watch out for cyclists, though; I was passed by two pedallers on their descent at tremendous speed; the authorities have sensibly at one point erected a crash barrier between the road and what is a terrifyingly steep drop on the right-hand side. Eventually the ground does level out and there are a few moments' respite, with gentler gradient, before a swing to the right and a final haul up to **Chew Reservoir**.

Pause here for a moment; you've earned a rest anyway, but it's worth considering the contrast between the popular easily accessible Dove Stone Reservoir and this one, surrounded by uncompromising moorland. No sailing clubs up here and still fewer branches of Starbucks. Your hitherto solid metal track ends at the south-west corner of the reservoir, but a clear path goes off to the left, along the south side of the reservoir. Follow this path which is narrow but clear, and then simply continue with it in pretty much the same direction beyond the reservoir, heading just north of east. Beyond the reservoir the path is much less clear on the ground, forging a sometimes tentative and less than whole-hearted trail through the tufty grass, heather and peat. You will be relieved to know that there are none of the peat groughs or channels which prove such a headache in the conquest of Kinder Scout just 15 or so miles south. But it's not easy, and you almost want some cyclists to have just passed by so you can identify their tyre marks in the mud! Just to add to the fun, the path does occasionally twist and turn, and has to negotiate the odd beck crossing. I suggest you take a GPS setting for grid reference SE 053 016, which is the junction for the **Black Chew Head** detour, just in case. Failing that, instinct will usually tell you which is the next step, but if you sink without trace into a morass of peat, never to surface again – well, you've probably got it wrong.

If all is well, however, you will arrive at the junction; in fact it's a fence with a stile, marking the boundary between Greater Manchester and Derbyshire. Here, don't cross the stile, but turn left to follow alongside the boundary fence for roughly a quarter of a mile – I say roughly, because the going is difficult in places, and you may need to detour away from the fence in order to make progress. However, it is never impossibly difficult, and you are rewarded with arrival at a small cairn and post which appears to mark the county high point – grid reference SE 056 019. That said, this is part of a huge plateau rather than a satisfying hill or mountain top and, looking around you, you will see one or two tufts of high grass which appear to be on slightly higher ground. I spent a distinctly nerdish few minutes bobbing around them, with my GPS device poised in height-indicator mode, trying to ascertain if any of these tufts 'beat' the post and cairn. That's the trouble with county high points on plateaux. I came to the conclusion that a tuft fractionally to the west of the post and cairn just took the honour, but it's hard to tell and not worth worrying about too much. The views are limited by the size of the plateau, but from certain points you can look back to Chew Reservoir while ahead; eastwards, you can see the starker hillsides plunging down towards Crowden Great Brook, signifying your proximity to the Pennine Way.

Retrace your steps along the boundary fence to the stile – the fence will certainly be a very welcome prop in mist. If you have already walked the Pennine Way and therefore visited Black Hill before, you could simply turn right and retrace your steps to Greenfield via Dove Stone Reservoir. However, if you are up for

Black Hill, the summit of West Yorkshire, either as a first-timer or returning visitor, turn left to cross the stile and continue along the path. Suddenly the path is wider and also cairned – what luxury! Soon it begins to descend and ahead you can see the ground falling away dramatically. Take great care as you drop down steeply to one of the most dramatic T-junctions of footpaths in Britain, the meeting of your path with the Pennine Way. There's no signpost to announce it, but you'll know when you've reached it, as you've effectively arrived at a cliff edge and, as you turn left to follow the **Pennine Way** north-eastwards, you're looking down to your right at an almost sheer drop towards **Crowden Great Brook**; looking back (for goodness sake stop before you do) you can see the brook as it flows into the Longdendale Valley.

Now proceed with immense care along the path, which while well defined is narrow and often rocky, and, as stated above, one false move or stumble could be the end of you. It's terrifying but exhilarating as well. The outcrops of gritstone are the Laddow Rocks, the steep sides and overhangs providing potentially fertile ground for climbers. As you continue, the danger of an early grave recedes and the character of the walk changes again, as the path makes its way down the steep hillside towards the brook. The path becomes stonier but is still very visible, and there is a 'shut-in' feel as the hillsides seem to get closer and closer together. The descent culminates in two stream crossings in close succession.

Beyond the fords, the path, still heading north-eastwards, strikes out across open moorland onto Dun Hill, with Black Hill clearly visible on the skyline. A generation ago, this was regarded as one of the grimmest parts of the Pennine Way. Wainwright described it as a 'wet and weary trudge', as the path, for want of a better expression, struggled across peaty moorland, which seemed to remain squelchy in even the driest conditions; as Black Hill got closer, the ground became positively treacherous and when I walked this part of the Pennine Way in 1988, on a dry sunny day, I actually fell straight into one bog and even with no pack had great difficulty in heaving myself out. Things have changed now: it is a proper path with flagstones for much of the way, and you can enjoy the starkness and grandeur of the surroundings rather than worrying that one unlucky placement of a foot may see you sink into a terminal peaty abyss.

The climb onto **Black Hill** itself isn't hugely demanding and soon after gaining the hilltop, you see the trig point, nicely perched on a carefully crafted cairn. This is the highest point in West Yorkshire, although historically Black Hill was in Cheshire. The official high point grid reference is SE 078 046 but I would suggest conditions would need to be very bad for you to miss it. It certainly isn't the loveliest hill, being another plateau with humps and bumps inviting you to wonder if there are higher spots than the trig point itself; views are limited (in fact rendered virtually non-existent) by the size of the plateau, although the Holme Moss transmitting station just to the south-east makes an obvious landmark. However, it no longer holds the terrors it did in Wainwright's day, when he described it as a 'desolate and hopeless quagmire… a frightening place in bad weather… peat naked and unashamed.' Some things do change for the better.

Time now to head back, retracing your steps all the way to the point at which you joined the Pennine Way. With the help of the obvious path it is a very straightforward walk south-westwards, across the grass of Dun Hill back to the fords, and thereafter the going gets slower as you pick your way up the hillside with Crowden Great Brook to your left. Then, having completed the ascent, the **Laddow Rocks** come into view, the ground falls away to your left and, again, you need to concentrate hard on where you're putting your feet, especially with such an enticing view ahead. At length you reach the point where you joined the Pennine Way but this time you continue along the Pennine Way towards **Longdendale**, the valley you can see ahead, and now embark on a very tough descent, veering south-eastwards. While the path is clear, there are a number of very steep stony sections where you have to be very patient and very careful; at the end of a long day, with custard cream supplies drying up and a cheese-and-pickle-sandwich famine looming, it would be all too easy to get careless in a rush for the finishing line. Assuming you are still in one piece, you continue along a gentler course, taking care not to be sucked away onto one of the paths leading off to the left. Eventually you find yourself on more fertile ground, crossing fields, the course of the Pennine Way very clear with just a couple of gates to negotiate. Veering to fractionally east of south, you drop down to arrive at a T-junction with a lane. **Crowden**, with its youth hostel, is signed to the left; unless you're staying at the hostel, turn right to follow the lane which rises gently then drops to the **A628**, another classic trans-Pennine highway.

Cross straight over the road with care, and bear right to follow the Pennine Way-marked path which proceeds parallel to the A628 through woods, with **Torside Reservoir** to your left. At the end of the reservoir, one of five all strung out along the Longdendale Valley, turn left as signed to follow a clear path along the reservoir bank. Immediately beyond the reservoir there's a path junction. You say farewell to the Pennine Way here, as it veers away to the left; instead you turn right along a path which is separated from the reservoir by trees. In a couple of hundred yards – just beyond the trees but before the path joins the reservoir – look out for and take a path going away to the left under a tunnel, above which is the course of an old railway, now the **Longdendale Trail**. The path under the tunnel isn't well signed and is easily missed so watch carefully – and if you want extra insurance, use your GPS to locate it, grid reference SK 053 981.

Emerging from the tunnel you reach a footpath junction, turning right and going forward to a field; follow the path diagonally uphill through the field, looking out for a stile at the very top giving access to the **B6105**. Join the B6105 via the stile and turn right to follow this road all the way to Glossop, a distance of roughly 3 miles, via a spectacular hairpin bend in the road known as the **Devil's Elbow**. **Glossop** is a pleasant town with an excellent range of amenities and a good range of B & Bs. The one I stayed in, however, was probably unique, having hosts who insisted on sitting me down the moment I arrived, and offering me tea, and either home-made raspberry and almond cake or home-made blackberry and vanilla muffins. People shouldn't have to make choices like that after 17 miles of walking.

Devon

High Willhays – 621 metres / 2,039 feet – SX 580892

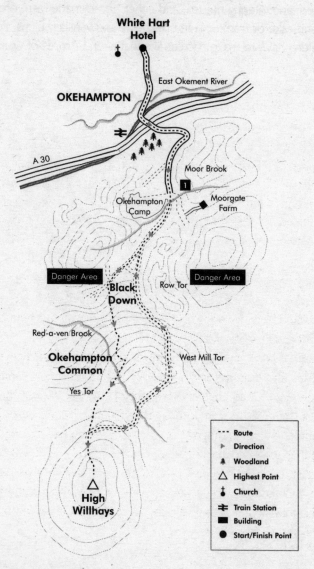

White Hart Hotel

East Okement River

OKEHAMPTON

A 30

Moor Brook

Okehampton Camp

Moorgate Farm

Danger Area

Row Tor

Danger Area

Black Down

Red-a-ven Brook

West Mill Tor

Okehampton Common

Yes Tor

△
High Willhays

--- Route
▶ Direction
♣ Woodland
△ Highest Point
♱ Church
⇌ Train Station
■ Building
● Start/Finish Point

Length: 9 miles. NOTE: The walk could be shortened to 6 miles if you get a lift or taxi up the road leading onto the moor
Start and finish: The White Hart Hotel, Okehampton
Public transport: Regular but infrequent buses serving Okehampton on the Exeter–Bude route
Refreshments: Okehampton (P, C, S); none en route
Difficulty: Strenuous
Rating: ****

Now you're tor-king

Considering what a large area Dartmoor covers, it is perhaps surprising, although pleasantly so, that its highest point is so close to civilisation. That said, the summit, not only of Dartmoor but of Devon and indeed southern England (this is the highest ground in England south of the Black Mountains), isn't logistically as straightforward as one might like. If you miss the bus from Exeter, you're likely to have to wait about four hours for the next and, having finally emerged from the vehicle and hauled yourself up onto the moor, you may find access prohibited. The course of this walk takes you through the Okehampton military range and, on occasion, the area is closed for firing (though generally not at weekends or in the school summer holidays).

Even if you find yourself on the moor without any red flags in sight, you may find that visibility is severely affected by the conditions. Mist and low cloud are very frequent on Dartmoor, and the fact that it's hot and sunny in Torquay barely thirty minutes away is no guarantee that in attempting this walk you'll be able to see anything more than the hand in front of your face. For this reason it is highly advisable to have a compass or GPS device. It's all very well to say come back another day if you're living or holidaying in the area, but this may be a less palatable prospect if you've travelled on the overnight train from Doncaster.

Dartmoor does indeed deserve more than just one day trip. It is the largest area of wild country in southern Britain, characterised by granite tors – rocky, bare hills – but also boasting large tracts of heather, blanket bog and patches of forest. It is exciting and challenging walking country. The variety of wildlife is huge: besides Dartmoor ponies, you may see foxes, adders, buzzards, wheatears, pied flycatchers and kestrels. This walk may not take you into the heart of Dartmoor – unless of course you go wrong – but it will give you a snapshot of its treasures.

The first part of the walk involves an uphill road slog of 1½ miles, and you could be forgiven for using a taxi to take you to point ■ below. However, for those who wish to walk from Okehampton, here goes. From the **White Hart Hotel** in the centre of Okehampton, walk away from the main street up George Street, adjacent to the hotel. The road bends slightly left; you see a church which is on the left, and more or less opposite the church you turn right up Station Road, and follow it uphill. There's a left turn signed to the old Okehampton station, but don't follow this; rather, carry straight on uphill, passing over the old railway and also the **A30**. There's a very sharp right-hand bend and then it's a straightforward road walk until you reach a small parking area on the right-hand side and the public road effectively ends ■. A right turn here, which you do not take, leads to **Okehampton Camp**, while roads leading away to the left are accessible to vehicles on a permissive basis only. Bear left and then immediately right along a tarmac track, with **Moor Brook** immediately to your left and a wall to your right. Keeping the modest **Row Tor** to your left, remain on the tarmac track up to a junction, with the tarmac track veering sharply left and a rougher track continuing ahead. Go straight over onto this rougher track, keeping **West Mill Tor**, appreciably higher than Row Tor, to your left. Follow this rougher track onto **Black Down**, as far as a junction of paths level with a col between West Mill Tor and its neighbour Yes Tor to the right, higher still than West Mill Tor. Turn left at this junction.

You now follow what is quite a well-defined path fairly gently uphill across the moor. The gradient then gets stiffer and the ground underfoot squelchier, as you make your way up to the col between West Mill Tor and Yes Tor. When the ground levels out, look carefully for a crossroads of paths more or less level with the stones on West Mill Tor, which are to your left. Turn right here and now follow a path towards Yes Tor; it's fairly faint in places, but the path is more clearly defined up the hillside, so simply use that as a line. Initially the going is quite easy and remains so as far as **Red-a-ven Brook**, which you have to ford, taking care as the stones around the brook may be quite slippery. Beyond the brook is the hardest work of the walk, as you climb very steeply to the summit of **Yes Tor** (GPS – SX 580 901), but you'll be amply rewarded. The summit is marked not only by stones but a trig point, and the views are astonishing, especially over Dartmoor but also northwards over mid-Devon towards Exmoor. In many ways it's a shame that this isn't the summit of Devon; it's a much more satisfying summit than High Willhays, but is dwarfed by it by an infuriating 2 metres!

It's only when you reach the summit of Yes Tor that the summit of High Willhays (GPS – SX 580 892) becomes apparent and the path to it, heading just west of south, is very obvious. Thankfully the col separating the two peaks is extremely shallow so the going is very easy. You descend gently and, at the bottom of the descent, look out for a clear track going away to the left; don't follow it yet, but mark it, as you'll need it for the return journey. The track, in the meantime, climbs up, again quite gently, to arrive on the **High Willhays** plateau. There is a fair array of summit furniture but the proper summit is very clear, marked by a large cairn. I conquered High Willhays very early one morning and found it coated in mist, with no views whatsoever, so returned the next morning. It was a beautiful, clear, sunny morning, the rising sun coating Yes Tor with orange, but no sooner had I come off Yes Tor en route for High Willhays than cloud swept up from the west to smother the roof of Devon yet again. The cloud did relent to allow me to enjoy the views across Dartmoor, but the mist certainly did make the surroundings more atmospheric, the rocks and piles of stones like big giants guarding this moorland plateau. It certainly felt very much more remote than Yes Tor. That said, I think you might still be left wishing that Yes Tor was your ultimate objective.

Now you need to make your way off the top, and return to the junction with the clear track referred to in the paragraph above (GPS – SX 580 899); in clear weather this will be very easy, but in mist it could be a great deal harder. Having reached the track at the col, turn right to follow it. It drops quite gently, keeping Yes Tor to your left, and reaches the same beck that you forded earlier; again you need to ford it, and then continue on the clear stony track. Even if the mist prevented you enjoying the views on the summits, you should be luckier now, the views quite magnificent, not only to other tors of Dartmoor and their rock-strewn tops, but the rolling green fields of mid-Devon stretching out forever. The journey may be enlivened even further by the sight of Dartmoor ponies. What you don't want, of course, is to turn back to the summit of High Willhays and find that the mist which obstinately refused to budge for the two hours you waited up there has suddenly lifted – with the last bus due imminently.

The track continues very obviously, keeping West Mill Tor to the left and Row Tor to the right; don't be tempted onto a track snaking to the right on the nearside of Row Tor. The track becomes tarmac, and it's now simply a matter of following it back to the top end of the road coming up from Okehampton, enjoying good views back to West Mill Tor and Yes Tor. Then it's back down the hill to Okehampton, be it by taxi or on foot. Even if you've chosen the wheeled option, you'll certainly have deserved your Devonshire clotted-cream tea. Which isn't to say that the dollops of cream and jam will not rather stick in your throat at the memory of having battled your way to the summit of Dartmoor through low cloud, driving rain and force-8 gale, while down in the town the sun is blazing and the locals are making gloomy noises about hosepipe bans and standpipes on street corners.

Lancashire

Gragareth – 627 metres / 2,056 feet – SD 688793
Green Hill – 628 metres / 2,059 feet – SD 701820

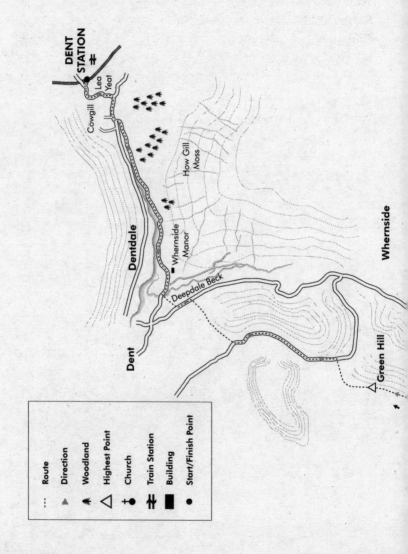

DENT STATION

Lea Yeat

Cowgill

How Gill Moss

Denidale

Whernside Manor

Deepdale Beck

Dent

Whernside

Green Hill

Route
Direction
Woodland
Highest Point
Church
Train Station
Building
Start/Finish Point

Length: 14 miles
Start: Ingleton
Finish: Dent station
Public transport: Regular buses serving Ingleton on the Settle–
Kirkby Lonsdale route; regular trains serving Dent on the Leeds–
Settle–Carlisle line
Refreshments: Ingleton (P, C, S); none en route
Difficulty: Strenuous, severe in places. NOTE: Because of the lack
of indications of paths on OS maps, and the unpredictability of the
weather, I have been more generous than usual in my provision of
grid references in the route description
Rating: ****

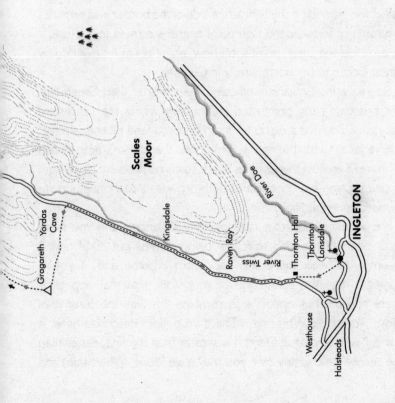

Boundary rider

'Twas all very simple in them days. Lancashire was just that – none of your Merseysides and your Greater Manchesters. A colossus of a county, encompassing Liverpool, Manchester, a goodly portion of the Lake District – and, in Coniston Old Man, a summit to be proud of. Now what have we? Two large metropolitan districts taking a huge slice off the west and south of the county, and Cumbria sweeping up the Lakeland glories including Coniston Old Man (how many more mountains did Cumbria *really* need?). Even though Lancashire still boasts many fine hilltops, nobody can be certain, thanks to border reorganisation, what its highest point should be. Officially, we're told, it's Green Hill. However, the hill itself straddles the border between Lancashire and Cumbria and, although a slight rise in the ground on the Lancashire side of the border wall provides a summit of sorts for the high point bagger's camera to capture, it doesn't feel like a high point somehow, especially as it's dwarfed by Great Coum to the north, firmly in Cumbria.

Step forward Gragareth, officially 3 feet shorter than Green Hill, but boasting a trig point, and indisputably within the Lancashire boundary. So what are you to do, in order to fend off criticism that you've failed to top the right summit? Well thankfully, Gragareth and Green Hill are less than 2 miles apart, so it's no problem to do both in one hit, and the conquest of both provides a really fine, if quite demanding, expedition.

It is an expedition that calls for careful planning and you need to decide which option to follow before setting out. One option is simply to walk there and back from Ingleton and, if you're staying in Ingleton either side of your walk, that may appeal. A more adventurous option is to combine this with the summit of North Yorkshire, Whernside. The third option, described here, is a linear walk ending at Dent; it is shorter than the first, easier than the second (and in any case you may have 'done' Whernside) and gets you back to the main rail network, but does involve a dubious descent off Green Hill, as I'll explain when we get there. I suggest you read the description carefully and then decide.

Ingleton is a delightful launching pad for your walk. On the attractive narrow main street there's a supermarket, an outdoor shop selling everything a walker could want or possibly need, and a couple of cafes – one providing me, on the eve of my walk, with a toasted and hot-buttered cheese scone, and a moist lemon drizzle cake, the ideal comfort food following a wet afternoon reconnaissance walk. There are lots of B & Bs, and the host of the one I stayed in couldn't have been more obliging about providing a before-hours feast of fruit juices, sugar-packed muesli, bacon, egg and toast. If you've time to spare before setting off you may also want to visit the well-signposted waterfalls to the north-east of the village, although as I dashed to the Co-op for extra supplies on the evening before I set out, it was hard to tell which was noisier out of the rushing Rivers Doe and Twiss or the rain that was bucketing from a leaden sky. So much for the evening outdoor picnic in the shadow of nearby Ingleborough; bring on the pre-packed chicken pasta salad in front of *Come Dine With Me* on More4.

You actually begin this walk in North Yorkshire and won't cross into Lancashire until you're almost in sight of Gragareth; in fact you will visit three counties in the course of this walk and, during the middle part of it, you'll be walking beside the boundaries firstly of Lancashire with North Yorkshire and then Lancashire with Cumbria. Your walk starts on the main approach to the village centre from the **A65**, where the road passes under a bridge which formerly carried the now defunct Clapham–Kirkby Lonsdale railway. Shortly beyond that bridge, turn left along a road signposted Thornton in Lonsdale. Cross both Rivers **Doe** and **Twiss**, then take a signed footpath turning to the right immediately beyond the sign for the waterfalls, as the road bends left. Follow the footpath through the trees, arriving at a kissing gate; pass through it and walk alongside the wall to your right, going through another gate and now veering gently north-west away from the wall, aiming for the right-hand one of two buildings you see in the fields ahead. Pass just to the left of this right-hand building and now veer northwards, aiming just to the left of a silver corrugated-iron building, continuing uphill to arrive at a gate and, beyond it, the **Ingleton–Dent road**. Turn right to follow this road. Before you continue, it's worth looking back for a splendid view of Ingleton.

You now follow the road along **Kingsdale** for roughly 3 miles, and after an initial steep climb it is very straightforward going. It's a narrow road and is generally very quiet – enabling you to enjoy the surroundings without having to dodge cars and trucks. To the right is **Kingsdale Beck**; when I walked along the road, there had just been very heavy overnight rain and the beck had flooded, making a very attractive scene indeed, which I enjoyed in the knowledge that I wouldn't have to negotiate the flood waters as part of my schedule. As you continue, you can see the road rising steeply ahead and, after the 3 miles of road walking, you reach a clump of trees to your left, with a layby opposite. Between the road and the trees is a gate which announces the land to be open access land – the grid reference is SD 706 790. Pass through the gate and walk up to the edge of the trees, where another gate provides access to Yorda's Cave and a very impressive waterfall. Yorda is a giant from Norse mythology, apparently with a penchant for stamping about and swallowing local infants, and his cave, the roof of which is 30 feet (9 metres) high in places, is well worth visiting if you've a torch and time to spare (although bear in mind your walk has hardly started). To progress, you need to bear left round the front of the woods and the outside wall, then, having passed them, veer right, north-westwards, steeply uphill, keeping the wooded enclosure to your right. Beyond the trees, as you continue to climb, you'll see a wall to your right, separating you from the waters of Yorda's Gill.

Continue uphill, passing through a gate in a crossing wall; ahead of you is the ridge on which both Gragareth and Green Hill are situated. Having passed through the gate, head diagonally left, aiming for another wall rising up the hillside, but you need to tread carefully and patiently, for the going is extremely soggy and there is no path as such. On reaching the wall, simply now follow parallel with and to the right of it; initially it's a rather squelchy uphill slog, then there's respite in the form of a short level section, before a big push for the top. It's one of the steepest climbs in this book, so take your time, pausing every so often to admire the magnificent views down to Kingsdale and beyond. You may well need to resort to hands as well as feet in places, but you're helped by footholds in the ground, and patience is rewarded when, after a gentler finale, you reach the very top of the ridge crossing the North Yorkshire–Cumbria boundary wall via a gate and stile.

Your way forward is to the right, alongside the boundary wall, but first you need to detour to **Gragareth**, the trig point of which can clearly be seen half-left across the grassy ridgetop – although if the mist obscures the view, the GPS reference is SD 688 793. There is a clear green path to the trig point from the wall, although after wet weather this can be very spongy. It's good to reach the trig point and it really does feel like a proper county summit, with excellent views down to Kirkby Lonsdale; in clear conditions you may be able to see as far afield as the Forest of Bowland, the Howgill Fells, the Lake District and Morecambe Bay, as well as the much nearer-at-hand Ingleborough. One feature of interest on the western side of the fell is a group of tall cairns known as the Three Men of Gragareth but, as they are some way to the west and getting to them requires you to lose much of the precious height you've gained, you could be forgiven for not detouring to see them.

Return to the boundary wall, believed to be one of the highest dry stone walls in the country, and now turn left to follow alongside it, heading just east of north. Although there's no path marked on

OS maps, there is in fact a path there, albeit it's not always clear. The problem is unlikely to be so much navigation as stepping round or over the numerous watery or boggy channels that decorate the ridgetop, but providing the weather is favourable, this is superbly enjoyable walking in classic watershed country, with streams flowing off the slopes to your right and left. As you approach **Green Hill**, you no longer have North Yorkshire across the other side of the boundary wall, but Cumbria; you're actually at the very north-eastern tip of Lancashire, with Cumbria immediately ahead of you and to the right of you. As well as excellent views to the side, there's a splendid hillside ahead on the skyline, which isn't Green Hill but Great Coum, dwarfing Green Hill completely. In fact, the 'summit' of Green Hill comes almost before you expect it; there's no big climb at all, just a slight rise in the ground, and at GPS reference SD 701 820 – about 1½ miles from where you joined the boundary wall – you're there, the high point being marked by a small cairn on a slight rise to the left. It's all a bit of an anticlimax. Again, though, the views are impressive, not only towards the Howgill and Lakeland fells to the north-west, but to Whernside and the Pennines to the east, although on the occasion of my visit, the wind was so strong that my enjoyment of the view was tempered by the need to concentrate on staying upright.

You may decide simply to retrace your steps to Ingleton from here. If you do, you will of course have marked the spot in the boundary wall where you came up from Yorda's Cave, and then enjoy, if that's the right word, a dramatic descent off the ridge, then a less steep but very wet descent to the trees, hitting the road and turning right to follow it back down to Kingsdale. (You could vary things a little at the end by following the road all the way to Ingleton via **Thornton in Lonsdale**.) However, rather than retracing your steps you could continue northwards beside the boundary wall, dropping down 78 feet (24 metres) or so to what is marked on the OS map as 'area of shake holes', grid reference SD 701 825.

The wall has crumbled here so can be crossed, but immediately adjacent to and in front of it is a wire fence. It is not barbed and is climbable, but you climb it at your own risk and, if you damage it, you will have to face the consequences (neither my publisher nor I accept any responsibility) – so take care and if in doubt retrace your steps. If you do get over safely, veer left to aim for the next crossing wall and then turn right to follow the wall side fractionally north of east downhill through the grass. As you descend, look back up at Green Hill, which from here is far more impressive in appearance than it was from above. It looks from here like a proper hill and not just a bit-part player in the story of the border ridge. Continuing to descend, you soon meet a stony track (grid reference SD 706 825) heading north–south, at right-angles to your line of descent; you'll need to cross another fence to access it, but I experienced no difficulty with this.

Once on the track, it is possible, providing you have the time and fitness levels, to access Whernside quite easily. To do this, turn right to follow the track for just over a mile back to the Ingleton–Dent road, then turn right to follow the road to a junction with a path at the next mapped field boundary on the east side of the road (grid reference SD 721 817). Turn left to follow this path, which rises just south of east to the summit of Whernside; to get back to **Ribblehead** station from there, turn left onto the ridge at the trig point, heading just east of north, and follow the directions given in this book's description of the highest point of North Yorkshire from the summit trig point onwards.

However, if you don't fancy this option, or the conditions aren't right, turn left rather than right onto the stony track at SD 706 825 and proceed northwards, then north-eastwards, then just west of north, to a signed junction with another track forking away to the left. You need to take the right signed fork here, descending via Nun House Outrake to reach the Ingleton–Dent road again. Please note that this stony track, all the way from SD 706 825 to the road (a distance of just over 2 miles), is very hazardous in places and floods after rain, giving you the impression that you're walking through a beck. There are usually options of walking along grassier channels to the right or left of the path itself, but it's slow going and will seem almost unfairly arduous after the exertions of the climb on and descent from the ridge. Be particularly careful towards the end, where the ground underfoot can be extremely slippery as you descend.

On arriving at the road, here Deepdale Lane – the last bit of the track before the road is slightly easier, as it's a driveway used by High Nun House – turn left to follow it briefly. However, look out in about a quarter of a mile, perhaps a little less, for a signed footpath going off the road to the right, at a stile just past a gate, grid reference SD 718 857. Cross the stile and follow the path north-eastwards over grass, initially along a right-hand field edge then straight on downhill and veering very slightly left, the line of the path discernible in the grass. You eventually arrive at trees at the bottom end of the field, with the rush of the waters of Deepdale Beck audible in the woodland. Follow a narrow path down to the beck, bearing left to follow alongside it and arrive at a road at Mill Bridge, the flow of water here very impressive after rain. Turn right to follow the road.

You now walk along this road for a little under 3 miles through **Dentdale**. Although this seems a lot of road walking, it's a very pleasant country road with little traffic, and the Dentdale scenery is delightful, with hills rising grandly from the valley all around. The highlight of the walk is the crossing of the River Dee at Ewegales Bridge. Immediately beyond this bridge, you reach a T-junction at which you turn right, soon passing the pretty church at Cowgill by a road junction and continuing to the next road junction at **Lea Yeat**, less than half a mile away. Here turn left as signed for what is a bit of a sting in the tail – a very steep climb indeed to **Dent** station, a bit of a shock after all the downhill walking!

Now, on arrival at the station, you hope that you won't have to wait too long for a train, but when one does arrive, you can be assured of a superb journey on the Settle–Carlisle line, enjoying the fells in comfort; either north to Carlisle via Kirkby Stephen and Appleby, past the Pennine giants Great Dun Fell and Cross Fell; or south to Settle over the Ribblehead Viaduct and past Pen-y-Ghent. But do check train times carefully, as rushing up the hill from Cowgill isn't a realistic proposition. Of course, just as bad as missing a train by two minutes, with the next not due for two hours, is the failure of an expected train to appear at all; since the station, at over 1,100ft (335 m), is the highest mainline station in the country, there may be very good reason for your train going AWOL. A helpful information board provides advice on what to do in that situation, although doubtless many walkers will have developed their own brand of coping strategies – especially those dogged every day by the non-appearance of the 7.42 from Sidcup to London Blackfriars.

Derbyshire

Kinder Scout – 636 metres / 2,088 feet – SK 086875

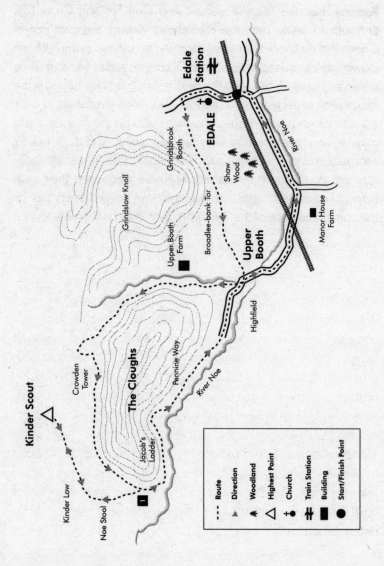

Length: 8 miles
Start and finish: Edale station
Public transport: Regular trains serving Edale on the Manchester–Sheffield line
Refreshments: Edale (P, C, S); none en route
Difficulty: Strenuous, severe in places. NOTE: This high point is set in the middle of the huge peat-covered Kinder plateau. In clear weather, when the peat is dry, you should have few problems, although you will still need a map and compass or (preferably) GPS navigator to be sure of finding the summit cairn. If the weather is bad, and/or the peat is waterlogged, the plateau becomes exceedingly dangerous, and in conditions of poor visibility a compass or GPS navigator is vital not only to assist in locating the summit but to get you safely back off the plateau afterwards
Rating: ****

Scout's honour

The summit of Derbyshire is at the heart of the Dark Peak area in the Peak District National Park. Contrasting with the greener limestone White Peak country further south, the gritstone landscape of the Dark Peak is much starker and more uncompromising, and correspondingly it provides much more of a challenge for walkers. Edale, with its handy railway station and splendid valley setting, provides the ideal base for an exploration of the Dark Peak. My first visit to Edale was as a prospective Pennine Way walker. I made for the visitor centre, and watched a film of a number of students tackling the Pennine Way and appearing to be close to throwing in the towel on day one. Feeling thoroughly demoralised, I decided to seek solace in a cup of tea in the youth hostel I was booked into – only to find it was another mile's walk from the village. Great start! Edale is indeed the start of the Pennine Way, father of all long-distance footpaths, which proceeds for a little matter of 256 miles to the Scottish border at Kirk Yetholm, and the early part of your walk overlaps with that route.

From **Edale station**, make your way up the road northwards, passing the village church and arriving at the centre of Edale village. Turn left off the road more or less opposite the **Old Nags Head Inn** along the clearly signposted **Pennine Way**; proceeding westwards, you head along the sunken Peat Lane, veering left at its end to enter fields. The Pennine Way is now a stone-paved path through the fields, and the Way is unmistakeable as you head south-westwards, climbing gently but steadily to below **Broadlee-bank Tor**. This is all good stuff and, providing the weather is fine, you may well wish you were striding on towards Scotland along the National Trail. The path is firm and clearly defined, providing beautiful views across the valley.

Sticking to the Pennine Way, you then descend along a clear path, avoiding the temptation to veer right onto a path going up into the hills, and arriving at **Upper Booth Farm**. Go forward through the farmyard to reach a T-junction with a metalled lane; turn right into the lane and cross the bridge over the **River Noe**, then just beyond the crossing you leave the Pennine Way and take the footpath which leads off to the right, and ascend on a narrow path through the trees above Crowden Brook. The path keeps just below the wall and heads almost due north towards the hills. Cross a footbridge in a rowan-shaded hollow and ascend the opposite bank of the clough ('steep-sided valley'); the path works along the side of the clough before descending to the brook as it narrows. Soon **Crowden Tower** appears on the skyline to the left. Choose the best route you can, scrambling over boulders and criss-crossing the stream; the easiest route slants up the hillside to the left, away from the stream, to reach the plateau to the right of the great buttress of Crowden Tower, which has been likened to a medieval castle. Turn left and scramble up the rocks to admire the view from the top of Crowden Tower, which extends down the steep-sided Crowden Clough to the long gully-split line of Rushup Edge.

You're now on the top of the Kinder plateau, more correctly **Kinder Scout** ('scout' in this context meaning 'projecting cliff', derived from the old Scandinavian word *skuti*), Now continue westwards/south-westwards along the broadly paved perimeter path, which leads between banks of peat towards the rock formations known as Woolpacks. Pass the throne-like **Pym Chair** on your right, and head west again on the perimeter track across the headwaters of the River Noe towards the prominent 'anvil' of Noe Stool. Keep on along the track for just under half a mile beside the remains of the wall to meet a path junction with the Pennine Way; the approximate grid reference is 079 864 and there is a large cairn ■.

Turn hard right (northwards) to rejoin the Pennine Way and, following an initially clear path, pass to the right of the untidy mass of stone known as **Edale Rocks**. Suddenly your hitherto very well-defined path becomes rather vague, but you need to aim northwards for the trig point at **Kinder Low**, perched neatly on one of the many stones around the edge of the plateau. Now, a combination of frustration and apprehension will grip the seeker after the summit of Derbyshire; apprehension at the mass of peat clothing the Kinder plateau, which can be delayed no longer, and frustration that the solid reliable trig point remains a maddening 9.8 feet (3 metres) shy of the highest ground. As you stand or sit nervously by the comforting landmark of the Kinder Low trig point, you may notice a change in the weather here, sunshine and warmth further down all too easily and quickly being replaced by rain, wind and mist.

Just over half a mile separates the trig point from the high point; a pathless, featureless half mile (to be precise, 0.54 miles), where skill with a map and compass or possession of a GPS navigational device is essential. The half mile is a peat wilderness and it becomes apparent where the 'dark' part of Dark Peak gets its name – although as for the other half, as Wainwright wryly put it, 'Nothing less like a peak could be imagined.' This extraordinary landscape, once covered in woodland, is effectively the result of activities of Stone Age and Bronze Age man, whose 'slash and burn' deforestation combined with over-grazing left the soil exposed to nature. Climate changes which took place over 10,000 years ago, and a 2,000-year period of wet weather, resulted in this exposed soil becoming waterlogged, a steady decay of vegetation and the loss of the capacity of the ground to sustain more than a handful of plants. The result is a vast expanse of peat moorland; erosion of the peat has produced hags or steep-faced peat islands, separated from their neighbours by groughs or water courses, which cut through the peat – all too often, right across the walker's direction of travel.

It is all uncompromising at best, formidable at worst, with an unpleasant propensity, in the worst weather and conditions, for swallowing walkers up to their waists and higher. John Hillaby, in his book describing his walk from Land's End to John o'Groats, found it profoundly depressing: 'A silent and utterly sodden world... Up there, alone, your equanimity depends on how many times you lose your way.' The Pennine Way used to follow a hideous course across the middle of the plateau, and the reward for reaching the spectacular Kinder Downfall on the far side of it was a quite ghastly walk across the peat moorlands of Featherbed Moss to Snake Road, where, as Barry Pilton in his book *One Man and His Bog* (his own Pennine Way journey) pointed out, many walkers gave up as the 'hypothetical path (crossed) a very real bus route'.

On a more cheerful note, the Kinder Low trig point is a great place to stop and admire what is an incredible view to the west and to reflect on a major landmark in the history of recreational walking in England. Down in the Sett Valley between the Kinder plateau and the huge Manchester conurbation is the little town of Hayfield, now a very popular launching pad for Kinder-bound walkers but also the start of the Kinder Trespass in 1932. On Sunday 24 April of that year, several hundred ramblers set out from Hayfield to claim the then privately-owned grouse moors for public exploration, and ended up fighting with gamekeepers who were trying to keep them off. Several of the leaders were arrested but the campaigning that day subsequently paved the way for the creation of the Peak District National Park, the first National Park in Britain. Meanwhile, in the mid-1930s one Tom Stephenson started pressing for a public right of way across the Pennines, and it was through his efforts that the Pennine Way opened thirty years later, starting at Edale. The plateau has its own distinctive wildlife, including not only the grouse, whose plaintive 'Go back!' cry is one of the most distinctive sounds of the moor, but also the peregrine, hen harrier, golden plover, snipe, mountain hare and, during the breeding season, the curlew; while the peat is decorated with cotton grass, and the peaty pools host bogbean and marsh cinquefoil, which flowers between May and July.

So, having gazed out at it, you need to go for it. In conditions of poor visibility it may assist to train your GPS navigator onto Kinder Low and note its precise grid reference (SK 07907 87065), which you'll need for the walk back. Now set your GPS navigator to grid reference SK 08656 87569, and walk across the plateau (no path) to the little cairn which marks the summit. If you're not blessed with a navigator, you need to aim north-eastwards from Kinder Low, the Woolpacks well over to the right (east), and hope that a combination of clear visibility and good eyesight will enable you to pick out the cairn. How much you enjoy your walk to the high point itself will almost certainly depend on the conditions. When I walked out to it, the region was enjoying a very settled spell of summer weather and the peat was bone dry; the steep-sided groughs, with little or no water flowing through them, were no more than an inconvenience. Even after scaling a good few of the groughs there were only a few faint hints of brown on my newly purchased black jogging bottoms. Visibility, meanwhile, was good enough for me to pick out the cairn with ease (although the GPS navigator was essential to get me going in the right direction to start with) as well as the Woolpacks. It will be a very different matter if the weather is wet or misty, and your sense of direction, like your bottom half if you have the misfortune to hit one of the worst bogs, is liable to sink without trace.

But through determined forging up and down through the groughs, duly guided by compass or navigator (I really do not advise your trying to do it without one of these), you will reach the summit cairn. It has to be said there are some nearby tufts of heather which appear to slightly exceed the height of the cairn; in fact, it really is very hard to see that it is higher than any number of tufts and other mini-rises in the vast acreage of peat which surrounds you. If you weren't so thrilled that your efforts with compass or GPS, brilliant intuition or psychic genius had got you to this spot, it might feel a bit of an anticlimax.

Now, resetting your navigator, return to Kinder Low the same way, and rejoin the Pennine Way, heading back past Edale Rocks (keeping them to the right) and regaining a clear path, but when you reach the large cairn at **1** above don't bear left back towards the Woolpacks but go straight on along the path, rising a little then veering left (eastwards) and beginning to descend away from the plateau. You arrive at a path junction, and here you bear left with the main path to follow steeply down to the packhorse bridge over the River Noe. This is a lovely descent, using the path known as **Jacob's Ladder**. The Pennine Way uses what was an important cross-Pennine trade route, taking salt from Cheshire to Yorkshire and wool from Yorkshire to Cheshire. Ponies going uphill towards Kinder followed a zigzag track up the hillside; one of the jaggers or herders is reputed to have taken a short cut up the steepest slope (now taken by the Pennine Way) to give him sufficient time for a smoke before the horse caught up with him! The packhorse bridge, as well as being a proud sturdy construction and a perfect spot for a picnic or just a rest and a drink, has a setting which is near perfection, with a glorious backcloth of a lush green hillside which, in the July morning sunshine in which I was fortunate enough to witness it, provided me with that wonderful feeling of not wanting to be anywhere else.

Beyond the bridge you join a clear track which heads south-eastwards, passing the buildings of Lee Farm and an information shelter, to arrive back at **Upper Booth**. On your return to Upper Booth, you have a choice. You could retrace your steps back to Edale via the Pennine Way, remembering to bear left in Upper Booth through the farmyard. But, if the weather is against you and/or you are in a hurry, you could continue along the road to **Barber Booth** to a T-junction; by turning left and following the road north-eastwards you'll soon be back at Edale station. I suggest, however, that providing the weather is on your side, you would need to be in a tearing hurry to take the road route back to the station from Upper Booth, as there are plenty more great walks you could do from Edale. But before thinking about venturing out again, relax and enjoy the village. Treat yourself to a pint in the renowned Old Nags Head, or enjoy a slice of celebratory gooey chocolate cake in the cafe, as I did, now only too glad not to have 256 more miles in front of me.

Herefordshire

Black Mountain (Ridge South of Hay Bluff) – 703 metres / 2,306 feet –
SO 255350

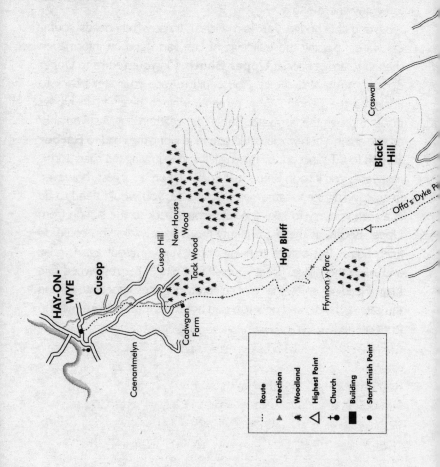

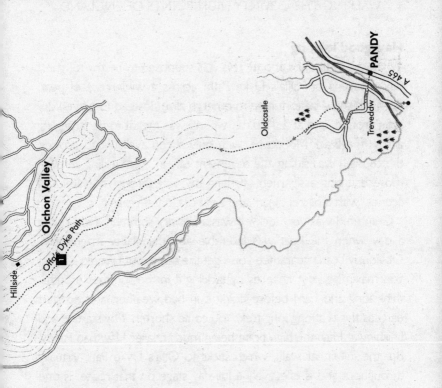

Length: 17½ miles

Start: Pandy

Finish: Hay-on-Wye (Hay from now on)

Public transport: Regular buses serving Pandy on the Hereford–Cardiff route; regulare buses serving Hay on the Brecon–Hereford route

Refreshments: Pandy (P); Hay (P, C, S); none en route

Difficulty: Strenuous, severe in places. NOTE: You should seriously consider postponing your walk if the weather is bad. Much of this walk is very exposed, leaving you absolutely at the mercy of the elements, there are limited opportunities for escape should things turn really bad, and you will miss out on what are some of the best views in this book

Rating: *****

Hay, good looking

What was all the fuss about? This was supposed to be my toughest day's walking on Offa's Dyke Path, across a wilderness of peat, from which I'd be fortunate to emerge alive. Instead I enjoyed dry solid ground, and at 2.30 p.m., when I was meant to be struggling across the Black Mountains, with only sheep available to provide directions, I was sitting at a pavement cafe in Hay tackling an even more daunting assignment, fighting my way through a plateful of scones, with a barrel of jam and a vat of clotted cream.

Granted, I was very lucky. It was a hot dry summer, and I chose a day when the heat was tolerable and the clarity magnificent. Obviously I can't guarantee you'll get the same, but I would suggest you maximise your chances by tackling it in the summer months, think long and hard before doing it in bad weather, and do start early as this is a long long trek. You could shorten it by starting and finishing at Hay, the high point being much nearer Hay than Pandy. But the full linear walk, which sticks to Offa's Dyke Path virtually throughout and is effectively a full-day stage on that route, is one of the finest pieces of ridge walking in Britain outside the Lake District. Assuming you follow the route suggested below, some careful planning is needed. If you're reliant on public transport and doing this as a one-off day excursion (although you could split it into two days if push came to shove), I do seriously recommend you travel down the day before. Staying the night at Pandy, and having reached Hay, make arrangements to stay at least a night there before getting the bus back. This is a walking experience to savour and celebrate, and indeed you may enjoy it so much that you decide to return to walk the whole of Offa's Dyke Path. It's one of the best-known and best-loved National Trails, running for 177 miles from Sedbury, near Chepstow on the Bristol Channel, to Prestatyn on the north Wales coast, and following as faithfully as possible King Offa's remarkable defensive construction, believed to date back to the late eighth century. Ironically you won't actually see any of the Dyke itself between Pandy and Hay, but (save for the section around Hay Bluff, described below) simply follow the Offa's Dyke waymarks and you won't go wrong.

So to business. From the **A465**, the main road through Pandy, make your way to the **Lancaster Arms** (you may well have stayed the night there!) and cross a stile just south of the pub on the right, on a byroad leading away from the main road. Walk just north of west through the meadow, cross a footbridge over the River Honddu and then continue over the railway, going forward to reach a road junction. Cross straight over onto a minor road and follow it, passing the farm of **Treveddw**, and then bearing right, cutting off the road corner and heading north-westwards over a field to arrive back at the road. Bear right to follow the road on, continuing along it for half a mile. At the crossroads junction after a quarter of a mile or so, turn right and go downhill. Despite the fact that you may feel you're taxiing prior to the climb onto the ridge, the views even at this stage are good, particularly to the very distinctive mountain to the south known as the Skirrid (this is the easily pronounceable English name; the Welsh call it Ysgyryd Fawr.) For a long time this peak was a destination for pilgrims, owing to the large cleft in the peak said to have been made by the earthquake following Christ's crucifixion.

Having descended along the road, fork left onto a sunken way which takes you uphill. Head for the west edge of a group of pine trees above you, at the south corner of the Iron Age hill fort of Pentwyn; you pass through the middle of the fort, arriving at its northern corner. Now take care to head for the east edge of a sizeable walled enclosure described as 'the Castle', beyond which the route becomes clearer, climbing steeply and forming the start of your 10-mile ridge walk, which will reach its thrilling climax at Hay Bluff. Shortly you reach a trig point at 1,520 feet (464 metres), but don't be deceived, for although you're getting there, there's still roughly another 780 feet (240 metres) of climbing to undertake. Continue north-westwards to the summit of **Hatterall Hill**, from which on a clear day there should be views to Llanthony Priory to the north-west; it dates back to the start of the twelfth century but the Augustinian monks who settled there found the surroundings uncongenial and many decided to move to Gloucester. A little further up the valley, at Capel-y-ffin, there are the remains of the more recent Benedictine abbey of St Anthony. Keep on along the ridge until you get almost level with Llanthony Priory, roughly 5 miles from Pandy, reaching a path crossroads **1**. Here is one of a number of paths providing escape routes off the ridge, should the weather close in; turning left off the ridge will take you down to the beautiful Vale of Ewyas and, although you won't find a settlement of any size there, it'll be easier for you to get help if needed and there's a road. But don't expect a bus; if you see one, it's a bad sign, as the chances are you're hallucinating.

Assuming you don't need to escape, however, on the ridgetop it's now straightforward walking up the long ridge leading from Hatterall Hill, heading north-westwards. Although you're continuing to rise, the gradient has now eased, the walking becomes easier, and you can enjoy watching the sheep and Welsh moorland ponies as you walk through totally unspoilt heather moorland, dotted with crowberry and bilberry. To your left you gaze across the heart of the Black Mountains, while to your right there's an extensive area of fine border countryside. Between your ridge and the mountains to the left lies the lovely Vale of Ewyas, as stated, although the width of the ridgetop does have the effect of restricting the views. Moreover, the surface of the ridgetop is rough. You pass a trig point about half a mile from the crossroads junction indicated at **1** above, at a height of 1,804 feet (552 metres), and now just keep going along the flat ridgetop. There's a real sense of remoteness, and it was quite a surprise to meet a walker who carried only a stick, a flask and a guidebook, and said his wife was carrying his equipment by car. She'd met some other Offa's Dyke Path walkers whose kit up till then had been carried by taxi and she was now carrying it also – not rucksacks but bulky suitcases and holdalls. It would have been interesting to watch their progress along the path if their transport had let them down at any stage.

There's a further trig point at 2,000 feet (610 metres), roughly 2½ miles from the last, and still you climb until, approximately 3 miles from this further trig point, you reach the highest point of all. Sadly there's no trig point to mark your achievement but you can check your arrival there using your GPS navigator, grid reference SO 255 350. It is actually on the border of Herefordshire (England) and Powys (Wales), so if you want to be pedantic and make sure you're in Herefordshire, keep to the right-hand edge of the ridgetop at this point. Not only is it the highest point in Herefordshire, but it's the highest point on the **Offa's Dyke Path**, and for good measure you're also on the eastern fringes of the Brecon Beacons National Park. The views aren't the best; as stated above, the ridgetop is wide, so you don't get the panoramas you might have hoped for, but don't despair, for you'll get your reward in just 1½ miles. To your left is the 2,260 feet (688 metres) summit of the Twmpa, now separated from your ridge by the Gospel Pass, and to your right there's now a parallel ridge climaxing in the 2,100 feet (640 metres) summit of Black Hill.

Shortly beyond the high point the view opens out, and you should see straight ahead of you the trig point marking the top of Hay Bluff and the end of the ridge. There's a short descent at **Llech y Lladron**, then at grid reference SO 254 356 there's a path junction where you take the fork heading north-westwards to **Hay Bluff** and its trig point, about 1½ miles from the high point. The view from here is stupendous, and a great reward for your efforts of the past 10 miles; you can clearly see not only the Twmpa and Black Hill, but the town of Hay, the Wye Valley, the Black Mountains and the

Brecon Beacons. Beyond the trig point, the path, continuing north-westwards, descends steeply (a drop of 600 feet [182 metres] in half a mile) and drops down across a common to a metalled road, with a prehistoric stone circle just across it. Turn right and follow the road for half a mile, then fork left just beyond a bend in the road, where a wall angles away from it. Now, sticking to Offa's Dyke Path, continue just west of north, then northwards across a grassy common with **Tack Wood** to your right. Reaching the northernmost point of the common, with woodland closing in to your right and your left, you go forward through a gate into a lane.

You pass **Cadwgan Farm**, and 350 yards or so beyond you go over a stile and drop down through two fields to a lane, again keeping Tack Wood to the right. Cross straight over and continue to descend, heading in pretty much a northerly direction, to reach a road. Turn left and follow it for a couple of hundred yards to just beyond a right-hand bend, turning right here (northwards) and following a really lovely path along the west side of Cusop Dingle with the village of **Cusop** just across the other side of it. Veering north-westwards, you now head for the town of **Hay** which is directly in front of you. You pass through a series of kissing gates and arrive at the town by the main car park.

Once a fortress on the border between England and Wales, Hay boasts Norman castle ruins and thirteenth-century town walls, and enjoys both bygone charm and a superb range of amenities. But it's best known for its books. In 1961 Richard Booth opened a huge second-hand bookshop and many others followed, so the place is now a Mecca for second-hand and antiquarian books, and a major literary festival is held here every year. There's a particularly good range of children's books and if you've a weakness for recalling the juvenile literature of yesteryear, prior to the takeover of children's minds and pockets by the Nintendo Wii and Xbox 360, you may well wish to factor in extra time in Hay before heading home. It would indeed be unfortunate to miss the last bus, having lost all track of time since rediscovering and lovingly re-reading from cover to cover that gem of scholarly wisdom, the *Whizzer and Chips Christmas Annual 1970*.

North Yorkshire

Whernside – 736 metres / 2,414 feet – SD 738814

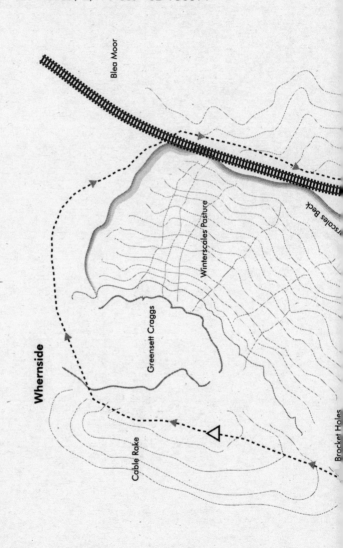

Blea Moor

Winterscales Pasture

Winterscales Beck

Greensett Craggs

Brocket Holes

Whernside

Cable Rake

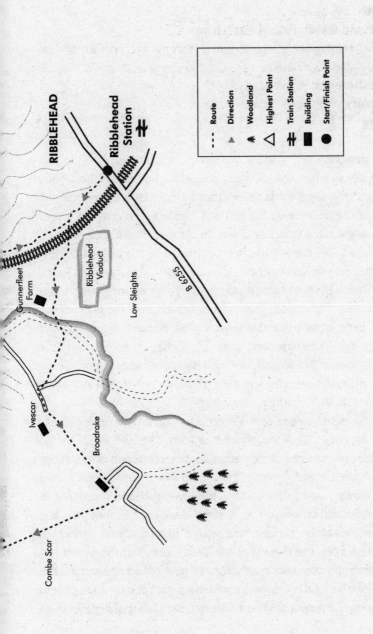

Length: 7½ miles
Start and finish: Ribblehead station
Public transport: Regular trains serving Ribblehead on the Leeds–Settle–Carlisle line
Refreshments: Ribblehead (P)
Difficulty: Strenuous, severe in places
Rating: ****

Peak practice

Firstly, get the right hill. Some guides state that the highest point of North Yorkshire is Mickle Fell, but a closer look at the map will show boundaries have changed and Mickle Fell is now no longer in Yorkshire. Don't despair if you've climbed Mickle Fell, though, (and lived to tell the tale) as this happens to be the highest point in Durham. So you've now homed in on North Yorkshire and found that Whernside is its highest point; you go to the map, and there it is – Great Whernside, just north of Kettlewell in the heart of the Dales. Except that's the wrong hill as well, because what you want is plain old Whernside, and poor old Great Whernside isn't the highest point of North Yorkshire or indeed any other county. So be aware of that before setting out from home – rather than in the pub in Kettlewell after climbing the wrong hill.

Having identified the right Whernside, you'll find that logistically it is a lot easier than somehow one feels it should be. If, in the days before, the rail authorities had not reopened the stations between Settle and Appleby, this would indeed have been a very much harder walk to plan. Now, however, with the reopening of Ribblehead station, all you really need is some stout footwear and a decent weather forecast, and you're halfway there. In fact, as you'll see from the brevity of the description that follows, it is a very straightforward walk, although it's best not to attempt it if the weather is bad. Of course you could make it harder for yourself, and combine your ascent of Whernside with the scaling of Ingleborough and Pen-y-Ghent, which with Whernside make up the so-called Three Peaks of Yorkshire and provide one of the best 'challenge' walks the country has to offer. Another option is to combine the conquest of Whernside with that of the summit of Lancashire, and the description devoted to Lancashire tells you how that might be done. But, as far as the description below is concerned, let's keep it simple and get you back to Ribblehead in the daylight.

You begin by walking down the station approach slip road to the **B6255** Hawes–Ingleton road. Turn right onto the road and pass the pub, then very shortly bear left along a signed bridleway; proceed on the wide bridleway north-westwards, parallel with the railway, then veer left under the **Ribblehead Viaduct**. This magnificent construction was completed between 1870 and 1875, but a little more than a century later, British Rail, which then owned the Leeds–Settle–Carlisle line, felt that the cost of doing necessary repair work to the viaduct was too great and decided to close the entire line. However, the line was saved, and between 1988 and 1991 the viaduct was restored; there's a plaque beside the bridleway close to the viaduct acknowledging the support of various bodies which enabled the restoration to take place.

Go forward north-westwards along the bridleway, veering westwards to **Gunnerfleet Farm** and passing the farm buildings to reach a T-junction with a track. Turn left onto it, then very shortly bear right along a signed footpath, keeping a wall to the right; go over a ladder stile and into the next field, going half-left across this field aiming for a little gate in the wall. Proceed through the gate into the adjacent field and follow the wall, heading north-westwards uphill. Use stone slabs to cross a wall and go forward across the next field, the path indicated by the darker grass, bringing you to the buildings of **Ivescar**. Ignore a signed bridleway going hard left but go forward into the farm area itself, and arrive at a clear bridle track pointing north-east/south-west. Turn left onto it, heading south-westwards, ignoring an early fork to the right. The track is well defined initially; it reaches a gate and veers gently right, and is then rather less well defined as it veers gently left and goes forward to another gate. Beyond it, continue in pretty much the same direction to reach the buildings of **Broadrake** which are to your right and, sticking to the same direction, continue beyond Broadrake across a field to reach a signed path junction. Turn right here along the path signed Whernside 1¾ miles.

The taxiing is now over, and you begin the assault on Whernside on what is a very clear path indeed, narrow but easily discernible all the way up. It is narrow, rocky and exceedingly steep in places, but the views just get better all the time. Eventually, it veers to the right, the gradient lessens and you find yourself on the ridge. It's then a very exciting ridgetop walk to the summit trig point and, although the trig point itself is just behind a wall, you certainly won't miss it however bad the weather is. The views are magnificent; Pen-y-Ghent and Ingleborough are the most distinctive and conspicuous features, but the Ribblehead Viaduct is also clearly visible, while to the north-west the verdant Dentdale provides a fine contrast to the stark steep hillsides.

Continue on beyond the summit along the ridge, sticking to the obvious main path, then within sight of the pools known as Whernside Tarns, you veer north-eastwards and drop down steeply round the side of **Knoutberry Hill**. Veering south-eastwards, you keep on an obvious path which continues to descend and arrives at a T-junction of paths. Turn right to follow the path south-eastwards, looking out for a lovely waterfall just to your right. Shortly you reach the railway and cross over it, but immediately to your right is a remarkable feature, a stone aqueduct carrying the stream that flows from the waterfall. Now keeping the railway to your right, and enjoying superb views to Ingleborough ahead, continue downhill past the **Blea Moor** signal box, arriving at a junction with the bridleway you were on at the start, close to the viaduct. You've come full circle and it now simply remains for you to turn left onto the bridleway and walk back to Ribblehead station.

Standing on the station reminds you of what it used to be like on station platforms before the advent of automated departure boards telling you how late your train is. There's no such luxury here, and thus I had no way of telling if I was going to be waiting five minutes because of a sheep on the line at Garsdale, or five days because of blizzards that had engulfed Appleby. Of course, if British Rail had had their way, I'd still be waiting there now.

County Durham

Mickle Fell – 788 metres / 2,591 feet – NY 806245

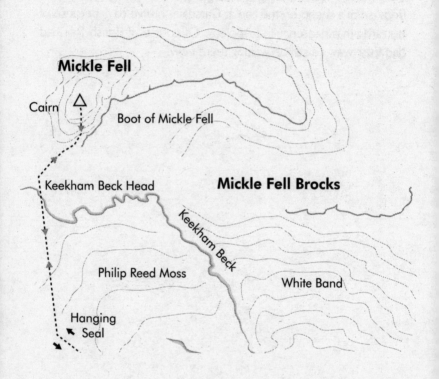

Length: 7½ miles
Start and finish: Durham/Cumbria boundary sign on B6276 Middleton–Brough road
Public transport: None. NOTE: The nearest settlement served by public transport is Middleton-in-Teesdale, to which there are regular buses from Barnard Castle, some of these buses starting their journeys in Darlington
Refreshments: None
Difficulty: Severe. NOTE: It is imperative that you read the introductory paragraphs below before attempting this walk
Rating: ****

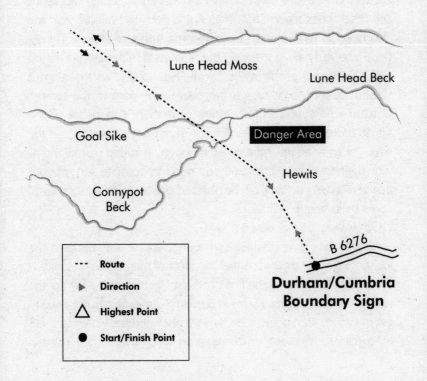

Lune Head Moss

Lune Head Beck

Goal Sike

Danger Area

Hewits

Connypot Beck

B 6276

Durham/Cumbria Boundary Sign

---   Route

▶   Direction

△   Highest Point

●   Start/Finish Point

Permission to peak, sir

You could be justified in thinking somebody up there doesn't want you to conquer Mickle Fell. It may not be the highest county high point in England, but there are more challenges involved with this expedition – and that is what it will be – than with any other in this book.

The problems can be divided into three. To begin with, there is no public transport within 8 miles of the start of this walk, so you have a choice between your car, a taxi or a very high walking mileage for the day; with no amenities whatsoever in those 8 miles, or on the described walk itself, splitting the walk into two days isn't an option either unless you choose to camp. Secondly, the route to Mickle Fell involves entering onto land using for military firing; access to the land is only available for walkers at certain weekends and other times at very short notice, and even on available days you also need to have written permission to gain that access. Thirdly, once you've finally got there, the walk itself, although posing no real navigational problems, is exceedingly tough, with numerous streams to ford, peat hags to negotiate and, close to the summit plateau, almost vertical climbing; and since there's no mobile phone signal, there will be real problems in summoning assistance in the event of an accident. Moreover, although, as stated, route finding won't generally be a problem, you need to be quite sure of your bearings to get you back off the plateau because, without these, you could be in severe difficulties.

Otherwise, it's a doddle.

All that said, it is doable, as I found, and it was perhaps the logistics involved that made the conquest of this one so fantastically rewarding. I addressed the first problem – getting to the start of the route – by Googling taxi firms in Barnard Castle, and found a taxi to get me to the start point, then having concluded the walk, did the 8 miles back to Middleton-in-Teesdale on foot. (There's little point in giving you the taxi driver's mobile; for all I know when you read this he may have retired on the profits of ferrying walkers where buses fear to tread, and now be driving taxis in the Maldives.) The second entailed some telephone and email correspondence with the military firing range office on 01768 343227; they are extremely helpful, or were to me anyway, and the permit was supplied to me electronically. I wasn't challenged during my walk at any stage, which suggests that you might get away without seeking permission, but it's a very long way to go only to be turned back.

NOTE: The terms of the permission made it clear that I was required to follow the boundary route, as described below, and I will assume that this will be the route stipulated for you as well. I have read an account of a climb of Mickle Fell using a longer route from the B6276 but along a track a little way to the east of the boundary route. It's clearly marked on maps, but whether you consider it worth taking the risk if you decide to walk it without permission is a matter for you.

As for the terrain, my previous conquest of the Pennine Way proved to be ideal training and enabled me to cope with the peat, slippery beck stones, long grass and deep heather; remember the wise words of Wainwright, "watch where you are putting your feet", and be careful. One rushed step and you could find yourself stuck halfway up the fellside until the next time a walker has permission to walk it and comes upon your prostrate person. Which, if that permission is several weeks later, may not be in exactly mint condition.

Well, here you are. The taxi should have taken you to the Durham/ Cumbria border on the **B6276** Middleton–Brough road; there's a cattle grid marking the border, but in any case the border signs are clear enough. Your taxi driver has relieved you of most of the paper money in your wallet, you've hopefully remembered to gather your cagoule, GPS device and permit from the foot well, so off you go. Facing the Cumbria side of the border, observe the various warning signs on the far side of the wall, and walk to the enclosed path you see between a stone wall and a fence heading immediately to the right, north-west away from the road at the county boundary. To access it, you'll have to climb over a wire fence; no stile is provided so this will be your first gymnastic endeavour of the day, and it won't be the last either.

Once on the enclosed path, you begin with an uphill trudge through rough grass, albeit there is a semblance of a path in places, then annoyingly you drop down, losing some of the precious height gained. As you descend, the stone wall is still with you to the left, but you arrive at another crossing fence, which you have to climb over, and at this point the stone wall dives off to the left. Continue in the same direction you have been following beyond the fence crossing, keeping a wire fence to your right, and very shortly pass through a gate in that fence and continue north-westwards beside the fence, now keeping it to your left. This will be your 'crutch' for much of the way and it will be invaluable in mist. In clear conditions, you can see Mickle Fell ahead, and excitement wells up, or should well up, as each step brings you closer to the mountainside.

You rise again, then begin to descend, the wire fence veering slightly left; a sign indicates the point at which you enter the military firing range (there's no gate though). You have to cross a beck, using a footbridge provided, then return to the fence and keep walking beside it. The going is reasonably easy for a time, but tends to become rougher, with further becks to cross, and there are some peat hags and very spongy grass, which should be negotiated with care. Better to take a long way round than risk injury; as long as you remember you need to get back to the fence, the exact choice of route is up to you. You come to a wide beck which you need to ford with care, and immediately beyond it the ground rises very steeply beside the fence, with the beck down below you and parallel with you to your right. Now notice a fence coming in from the left to meet yours: just over 2 miles from the start, this is **Hanging Seal** and a key point on your walk. **Mickle Fell** is now that much closer and you can start to feel you really will make it.

Turn right with the fence and – continuing to keep it to your left – follow it steeply downhill, the fence then veering sharp left and shortly right again, now heading northwards towards the fellside; keep following alongside it all the while. As a navigational aid, it could hardly be bettered, but the going looks easier than it is; the ground is often very squelchy, there's rarely a path and there are many obstructions in the form of peat hags and long tufty grass. Just be very careful. Although you won't see many other souls about – I was absolutely on my own when I was here on a Saturday morning in August – you will have company in the form of grouse, whose legendary 'go back' call hardly inspires you for the fight! You see the fence rising and, keeping it as your faithful companion, you rise with it; the way ahead is clear, but the gradient is severe in the extreme and you will undoubtedly need your hands to assist you. It's worth stopping frequently to get your breath back and admire the views which are opening up to the south. Towards the top, the fence veers to the right and you stick with it, the gradient getting even tougher; but just when you think you can take no more, you reach a crossing fence and a stile in the middle, and suddenly, you're there, on the summit plateau. You've pretty much made it. For reasons which will become apparent, I suggest that once your heartbeat has come back to slightly below 300 beats per minute, you mark this stile on your GPS device.

Turn half-right now and make your way across the plateau; if you've a GPS device, key in NY 806 245, which is the grid reference for the large summit cairn. Soon, luxury of luxuries, there's a green path which will feel like the royal red carpet, taking you unerringly to the cairn. Now the views open up in all directions and you can permit yourself a gasp; not only have you the southward views but the whole of the **Mickle ridge** opens out dramatically to the east. Although the terms of the permission may say you need to walk straight back from the summit, you may not be able to resist a walk along the ridge, but again that's a matter for you and your conscience. Perhaps the most impressive and captivating view is to the north, with the Cow Green Reservoir – which may bring the Pennine Way memories flooding back – clearly in view. Looking to the north-west, you should be able to see the golf ball on Dun Fell, a key landmark on the Pennine Way, just short of its highest point at Cross Fell. While the views southwards have been excellent all the way up, they are truly magnificent once you're on the top, a stunning mix of moorland, valley and mountain scenery. I found myself on the peak as a strong weather front was approaching from the south-west, and could see the black cloud enveloping the distant hilltops and sending columns of wispy white cloud ahead of it, dropping down onto the hills like thick plumes of smoke. It sent a powerful and potent message, which was – I'm going to get wet.

Now you will understand the need to have taken a GPS reading at the stile just as you reached the plateau, because you now need to head back to it. If you've been up there a while, it will be very easy for you to lose any sense of direction and to forget which way you've come; in mist, you could find yourself in a real Mickle pickle. If you've not got a GPS device or compass – well, you probably shouldn't be up here at all, but hopefully you will have found some other landmark to guide you back to the stile, or else resorted to the Hansel-and-Gretel method of a line of stones. Once you've reached the stile, you cross over it and now begin a precipitous descent, taking the greatest care. Initially don't forget the need to bear round to the right but soon proceed in a clear southerly direction, keeping your trusty boundary fence to your right; it's a very steep descent indeed, but immensely satisfying to see the fence stretching ahead, leading you back to civilisation. You'll know you're getting close to Hanging Seal when the fence kinks to the left then the right, and climbs very steeply uphill.

This uphill climb indeed brings you to the Hanging Seal junction of fences, and it's here you now turn sharp left to head south-eastwards, clinging limpet-like to the fence as before. Initially there's a sharp drop and a beck to be forded – if you want to avoid getting your feet wet, choose your stepping stones carefully! – and the going remains fitful and somewhat tortuous as you choose your best way round the various obstacles nature has thrown in your path. Things do get easier, and once you've crossed the footbridge – helpfully labelled 'USE AT OWN RISK' – the worst is over. You come out of the military firing range area, the fence veers to the right, and you then drop down to the fence crossing; the wall comes in from the right, and you're back on the enclosed path again. You climb briefly, then it's a long descent back to the road, although even when you hit the road, you can hardly be said to be in civilisation. Unless you've brought your car, you'll need to have arranged a taxi or take the long walk back to **Middleton-in-Teesdale**. Having taken the taxi one way, I walked the 8 miles and two and a half hours back to Middleton, through an extraordinary thunderstorm; it lasted several hours, never peaking, and although the lightning was only very faint, the thunder was booming around me without ever moving in any particular direction. Of course I knew why: I'd conquered Mickle Fell, and somebody up there didn't like it.

Northumberland

The Cheviot – 815 metres / 2,676 feet – NT 909205

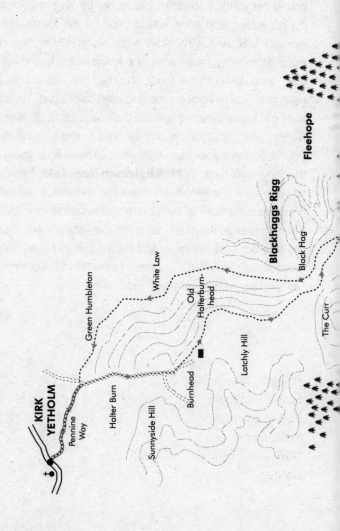

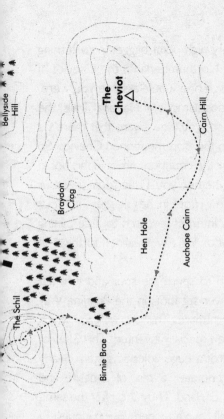

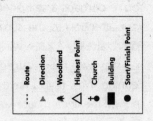

Route   ⋮
Direction   ◀
Woodland   ◀◀
Highest Point   △
Church   +•
Building   ■
Start/Finish Point   ●

Bellyside Hill

The Cheviot

Braydon Crag

Cairn Hill

Hen Hole

Auchope Cairn

The Schil

Birnie Brae

Length: 20 miles
Start and finish: Kirk Yetholm
Public transport: Regular buses serving Kirk Yetholm from Kelso
Refreshments: Kirk Yetholm (P); none en route
Difficulty: Strenuous, severe in places
Rating: ****

Border terrier

You're perhaps a seasoned county high point bagger, now turning your attention to the summit of Northumberland, the Cheviot. If you're already a keen walker, which one would assume you were, you may well have walked that most famous of National Trails, the Pennine Way. If you have done so, you'll be aware that there's a spur off the linear route leading to the aforementioned Cheviot. So it follows that if you want to bag all the county summits in this book, you need to remind yourself whether you undertook the spur route. If you did, you can sink a few more inches deeper into your armchair and confine your day's Internet research to ascertaining the cheapest way to fly to Barbados for a well-earned fortnight in the sun.

But if you were foolish enough to spurn the spur and turn left for Auchope Cairn, or you've never set foot on the Pennine Way before, prepare for a logistical nightmare. This is a walk for which the word 'remote' might have been specially invented. The Cheviot Hills, created by the outpourings of a huge volcanic system nearly 400 million years ago, which generated a mix of andesite and granite, are among the loneliest in England. They also offer the same unappetising menu of peat that will have attended your conquest of Kinder Scout. The nearest bus stop is 10 miles away, the nearest railway station at least two lengthy bus rides away, and the terrain and climate are at best inhospitable, at worst presenting a challenge which may prove beyond all but the bravest and best prepared – and sometimes beyond them, too. So as you scan your computer screen for cut-price rail and air fares, and bus connections to base camp, you will curse your walking companion for persuading you to miss out the spur route when walking the Pennine Way in order to be sure of getting down to your B & B in time for *The Weakest Link*.

Essentially it comes down to two options. One is to start from Byrness and walk to Kirk Yetholm, following the traditional final leg of the Pennine Way. This was how I came to conquer the Cheviot. It involved staying the previous night in Byrness (having walked all the way up the Pennine Way from its start point at Edale in Derbyshire) and getting going at 5.35 a.m., reaching the summit of the Cheviot some six and a half hours later, and arriving in Kirk Yetholm twelve hours after starting from Byrness. There are a number of Pennine Way walking guides which will provide the route to follow, although at least one guide recommends missing the Cheviot altogether if the weather is bad. Including the Cheviot, it's a walk of some 27 miles in length, and that itself may be more than many walkers can manage in a single day; there are ways of breaking it up, but nobody has devised one which eliminates the need either to detour a substantial number of extra miles for off-route accommodation or to go equipped with a tent which will withstand driving rain and force-9 gales.

The other possibility, which I have described below as the optimum way of conquering the beast, is to find your way to Kirk Yetholm and walk to the Cheviot via the northernmost section of the Pennine Way, then walk back again. This is still a 20-mile trek, although you could shave off a little if you were lucky enough to get a lift or find a taxi for the road section at the Kirk Yetholm end. There simply are no other route-shortening options – other, I suppose, than chartering a helicopter, which might make something of an inroad into your county high point bagging budget.

But let's assume you've made it to Kirk Yetholm. From the road junction in the centre, join the **Pennine Way** by following the road heading south-eastwards away from the **B6401**, and in 1 mile you reach a cattle grid where the old and new routes of the Pennine Way diverge. Continue on along the Burnhead Farm access road, sticking to the old Pennine Way route, heading just east of south with **Halter Burn** your constant companion to your left. Shortly before the buildings of the hamlet of **Burnhead**, roughly 1 ½ miles from the parting of the old and new Pennine Way routes, the road kinks left and right, and it is here that you cut round the near (north) side of the buildings. You're still on the Pennine Way, albeit this represents a slight re-routing from the original.

Just east of the buildings of Burnhead you veer left, following a farm track with **Latchly Hill** to your right. Now contouring the lower slopes of Latchly Hill, you head south-eastwards, fording Latchly Sike, still keeping Halter Burn to your left; then veer right, southwards, past the ancient settlements at **Old Halterburnhead**, the track becoming a path. Now head southwards and, in roughly half a mile from Old Halterburnhead, you reach a junction with a track. Turn left to follow this track uphill, over the col between **Black Hag** to your left and the **Curr** to your right. Veering eastwards, you're united with the new Pennine Way route immediately below Black Hag and **Corbie Craig**. Turn right at the path junction, keeping Corbie Craig just to your left, and shortly reach another fork junction of paths. Take the left one to shortly arrive at a ladder stile and the England/Scotland border wall. Now head south-eastwards following the border fence, climbing steeply to reach the **Schil**, the first (or last!) major summit of the Pennine Way. It has a rocky tor on the summit, and is described by Wainwright as forming the most attractive mountain-top in the Cheviots, with splendid views to the Scottish lowlands and the North Sea. It's certainly a great deal more rewarding scenically than your ultimate objective, I'm sorry to say…

The going is now clear as you follow the border fence beyond the Schil south-eastwards, veering south-westwards and then just east of south. This is superb ridge walking with magnificent views. Roughly 1½ miles from the Schil you arrive at **Red Cribs**, and from here there is a really stupendous view down College Valley, looking just east of north. It's at this point that you veer decisively eastwards, then just south of east; to your left is **Hen Hole**, a hanging valley which was formed when the glaciers retreated 10,000 years ago.

You pass a mountain refuge hut, which may prove a life-saver if conditions are bad, and go forward to **Auchope Cairn**, where there's a small stone shelter.

Thus far you've been walking on firm dry grass, but here the surface deteriorates as you veer more clearly south-eastwards to reach a stile and a meeting of fences. It is here that the Pennine Way spur route to the Cheviot begins. Bear left to head just north of east to the 2,545 feet (775 metres) summit of **Cairn Hill**, then veer left, north-eastwards, to the trig point marking **the Cheviot**, the summit of the Cheviots and of Northumberland. There is now a proper flagstone path to the summit, but in former years when such luxuries had not been conceived, this was one of the most unpleasant pieces of walking imaginable. I undertook this walk with three hardy companions in 1988, and my log records that the walk to Cairn Hill was 'a bit gruesome in places but not bad', while the walk on to the Cheviot was atrocious and we all got into difficulties with the peat. I had to be pulled out on one occasion, but one of my companions went in above his waist and it took two of us to pull him out. The trig point was surrounded by black peat and we ended up actually crawling through it to reach the summit column. One would have hoped that the reward for one's exertions, not only on the spur route but the hike from the start, would be a stunning view, especially given the great altitude, but sadly this wasn't, and indeed isn't, the case. There really isn't a view to speak of. Wainwright, in his *Pennine Way Companion: A Pictorial Guide*, wrote that the Cheviot stands 'wholly in England and, after experiencing it, one can readily understand why the Scots wanted no part of it'.

You now need to retrace your steps, returning firstly via Cairn Hill to the main route of the Pennine Way, then bearing right to follow it north-westwards to Auchope Cairn, veering just north of west past the mountain shelter to Red Cribs and the stunning view to College Valley. Now you veer right, just west of north, beside the border fence and along the ridge, enduring a steep ascent to the Schil, doubtless wishing that had been your objective and not the Cheviot; the view is just so much better. As you descend from the Schil, sticking to the border fence, look out for a number of tors to your right, the remains of a small circlet of hardened rocks known as metamorphic aureole. You proceed north-westwards to the ladder stile you crossed earlier, passing from England into Scotland and arriving at two path junctions in quick succession, turning right at the first. The second is the junction of the old and new Pennine Way routes. You could retrace your steps all the way along the old route, forking left and almost immediately right, continuing via Old Halterburnhead and Burnhead, beside Halter Burn and then along the road to reach Kirk Yetholm. However, if you're not too tired, both physically and mentally, you may wish to use the new Pennine Way route, which keeps with the border ridge for a little while longer.

If you decide on the latter, take the right rather than left fork from the junction of the two routes and continue northwards along the ridge past Steerrig Knowe, sticking to the grassy **Steer Rig**. The path now veers gently left, just west of north, and climbs to White Law, from which there are excellent views to the Lammermuir Hills. If these sound familiar, it may be because you'll have had to negotiate them towards the end of your walk along the Southern Upland Way, one of the principal Scottish long-distance routes. Back on your Cheviot–Kirk Yetholm walk, you veer north-west from White Law to reach a ladder stile, then right, northwards, heading downhill beside a wall. In half a mile or so you reach a junction with a signed track at Stob Rig, and here you need to turn left, finally leaving the England/Scotland border, along a track which wanders round the south-west slopes of **Green Humbleton**. Almost directly beneath Green Humbleton the path forks, and you need to take the right fork, dropping down to **Shielknowe Burn** and keeping it just to your left. You cross Halter Burn, and almost immediately reach the cattle grid and road, here reunited with the old Pennine Way route. Turn right onto the road, which you follow for 1 mile to reach Kirk Yetholm. Congratulations – you've made it.

This is of course the finishing line for the Pennine Way, too, and as you near the end you may meet a sweaty, heavily laden walker gasping, and panting and wheezing his way along the road, every step a monumental effort, as his blistered feet crash against the hard unyielding tarmac surface. Do find time to wish him luck for the remaining 255 miles to Edale.

Cumbria

Scafell Pike – 978 metres / 3,210 feet – NY 215072

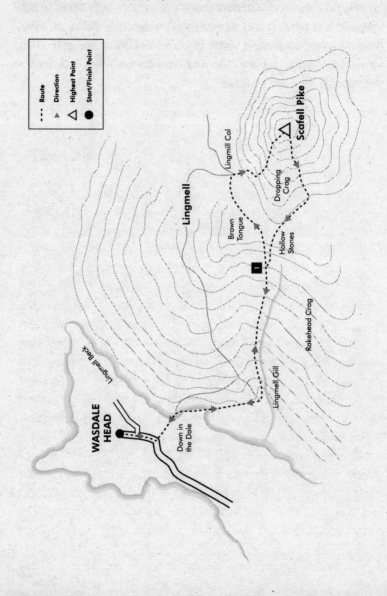

Length: 7 miles
Start and finish: Wasdale Head
Public transport: Regular, but infrequent, buses serving Gosforth on the Whitehaven–Millom route. NOTE: There is also at the time of writing a hybrid bus/taxi service from Gosforth to Wasdale Head. Check the Internet or tourist information offices for more details
Refreshments: Wasdale Head (P); none en route
Difficulty: Strenuous, severe in places
Rating: *****

Top of the tops

This is it. The high point of all county high points. The daddy of them all. The summit not only of Cumbria but of England. It doesn't get any higher.

Cumbria as we know it today has absorbed the whole of the Lake District, but it wasn't always thus. Prior to 1974, the Lake District straddled two counties, Cumberland and Westmorland, with Scafell Pike being the summit of Cumberland and Helvellyn the highest point of Westmorland; were this book being written back in those days, I'd thus be guiding you up Helvellyn as well. Not that you need an excuse to climb Helvellyn – it's a fantastic walk, in some ways a more challenging assignment physically than the conquest of Scafell Pike, and there's no reason why you couldn't incorporate walks up both into your Lakeland sojourn. You can then say that you've done both the historic county high points of Cumberland and Westmorland. But now, with Cumberland and Westmorland rolled up into Cumbria, there can only be one county high point, and Scafell Pike (not Sca fell – that's another mountain) is it.

Scafell Pike is a real mountain. It's a rough, rugged beast, one of three summits rising from the main spine of an elevated ridge which keeps above 2,800 feet (853 metres), ending in the cliffs of Great End, and part of a range which includes Sca fell (at 3,162 feet [964 metres], one of the 'big four' Lakeland peaks, but not to be confused with its neighbour). Unlike, say, Great Gable in the Lake District, or Buachaille Etive Mor close to the West Highland Way in Scotland, it is not at all distinctive, with many other mountain and fell tops in close proximity, and on only one side is there an uninterrupted fall to valley level. On all the others, there are intervening mountains. While there are no tarns on the dry, stony mountain surface, crags are evident on all sides, and sizeable areas of the upper slopes are covered by piled-up boulders, a legacy of volcanic eruption. Wainwright says: 'The landscape is harsh, even savage... there is no sentiment about Scafell Pike.'

Navigationally, the walk described below is not that difficult. There are good paths throughout, there are no real route-finding problems and it isn't a particularly long walk. That said, there are two aspects to it which will cause you headaches. The first is actually getting there. I cheated by driving to the start point, but if you are dependent on public transport, there is only an infrequent bus service to Gosforth, the nearest village, and then you're faced with either a 10-mile road walk, or a taxi ride. At the time of writing there is a sort of hybrid bus/taxi service which operates three days a week and requires pre-booking, but it's clearly more economical than a normal taxi ride. Whatever you decide, do check before setting out, or you could find yourself getting to know Gosforth better than you ever intended or indeed wished to. The second difficulty is picking a decent day to do it, which sadly not even the most advanced computer equipment can help with. Whatever time of year you do it, you can never be certain of good weather, and one thing you'll quickly learn about Lakeland is that it has its own microclimate and the weather forecast is rarely reliable. Notwithstanding the BBC's assurance that the day of your proposed climb will be lovely and sunny across England, the best forecast is to wake up on the morning, pull back the curtains of your hotel bedroom, and if you see large drops of water falling from a leaden sky and hurling themselves against your window... well, it's probably raining.

I've chosen Wasdale Head as the start point because it affords the quickest and easiest ascent, but it is by no means the only way of getting up Scafell Pike. There are popular routes also from Borrowdale via Sty Head or Esk Hause, but they are longer (6 miles and 5½ miles each way, respectively) and more challenging. While I accept that getting to Wasdale Head if you've not got your own car is more problematic than getting to Borrowdale, the walk as described below is better suited to less experienced walkers whose priority is the conquest of the mountain, and it is also safe, being well defined and well cairned. The description below is based on your wanting to do Scafell Pike and that alone, but it should go without saying that there is an abundance of options, and if you fancied some more adventurous walking then, providing you've the necessary equipment, don't let me stop you. If you're a seasoned Lakeland visitor you'll probably have climbed Scafell Pike previously and can skip this section anyway!

Your start point, at Wasdale Head, is literally the end of the road; the narrow lane which hugged the shores of Wast Water, and which you would have followed to get here from Gosforth, comes to an abrupt end in the village. You actually need to leave the village and backtrack southwards along the road for a couple of hundred yards, to a point where the road bends sharply right with two footpaths going off to the left, one straight on southwards, the other to the left, south-eastwards. Take this latter path, crossing a meadow; it's a deceptively easy start. Harder work comes when, having shortly crossed **Lingmell Beck** by a footbridge, you veer round to the right, southwards, and follow a path which contours the slower slopes of Lingmell Fell. But you're still really just taxiing. As you approach **Lingmell Gill**, and just over half a mile from your crossing of Lingmell Beck, you veer sharply left. Pause every so often, not only to get your breath back but also to enjoy increasingly impressive views back to Wast Water and the surrounding mountains. Now head just north of east, parallel with Lingmell Gill, climbing more steeply.

You reach a confluence of streams, crossing the left-hand one and walking between the two, and the going is now definitely a lot tougher as you head eastwards then south-eastwards up **Brown Tongue**. It's hard work and again you need to be patient. You veer more eastwards and, continuing on an excellent path, reach an important junction of paths ■ where you keep straight on (in other words the left of the two paths), arriving at a set of boulders known as the **Hollow Stones**. You've now climbed to 2,000 feet (610 metres) (Wasdale Head was 75 feet [23 metres], so well over half the climbing is done). This is a good place to stop and look to the right, towards the magnificent Scafell Crag, which separates Scafell Pike from its neighbour mountain Sca fell. Now you veer in a more north-easterly direction below Pikes Crag, following a clear cairned route to arrive at **Lingmell Col** (roughly 2,400 feet [732 metres]). You can really start to feel excited and believe that you're going to make it. At Lingmell Col you veer round to the right, south-eastwards, for the final assault on the summit via **Dropping Crag**. Description is now unnecessary as you continue upwards for a further 800 feet (244 metres) across stones and past numerous cairns, to arrive at the summit, not only of this walk and of Cumbria, but of England.

How you feel when you reach the top will depend on the conditions and the difficulty you experienced on your way up. You may have been unfortunate with the weather, and may reach the top in rain or thick mist. Being a walker you will be an optimist at heart, all the way up you will have fondly believed that the incessant drizzle and pea-souper that has dogged your every step from Wasdale Head will miraculously have lifted as you reached the top, and you will doubtless feel cheated and intensely disappointed when they have not. But you may have chosen a day of sunshine and clarity and, despite Wainwright's description of the summit – a 'barren desolation of stones… there is no beauty here' – you may be fortunate to enjoy stunning views. You will observe not only a vast number of Lakeland peaks as well as lakes, but Morecambe Bay, the Irish Sea, the Solway Firth, and even the Isle of Man and southern Scotland; on rare occasions you may even be able to pick out Snowdonia in Wales and the Mourne Mountains in Ireland. You may not be on your own; despite the logistical difficulty which may be involved in getting to base camp, you may well be sharing your experience with many other walkers; but enjoy the moment nonetheless – you've reached the roof not only of Cumbria but the whole country.

Having lingered on the mountain top you now need to get back. The easiest, and I have to say the safest course, is simply to retrace your steps, the cairns providing what could be vital assistance in mist; just remember to veer left (south-westwards) at Lingmell Col. However, in good weather there is another option. The well-cairned path you will have followed to the summit will bring you to another path heading north-east to south-west from **Scafell Pike**'s other neighbour Broad Crag. By joining this path and heading south-west you will reach Mickledore and a T-junction of paths immediately beneath the formidable Scafell Crag. If you turn right here and head north-westwards, descending past Black Crag, you will arrive at the junction of paths at ■ above, turning left to retrace your steps back to Wasdale Head. Wainwright recommends this variation 'to all but the most timid of pedestrians', but of course you need to find the path off the summit first. Which in mist could be a real problem.

So the job is done – what next? With my ascent having been completed much quicker than I expected, I thought I'd have a punt at trying to reach Sca fell from Scafell Pike via Lord's Rake. Bad move. I was beaten back by a treacherous scree slope, and ended up being forced most of the way back to Wasdale before finding a safe route up to Sca fell. So I wouldn't recommend that, not on the same day anyway; enjoy a night's stay at Wasdale Head and do it the next day. There's plenty more walking in Lakeland itself: having conquered Scafell Pike and Sca fell you could bag the other two of the Lake District Big Four, Skiddaw and Helvellyn, as suggested above. And, if the bug has well and truly bitten, you may want to seek out the summits of the counties of Wales and Scotland, but these are other stories, for other books, for another day.

But if this is indeed the final walk you do, having completed all the others described in this book, you can feel rather proud of yourself. Don't brag about it too much to your fellow drinkers at Wasdale Head, as there's bound to be someone there who'll boast of much more extensive conquests. Just sit and cast your mind back to the many great walks you'll have enjoyed on your way to this point. The majestic calm of Lewesdon Hill; the exhilarating high-level marches that brought you to Green Hill and Whernside; the many prehistory lessons en route to Milk Hill; the steely determination with which you studied your GPS navigator to bog-trot successfully to that infuriatingly just-a-little-bit-higher-than-Kinder-Lowtrig point summit of Kinder Scout; the formidable hands-and-knees ascent of Mickle Fell... Memories you will treasure forever. Memories of not giving up, of keeping at it – until at last you reached the top and could rise no higher.

Congratulations: you've conquered the summits of England.

Bibliography

Ayto, John and Crofton, Ian *Brewers Britain & Ireland* (2005, Weidenfeld & Nicolson)

Brandon, Peter *The Discovery of Sussex* (2010, Phillimore)

Hillaby, John *Journey Through Britain* (1968, Constable & Company)

Lawrence, Paul; Maple, Les; and Sparshatt, John *UK Trailwalker's Handbook* (2009, Cicerone)

Montague, Trevor *A to Z of Britain and Ireland* (2009, Sphere)

Pevsner, Nikolaus & Nairn, Ian *Buildings of England – Sussex* (1965, Penguin)

Pilton, Barry *One Man and His Bog* (1985, Corgi)

Plowright, Alan *Plowright Follows Wainwright* (1995, Michael Joseph)

Somerville, Christopher *Britain & Ireland's Best Wild Places* (2008, Allen Lane)

Somerville, Christopher *Never Eat Shredded Wheat* (2010, Hodder & Stoughton)

Spence, Keith *Companion Guide to Kent and Sussex* (1973, Boydell & Brewer)

Various *AA Book of Britain's Countryside* (1998, Midsummer Books)

Various *AA Book of British Villages* (1980, Drive Publications Ltd)

Various *AA Illustrated Guide to Britain* (1977, Drive Publications Ltd)

Various *National Trail Guides* (1989–present, Aurum Press)

Vinter, Jeff *Railway Walks GWR & SR* (1990, Alan Sutton)

Wainwright, Alfred *A Pictorial Guide to the Lakeland Fells (Western Fells)* (1966, Westmorland Gazette)

Wainwright, Alfred *Pennine Way Companion* (1968, Westmorland Gazette)

Walters, Jenny *County Highs* (February 2009, *Country Walking* magazine)

About the Author

David Bathurst was born in 1959 and has enjoyed walking throughout his adult life. He has walked all the official long-distance footpaths of Great Britain and also the entire south coast of England, and as well as writing guides to these routes, which have been published by Summersdale, he has written numerous guides to walking in Sussex and Kent. While not writing, David has undertaken numerous unusual fundraising events, including the recital of the entire works of Gilbert & Sullivan from memory and, in 2011, reading the complete King James Bible in six successive days. A lawyer by profession, he lives near Chichester in West Sussex with his wife Susan and daughter Jennifer.

Other walking books by David Bathurst include:

The Big Walks of Great Britain
The Big Walks of the North
The Big Walks of the South
Walking the South Coast of England

THE
BIG WALKS
OF GREAT BRITAIN

including South Downs Way, Offa's Dyke Path, The Thames Path,
The Peddars Way and Norfolk Coast Path,
The Wolds Way, The Pembrokeshire Coast Path,
The West Highland Way, The Pennine Way

DAVID BATHURST

THE BIG WALKS OF GREAT BRITAIN

David Bathurst

ISBN: 978 1 84024 566 0   Paperback   £9.99

From the South West Coast Path to the Great Glen Way, from the Cotswold Way to Hadrian's Wall, and from the Yorkshire Wolds to Glyndwr's Way, there are big walks here to keep you rambling all year round. And what better way to discover the landscapes of Great Britain, from green and gentle dales to majestic mountains and rugged cliffs?

An indefatigable walker, David Bathurst has unlaced his boots to produce this invaluable companion to the 19 best-loved long-distance footpaths. His appreciation of the beauty and history of the British countryside and his light-hearted style will appeal to experienced and novice walkers alike.

- The definitive guide to the national trails of England and Wales and the Scottish National Long Distance Walking Routes

- Detailed descriptions of the trails and a wealth of practical information, including amenities available

- Recommends historic and geographic areas of interest on or near the paths, from ancient burial mounds to flora and fauna

- Routes range in difficulty from the gentle 73-mile Great Glen Way to the massive 628-mile South West Coast Path

'Meaty, practical guide jam packed with walks that promise to keep you rambling all year round.'   THE SUNDAY EXPRESS

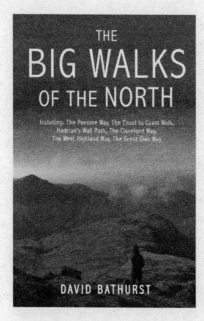

THE BIG WALKS OF THE NORTH

David Bathurst

ISBN: 978 1 84953 023 1

Paperback

£8.99

From the Great Glen Way to the Coast to Coast Walk, there is no better way to discover the spectacular diversity of northern Britain's landscape than on foot. Whether you enjoy exploring green and gently rolling dales or tackling rugged mountain paths, there are walks here to keep you rambling all year round.

Indefatigable walker David Bathurst has unlaced his boots to produce this definitive companion to the ten best-loved long-distance footpaths in the north of Britain, with each split into manageable sections. Combining practical, detailed descriptions with an appreciation of the beauty and history of the British countryside, this in an indispensable guide for experienced and novice walkers alike.

'Whether you're a keen walker set to tackle the 258 miles of the hauntingly beautiful Pennine Way, or if you are just looking to explore the beauty of your native surroundings, there is sure to be a route for you in this guide.'
REAL TRAVEL magazine

'David Bathurst is the knowledge on Britain's long-distance footpaths.'
ADVENTURE TRAVEL magazine

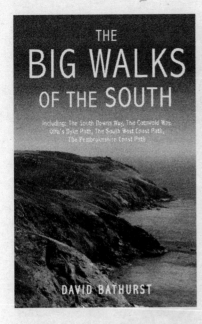

THE BIG WALKS OF THE SOUTH

David Bathurst

ISBN: 978 1 84953 024 8

Paperback

£8.99

From the South Downs Way to the Pembrokeshire Coast Path, there is no better way to discover the spectacular diversity of southern Britain's landscape than on foot. Whether you enjoy exploring green and gently rolling valleys or tackling rugged cliff-top paths, there are walks here to keep you rambling all year round.

Indefatigable walker David Bathurst has unlaced his boots to produce this definitive companion to the ten best-loved long-distance footpaths in the south of Britain, with each split into manageable sections. Combining practical, detailed descriptions with an appreciation of the beauty and history of the British countryside, this in an indispensable guide for experienced and novice walkers alike.

'A helpful pair of volumes for those looking to choose a suitable first or next long distance footpath from across Scotland, England and Wales. Easy to read.' WALKING WALES

WALKING THE
SOUTH COAST
OF ENGLAND

A Complete Guide to Walking the South-facing Coasts of Cornwall,
Devon, Dorset, Hampshire (including the Isle of Wight),
Sussex and Kent, from Land's End to South Foreland

DAVID BATHURST

WALKING THE SOUTH COAST OF ENGLAND

David Bathurst

ISBN: 978 1 84024 654 4   Paperback   £8.99

For this detailed guide to some of the best walking in Britain, David Bathurst has walked over 700 miles of coast, taking in breathtaking natural landscapes and significant landmarks on the way. With rugged cliffs and ancient cathedral cities, historic ports and wonderful wildlife, there's something for everyone; whether you're a seasoned hiker ready to take on the entire walk, or a summertime stroller who wants to experience these rewarding rambles in smaller doses.

Includes:

- A complete guide with detailed descriptions of the route

- Useful information about the geography and history

- Practical advice regarding navigation and local amenities

- Recommendations for top ten weekend walks

This invaluable guidebook is a must-have for anyone going walking on England's south coast.

'there's something for everyone, from seasoned hikers to summertime strollers'
BEST OF BRITISH magazine

'If you… decide to put the dream into action then you should read David Bathurst's excellent book… It takes you along the walk in a way you can follow as a guide and enjoy as an armchair read.'   walkscene.co.uk

Have you enjoyed this book?
If so, why not write a review on your favourite website?

If you're interested in finding out more about our travel books
friend us on Facebook at **Summersdale Traveleditor** and
follow us on Twitter: **@SummersdaleGO**

Thanks very much for buying this Summersdale book.

www.summersdale.com